RHEUMATOID ARTHRITIS

National clinical guideline for management and treatment in adults

Published by

Royal College
of Physicians
Setting higher medical standards

Royal College of Physicians

The Royal College of Physicians plays a leading role in the delivery of high-quality patient care by setting standards of medical practice and promoting clinical excellence. We provide physicians in the United Kingdom and overseas with education, training and support throughout their careers. As an independent body representing over 20,000 Fellows and Members worldwide, we advise and work with government, the public, patients and other professions to improve health and healthcare.

National Collaborating Centre for Chronic Conditions

The National Collaborating Centre for Chronic Conditions (NCC-CC) is a collaborative, multiprofessional centre undertaking commissions to develop clinical guidance for the National Health Service (NHS) in England and Wales. The NCC-CC was established in 2001. It is an independent body, housed within the Clinical Standards Department at the Royal College of Physicians of London. The NCC-CC is funded by the National Institute for Health and Clinical Excellence (NICE) to undertake commissions for national clinical guidelines on an annual rolling programme.

Citation for this document

National Collaborating Centre for Chronic Conditions. *Rheumatoid arthritis: national clinical guideline for management and treatment in adults.* London: Royal College of Physicians, February 2009.

ISBN 978-1-86016-359-3

ROYAL COLLEGE OF PHYSICIANS
11 St Andrews Place, London NW1 4LE
www.rcplondon.ac.uk

Registered charity No 210508

Typeset by Dan-Set Graphics, Telford, Shropshire

Printed in Great Britain by The Lavenham Press Ltd, Sudbury, Suffolk

Contents

DEVELOPMENT OF THE GUIDELINE

THE GUIDELINE

Royal College
of Physicians
Setting higher medical standards

——————————— Corrigendum ———————————

Rheumatoid arthritis

National clinical guideline for management and treatment in adults

Readers are asked to note the following amendments to the Royal College of Physicians of London publication: *Rheumatoid arthritis: national clinical guideline for management and treatment in adults*, February 2009.

1 Page 18, Figure 3.1 Diagnosis and treatment of rheumatoid arthritis, section: treatment – for people with RA, symptom control, line 12
The brackets and words 'other than etoricoxib 60 mg' should be deleted. The amended recommendation should read as follows: 'The first choice should be either a standard NSAID or a COX-2 inhibitor'.

2 Page 180, Recommendation 30, line 2
The brackets and words 'other than etoricoxib 60 mg' should be deleted. The amended recommendation should read as follows: 'When offering treatment with an oral NSAID/COX-2 inhibitor, the first choice should be either a standard NSAID or a COX-2 inhibitor'.

With thanks for your cooperation and apologies for any inconvenience caused by these printing errors.

Royal College of Physicians, 11 St Andrews Place, Regent's Park, London NW1 4LE
Tel: 020 7935 1174 / Fax: 020 7486 5425 / Website: www.rcplondon.ac.uk

Guideline Development Group members

Dr Michael Rudolf *(Chair)*
Chair, NCC-CC; Respiratory Physician, Ealing Hospital NHS Trust

Dr Chris Deighton
Clinical Advisor, NCC-CC; Consultant Rheumatologist, Derby Hospitals
NHS Foundation Trust

Mrs Ailsa Bosworth
Patient and Carer Representative, Maidenhead

Dr Jane Hall
Senior Clinical Research Physiotherapist and Honorary Senior Lecturer RACE/Physiotherapy
Royal National Hospital for Rheumatic Diseases and University of Bath

Dr Alison Hammond
Reader in Rheumatology Rehabilitation, University of Salford

Ms Sheena Hennell
Consultant Nurse, Wirral University Teaching Hospital

Dr Patrick Kiely
Consultant Rheumatologist, St George's NHS Healthcare Trust, London

Dr Raashid Luqmani
Consultant Rheumatologist, Nuffield Orthopaedic Centre and University of Oxford

Dr David Morgan
General Practitioner (non RA specialist), Birmingham

Dr Rachel O'Mahony
Senior Research Fellow, NCC-CC

Mrs Enid Quest
Patient and Carer Representative, Bristol

Mrs Isabel Raiman
Community based nurse, Brighton and Hove City Teaching PCT

Mrs Alison Richards
Information Scientist, NCC-CC

Professor David L Scott
Consultant Rheumatologist, Kings College Hospital

Ms Jaim Sutton
Project Manager, NCC-CC – until March 2008

Mr Jonathan Tosh
Health Economist, ScHARR, University of Sheffield

Ms Claire Turner
Senior Project Manager, NCC-CC – from April 2008

Dr Louise Warburton
General Practitioner (specialist in RA), Shrewsbury

The following individuals acted as either deputies for GDG members or were invited experts:

Ms Zara Bingham
Patient and carer representative (acted as a deputy for Alisa Bosworth at a GDG meeting),
Manchester

Dr Paul D'Orso
General Practitioner (non RA specialist), Birmingham
(acted as a deputy for Dr Morgan for one meeting)

Mr Colin Howie
Consultant Orthopaedic and Trauma Surgeon, Edinburgh New Royal Infirmary
(invited expert attended one GDG meeting)

Dr Anthony Redmond
Podiatrist & Senior Lecturer, University of Leeds (invited expert attended two GDG meetings)

Mr Andrew Robinson
Consultant Foot and Ankle Surgeon, Cambridge University Hospital NHS Trust
(invited expert attended one GDG meeting)

Dr Joanna Sheldon
Immunologist, St George's Hospital, London (invited expert attended one GDG meeting)

Acknowledgements

The Guideline Development Group is grateful to the following people for their valuable contributions to the development of this guideline:

- Dr Bernard Higgins, Director, NCC-CC
- Ms Jane Ingham, Assistant Director Implementation, NCC-CC
- Ms Jill Parnham, Assistant Director Operations, NCC-CC
- Mr Rob Grant, Senior Technical Advisor
- Dr Allan Wailoo, Senior Health Economist, ScHARR, University of Sheffield
- Dr Alan Brennan, Director of Health Economics and Decision Science, ScHARR, University of Sheffield
- Ms Susan Tann, Coordinator, NCC-CC

Preface

There are over 400,000 people with rheumatoid arthritis (RA) in the UK. Although this makes it a common disorder, there are numerous other conditions ahead of it in terms of numbers, and indeed as causes of excess mortality. What this does not capture however, is the dreadful morbidity associated with the disease. The synovitis of RA affects multiple sites causing widespread pain, and the subsequent destruction of the joints can lead to severe disability affecting all aspects of motor function from walking to fine movements of the hand. Furthermore, RA is not simply a disease of the joints but can affect many other organs causing, for example, widespread vasculitis or severe lung fibrosis. More recently it has become apparent that RA is associated with an increased prevalence of coronary artery disease and significant increased risk of premature mortality.

Fortunately there are a considerable number of disease-modifying and anti-inflammatory agents which can significantly reduce the impact of RA. Some of these, for example corticosteroids, sulphasalazine or methotrexate, have been available for many years, and rheumatologists are well used to balancing the benefits and side-effects of these drugs. More recently, targeted disease-modifying and anti-inflammatory therapies, particularly the anti-TNF agents, have emerged, and have proved effective in many patients. While it is encouraging that there is such a wide range of treatment available, the choice brings with it difficult questions concerning the best sequencing of therapy. Moreover, the newer drugs are expensive. The high impact of the disease and the need to make best use of the available treatment make RA a highly suitable subject for a NICE guideline, which it is now my pleasure to introduce.

I have already touched on the exciting therapeutic options for RA, but this guideline addresses many other aspects of management. Because established RA has so many classical features it is easy to forget that at presentation the diagnosis may not be readily apparent, yet early intervention may be important. The guideline offers advice on this problem, including a consideration of the place of newer serological markers of the disease, particularly anti-CCP antibodies. The role of objective measures in the monitoring of disease activity is also considered, as an important component of achieving and maintaining control. The importance of non-pharmacological management of RA is also emphasised, including the many therapeutic interventions which are usually supervised by physiotherapists, occupational therapists and podiatrists; as is the crucial role of the multidisciplinary team including these professionals as well as specialist nurses and doctors.

As in all NICE guidelines, recommendations are based on best available evidence interpreted by a Guideline Development Group (GDG) whose members have expertise and experience in all aspects of managing RA. This GDG have been a huge pleasure to work with. They have shown enormous enthusiasm for the task and for working with NICE to produce the best possible guidance for those suffering from RA. They have done this with a tremendous group spirit and constant good humour, and they fully deserve the thanks which I now offer to them on behalf of all those working at the NCC-CC. I hope that their guidance is as influential as it deserves to be; I believe it should help to improve the care of all people with RA.

Dr Bernard Higgins MD FRCP
Director, National Collaborating Centre for Chronic Conditions

Acronyms, abbreviations and glossary

Acronyms and abbreviations

ABA	Abatacept
ACR	American College of Rheumatology (see ARA)
ACR20, 50, 70	ACR criteria 20, 50, 70
ADA	Adalimumab
ADL	Activities of daily living
AEs	Adverse events
AIMS	Arthritis Impact Measurement Scale
AL-TENS	Acupuncture-like transcutaneous electrical nerve stimulation
Anti-CCP	Anti-cyclic citrullinated peptide
Anti-TNF	Anti-tumor necrosis factor
ARA	American Rheumatism Association (now ACR)
ARMA	Arthritis and Musculoskeletal Alliance
AUC	Area under the curve
ARC	Arthritis Research Campaign
BMI	Body mass index
BSR	British Society of Rheumatology
CBT	Cognitive behavioral therapy
CI	Confidence interval (95% unless stated otherwise)
COX-2	Cyclooxegenase-2
CRP	C-reactive protein
CS	Corticosteroid
CsA	Cyclosporin A
CTX	Cyclophosphamide
CV	Cardio-vascular
DAS (DAS28, DAS32)	Disease Activity Score
DMARD	Disease modifying antirheumatic drug
EA	Electroacupuncture
EQ-5D	EuroQol 5-dimensional outcomes questionnaire
EOW, eow	Every other week
ESR	Erythrocyte sedimentation rate
ETN	Etanercept
EULAR	The European League against Rheumatism
EW, ew	Every week
GDG	Guideline development group
GI	Gastrointestinal

HAQ	Stanford health assessment questionnaire score
HCQ	Hydroxychloroquine
IA	Inflammatory arthritis, or Intra-articular
ICER	Incremental cost-effectiveness ratio
IFX	Infliximab
IM	Intramuscular
IRGL	Impact of Rheumatic Diseases on General Health and Lifestyle Questionnaire
ITT	Intention to treat analysis
IV/iv	Intravenous
JSN	Joint space narrowing
LASER	Light amplification by stimulated emission of radiation
MA	Meta-analysis
MACTAR	McMaster Toronto Arthritis Patient Preference Disability Questionnaire
MCP	Metacarpophalangeal joint
MD	Mean difference
MDT	Multidisciplinary team
MTP	Metatarsophalangeal joint
MTX	Methotrexate
MHRA	Medicines and Healthcare products Regulatory Agency
MI	Myocardial infarction
NCC-CC	National Collaborating Centre for Chronic Conditions
NHS	National Health Service; this guideline is intended for use in the NHS in England and Wales
NICE	National Institute for Health and Clinical Excellence
NS	Not significant (at the 5% level unless stated otherwise)
NSAID	Non-steroidal anti-inflammatory drugs
NRAS	National Rheumatoid Arthritis Society
OMERACT	Outcome Measures in Rheumatoid Arthritis Clinical Trials
OR	Odds ratio
OT	Occupational therapy or therapist
PIP	Proximal interphalangeal joint
PPI	Proton pump inhibitor
PPV	Positive predictive value
PUFA	Polyunsaturated fatty acid
QALY	Quality-adjusted life-year
QoL	Quality of Life
RAI	Ritchie Articular Index
RCT	Randomised controlled trial
RF	Rheumatoid factor
ROM	Range of motion

RR	Relative risk
RTX	Rituximab
SAARD	Slow-acting antirheumatic drugs
SAEs	Serious adverse events
SC/sc	Subcutaneous
SDAI	Simplified Disease Activity Index
SHS	Sharp/van der Heijde Score
SF-12	Short form (12 point) questionnaire
SF-36	Short form (36 point) questionnaire
SMD	Standardised mean difference
SR	Systematic review
SS	Statistically significant
SSZ	Sulphasalazine
TENS	Transcutaneous electrical nerve stimulation
TF	Transdermal fentanyl
TJR	Total joint replacement
TSS	Total Sharp Score
UA	Undifferentiated arthritis
UPA	Undifferentiated polyarthritis
VAS	Visual analogue scale
WMD	Weighted mean differences

Glossary

Biological drug/biologic	Type of DMARD which targets pro-inflammatory cytokines that are involved in joint destruction (particularly TNF-alpha and IL-1).
Clinically significant improvement	Some trials define a dichotomous outcome of clinically significant pain relief as having been achieved above a specific threshold on a pain score, e.g. pain VAS. However, there is no standard threshold and each such trial should be considered individually.
Cohort study	A retrospective or prospective follow-up study. Groups of individuals to be followed up are defined on the basis of presence or absence of exposure to a suspected risk factor or intervention. A cohort study can be comparative, in which case two or more groups are selected on the basis of differences in their exposure to the agent of interest.
Confidence interval (CI)	A range of values which contain the true value for the population with a stated 'confidence' (conventionally 95%). The interval is calculated from sample data, and generally straddles the sample estimate. The 95% confidence value means that if the study, and the method used to calculate the interval, is repeated many times, then 95% of the calculated intervals will actually contain the true value for the whole population.

Cochrane review	The Cochrane Library consists of a regularly updated collection of evidence-based medicine databases including the Cochrane Database of Systematic Reviews (reviews of randomised controlled trials prepared by the Cochrane Collaboration).
Cost-consequence analysis	A type of economic evaluation where, for each intervention, various health outcomes are reported in addition to cost, but there is no overall measure of health gain.
Cost-effectiveness analysis	An economic study design in which consequences of different interventions are measured using a single outcome, usually in natural units (for example, life-years gained, deaths avoided, heart attacks avoided, cases detected). Alternative interventions are then compared in terms of cost per unit of effectiveness.
Cost-utility analysis	A form of cost-effectiveness analysis in which the units of effectiveness are quality adjusted life-years (QALYs).
Disease modifying antirheumatic drug (DMARD)	Treatment that can reduce or prevent joint damage.
Established RA	Rheumatoid arthritis disease duration of longer than two years.
Incremental cost	The cost of one alternative less the cost of another.
Incremental cost effectiveness ratio (ICER)	The ratio of the difference in costs between two alternatives to the difference in effectiveness between the same two alternatives.
Larsen Score	Method of assessing radiographic joint damage cause by RA.
Manual therapy	A range of physiotherapy techniques where the affected joint (typically the hip) is manipulated and stretched beyond the range of motion that the person with osteoarthritis is able to use.
Meta-analysis	A statistical technique for combining (pooling) the results of a number of studies that address the same question and report on the same outcomes to produce a summary result.
Methodological limitations	Features of the design or reporting of a clinical study which are known to be associated with risk of bias or lack of validity. Where a study is reported in this guideline as having significant methodological limitations, a recommendation has not been directly derived from it.
Multivariate	Analysis of more than one variable at a time. Takes into account the effects of all variables on the response of interest.
Observational study	Retrospective or prospective study in which the investigator observes the natural course of events with or without control groups, for example cohort studies and case-control studies.
Odds ratio	A measure of treatment effectiveness: the odds of an event happening in the intervention group, divided by the odds of it happening in the control group. The 'odds' is the ratio of non-events to events.
p values	The probability that an observed difference could have occurred by chance. A p value of less than 0.05 is conventionally considered to be 'statistically significant'.

Quality of life (QoL)	Refers to the level of comfort, enjoyment and ability to pursue daily activities.
Quality-adjusted life-year (QALY)	A measure of health outcome which assigns to each period of time a weight, ranging from 0 to 1, corresponding to the health-related quality of life during that period, where a weight of 1 corresponds to optimal health, and a weight of 0 corresponds to a health state judged equivalent to death; these are then aggregated across time periods.
Randomised controlled trial (RCT)	A trial in which people are randomly assigned to two (or more) groups: one (the experimental group) receiving the treatment that is being tested, and the other (the comparison or control group) receiving an alternative treatment, a placebo (dummy treatment) or no treatment. The two groups are followed up to compare differences in outcomes to see how effective the experimental treatment was. Such trial designs help minimize experimental bias.
Recent-onset RA	Rheumatoid arthritis disease duration of up to two years. Within recent-onset RA, categories of suspected persistent synovitis or suspected RA refer to patients in whom a diagnosis is not yet clear, but in whom referral to specialist care or further investigation is required.
Rescue medication	In this guideline, this is an outcome recorded by some studies. The rate of rescue medication use is the rate at which participants had to use a stronger medication (typically for analgesia).
Self-management	A term used for aspects of RA care which a person can do for themselves with advice from the primary care team, eg GP, nurse, physiotherapist, occupational therapist and information leaflets.
Sensitivity analysis	A measure of the extent to which small changes in parameters and variables affect a result calculated from them. In this guideline, sensitivity analysis is used in health economic modelling.
Stakeholder	Any national organisation, including patient and carer groups, healthcare professionals and commercial companies with an interest in the guideline under development.
Statistical significance	A result is deemed statistically significant if the probability of the result occurring by chance is less than 1 in 20 (p <0.05).
Systematic review	Research that summarises the evidence on a clearly formulated question according to a pre-defined protocol using systematic and explicit methods to identify, select and appraise relevant studies, and to extract, collate and report their findings. It may or may not use statistical meta-analysis.
Technology appraisal	Formal ascertainment and review of the evidence surrounding a health technology, restricted in the current document to appraisals undertaken by NICE.
Univariate	Analysis which separately explores each variable in a data set.
Utility	A number between 0 and 1 that can be assigned to a particular state of health, assessing the holistic impact on quality of life and allowing states to be ranked in order of (average) patient preference.

DEVELOPMENT OF THE GUIDELINE

1 Introduction

1.1 Background

Rheumatoid arthritis (RA) is an inflammatory disease that exerts its greatest impact on those joints of the body that are lined with synovium, a specialised tissue responsible for maintaining the nutrition and lubrication of the joint. The distribution of joints affected (synovial joints) is characteristic. It typically affects the small joints of the hands and the feet, and usually both sides equally in a symmetrical distribution, though any synovial joint can be affected. In patients with established and aggressive disease, most joints will be affected over time.

The initial trigger for RA is unknown. There is evidence to suggest abnormalities in components of the immune system that lead to the body developing abnormal immune and inflammatory reactions, particularly in joints. These changes may precede the symptomatic onset of RA by many years. Whatever sets the pathology in motion results in a large increase in blood flow to the joint (giving heat and sometimes redness), proliferation of the synovial membrane with an increase in synovial fluid (swelling), and pain (due to stretching of pain receptors in the soft tissues around, and the bone on either side, of the joint). These features result in rapid loss of muscle around an affected joint, and this, along with pain and swelling lead to loss of joint function. If the inflammation of the synovial membrane cannot be suppressed it will result in increasing damage to the joint, due to the release of protein-degrading enzymes from inflammatory and other cells, and a conversion of parts of the synovial membrane into an inflammatory tissue called pannus which can invade the bone and cartilage at the margins of the joint. The degree of progressive damage is related to the intensity and duration of the inflammation. Damage to joints results in progressive deformity, disability and handicap. Other structures have synovial linings, such as tendon sheaths, and inflammation of these can result in tendon rupture. Consequently, suppression of inflammation in the early stages of the disease can result in substantial improvements in long-term outcomes for joints and other components of the musculoskeletal system.

Compounding this widespread inflammatory arthritis is the fact that RA affects much more than the joints, and is a systemic disease. In all patients the release of large concentrations of proteins that drive inflammatory processes (such as tumour necrosis factor-α (TNF-α)), result in symptoms of profound fatigue, with a feeling of ongoing influenza-like symptoms, and even fever, sweats and weight loss. Furthermore, other body organ systems may be affected by the inflammatory process, with dryness of the eyes and mouth (Sjögren's syndrome), and nodules (hard lumps particularly over extensor surfaces like the backs of elbows) affecting up to a third of patients.

More significant inflammatory manifestations may lead to serious pathology, such as fibrosis in the lungs, inflammation affecting the lining of the heart and lungs (pleural and pericardial effusions), or vasculitis. Vasculitis results in inflammation of the inner lining of the blood vessels and may lead to potentially devastating effects for whichever organ is supplied by the affected blood vessels. Examples of vasculitis are scleritis of the eye, a painful and potentially sight-threatening vasculitis, and peripheral neuropathy, where nerves are irreversibly damaged leading to weakness or sensory abnormalities. Inflammation of the joints can also be life threatening when it affects the neck, causing potentially unstable articulations between the bones, and inflammatory pannus. This combination of bone deformity and swollen inflammatory tissue can press on the spinal cord, leading to ischaemia and widespread neurological consequences affecting all four limbs, bowel and bladder function, or the respiratory muscles and centres in the brain stem that control respiration, potentially resulting in death.

Thankfully, these life-threatening inflammatory manifestations of disease are uncommon, and are possibly becoming rarer. However, it has become increasingly evident that the ongoing inflammation and loss of mobility can have other unforeseen circumstances for people with RA. Heart conditions such as ischaemic heart disease and cardiac failure have been shown to be more common in RA, and result in premature death for many patients. Atherosclerosis (where the inner lining of arteries become progressively thickened and impair blood supply to whichever organ is being served) is driven in part by ongoing inflammation, so that the people with the most active RA have the greatest risk of heart disease. Osteoporosis is also more common, due to reduced mobility, inflammation, and sometimes the drugs they are on (particularly steroids). People with RA are more prone to infections than the rest of the population, probably due to abnormalities in the immune system, and sometimes contributed to by medication (such as the immunosuppressant effects of steroids).

Clearly RA has the potential for not only widespread joint and soft tissue damage, but also inflammatory processes that can directly or indirectly affect most organ systems in the body, and result in premature death. Appropriate management therefore needs to address not only the impact on joints, but also focus on the whole body, the person suffering from the disease, their families and carers, and where appropriate their employers.

1.2   Definition

The most commonly used classification criteria for RA were drawn together in 1987 by a committee of the American College of Rheumatology[2] and published as 'The American Rheumatism Association 1987 revised criteria for the classification of rheumatoid arthritis' (see Table 1.1 for a summary). It is important to note that these are classification criteria and not diagnostic criteria. In other words, they were designed to facilitate communication between researchers, and ensure more robust research through reliable case definition, so that irrespective of where a study is taking place, everybody means the same thing by the term 'RA'. They are not diagnostic criteria (although commonly misnamed as such), because there are no diagnostic tests for RA that differentiate it from normality or from other types of arthritis. The diagnosis is therefore largely a clinical one, relying particularly in the early stages on the history and examination of the patient, with tests (blood or imaging) sometimes helping to confirm the most likely diagnosis.

The 1987 ACR criteria were not designed for clinical practice, although they do influence the way that clinicians think of RA, and do appear in national clinical guidelines. However, they are not useful in discriminating between RA and self-limiting disease in early synovitis that might evolve eventually into disease that fulfils the criteria for RA. They also exclude some individuals with a polyarthritis that does not quite fulfil the criteria, but whose disease closely resembles RA, and has a similar course and response to treatments.

For the purposes of this guideline, the guideline development group (GDG) accepted a clinical diagnosis of RA as being more important than the 1987 classification criteria for RA,[2] because an early persistent synovitis where other pathologies have been ruled out needs to treated as if it is RA to try to prevent damage to joints. Identification of persistent synovitis and appropriate early management is more important than whether the disease satisfies classification criteria.[3] The GDG was therefore keen to take a pragmatic approach and include consideration of all patients with a recent-onset or established inflammatory arthritis where other underlying pathologies had been excluded.

Table 1.1 Summary of 1987 ACR classification criteria for rheumatoid arthritis[2]

Patients must have four of the seven criteria:

- morning stiffness lasting at least 1 hour*
- swelling in three or more joints*
- swelling in hand joints*
- symmetric joint swelling*
- erosions or decalcification on x-ray of hand
- rheumatoid nodules
- abnormal serum rheumatoid factor.

*Must be present at least six weeks.

1.3 Prevalence and incidence

The first study to address prevalence of RA in the UK was published in 1961, where Lawrence estimated that 1.1% of the population of Leigh and Wensleydale had RA.[4] Using the 1987 ACR criteria,[2] Symmons and colleagues came up with a similar figure (0.8%) in a Norfolk population study.[5] This equates to approximately 400,000 people with this condition in the UK.

The incidence of the disease is low, with a second study from Norfolk showing a rate of 1.5 males per 10,000 population per year, and a figure of 3.6 for females.[6] This translates into approximately 12,000 people being diagnosed with new RA each year in the UK. These figures also illustrate another feature of RA in that the overall occurrence of RA is 2–4 times greater in women than men. The peak age of incidence in the UK for both genders is in the 70s, but with a long tail on either side, illustrating that all ages can develop the disease.[6]

The GDG categorised RA into two categories of disease duration: 'recent-onset' (disease duration of ≤2 years) and 'established disease' (disease duration of >2 years). The British Rheumatology Society also took this approach when developing their guidelines.[7] Within recent-onset RA, categories of suspected persistent synovitis or RA, or of early inflammatory arthritis, refer to patients in whom a diagnosis is not yet clear but where referral to specialist care or further investigation is required. Newly diagnosed RA refers to patients in whom the diagnosis has just been made, which will usually be patients with recent-onset RA.

1.4 Management principles

The drug management of RA can be considered under two headings. The first is the relief of symptoms, with pain relief being the number one priority for patients. The second is modification of the disease process so that radiological progression, which is closely correlated with progressive functional impairment, can be retarded or stopped.

The ultimate aim of management is to achieve disease remission for the patient. Disease remission has been defined in a number of different ways, including having scores below certain levels on disease activity indices (eg DAS28 <2.6). Each definition includes elements of a lack of signs and symptoms of disease activity and in others evidence that disease progression has been stopped. Where remission cannot be achieved, the aim should be to minimise disease activity in order to optimise the chances of preventing progressive damage to joints with subsequent disability. The longer the remission period, or the least amount of disease activity that can be achieved, the better the long-term outcome. Where the guidelines refer to sustained disease control, this suggests a minimum of six months of remission or minimal disease activity.

Analgesics and non-steroidal anti-inflammatory drugs (NSAIDs) can be helpful in relieving pain, where they are not contraindicated. Within the class of NSAIDs is a group of drugs that were originally developed with a safer gastrointestinal profile in mind. These are referred to as cox II-inhibitors. The GDG was asked to update the existing technology appraisals on these drugs, but as the group was aware that the recently published NICE guidelines on osteoarthritis (OA) management[7,8] addressed this issue, it was considered that the recommendations from the recently published OA guideline might also be relevant to RA management.

Conventional disease modifying antirheumatic drugs (DMARDs) include methotrexate, sulphasalazine, hydroxychloroquine, leflunomide and gold injections. These drugs can be helpful in slowing down the damaging component of the disease process; however, the precise modes of action are still subject to research.

The optimal sequencing of DMARDs remains a source of debate, and whether patients should be started on combinations of therapies or single DMARDs is also contentious. The GDG felt that this was an important area for detailed health economic analysis in an attempt to try to determine which DMARD strategy was most cost effective.

A group of drugs have been developed, labelled 'biological', because they consist of monoclonal antibodies and soluble receptors that specifically modify the disease process by blocking key protein messenger molecules (such as cytokines) or cells (such as B-lymphocytes). The development of biological drugs has been based on an increasing understanding of the disease pathology. The key drivers of RA include cytokines such as tumour necrosis factor-α (TNF-α), interleukin-1 (IL-1) and interleukin-6 (IL-6). An IL-1 receptor antagonist called anakinra had been appraised by NICE and rejected for use in the NHS as not being cost effective.[9] During the course of the guideline development the GDG was asked to update this technology appraisal (see section 7 of the guideline – pharmacological management).

In addition, the GDG was aware that during the development of this RA guideline, other single and multiple NICE technology appraisals were taking place on biological therapies for RA. These NICE appraisals were as follows:

- Re-appraisal of the use of anti-TNF in RA (an update of 'Guidance on the use of etanercept and infliximab for the treatment of rheumatoid arthritis').[1] This was published in October 2007 and is available from www.nice.org.uk/TA130

- Use of rituximab (a B-lymphocyte depletory) for the treatment of rheumatoid arthritis.*[7,10]
- Use of abatacept (a co-stimulation inhibitor preventing T-lymphocyte activation) for the treatment of rheumatoid arthritis.* [7,11]
- Technology appraisals looking at the sequential use of adalimumab, etanercept and infliximab, the use of certolizumab pegol and the use of tocilizumab for the treatment of rheumatoid arthritis. These findings were not published during the development of this guideline.

1.5 Health and resource burden

Rheumatoid arthritis can result in a wide range of complications for the individual patient, their carers, the NHS and society in general. The economic impact of this disease includes:
- direct cost to the NHS and associated healthcare support services
- indirect costs to the economy, including the effects of early mortality and lost productivity
- personal impact of RA and subsequent complications on patients and their families.

Although the course of RA is heterogeneous and variable, within two years of diagnosis patients usually experience moderate disability, and after 10 years 30% are severely disabled. Life expectancy in patients with RA is also reduced. For example, a 50-year-old woman with RA is expected to die four years earlier than a 50-year-old woman without RA.

Approximately one third of patients cease work because of the disease within two years of onset, and this prevalence increases thereafter. The total costs of RA in the UK, including indirect costs and work related disability, have been estimated at between £3.8 billion and £4.75 billion per year.[12] A survey by the National Rheumatoid Arthritis Society estimated that when a patient stops work due to RA, it represents an average loss of productivity equivalent to £287,544.[7,13] Clearly this disease represents a huge cost to the UK economy, and an enormous cost to individual patients.

1.6 Living with RA

The GDG discussed the impact of RA on people with the patient representatives on the guideline group. It is clear that RA impacts on every area of a person's life. The diagnostic label often comes as a shock, and affected people may be worried about the potential for a life of increasing disability.

If people with RA are asked to single out one symptom which causes the most difficulty, it is pain. This can be difficult for other people to sympathise with, particularly in the early stages of disease when external appearances may be minimal, and can therefore lead to feelings of isolation and depression. It can also be difficult for people to come to terms with having RA and to accept that their plans for the future, which until being diagnosed they had taken for granted, may have to be modified considerably.

---

* See section 10 for the wording of these recommendations.

RA potentially changes relationships with others, impacting on ability to remain in work, and therefore affecting the finances and independence of the individual and their family. It can be reassuring to know that, if diagnosed early and treated with effective therapies, disability is much less likely to happen.

2 | Methodology

2.1 Aim

The aim of the National Collaborating Centre for Chronic Conditions (NCC-CC) is to provide a user-friendly, clinical, evidence-based guideline for the National Health Service (NHS) in England and Wales that:

- offers best clinical advice for the management and treatment of rheumatoid arthritis (RA) in adults in primary and secondary care
- is based on best published clinical and economics evidence, alongside expert consensus
- takes into account patient choice and informed decision-making
- defines the major components of NHS care provision for RA
- details areas of uncertainty or controversy requiring further research
- provides a choice of guideline versions for different audiences.

2.2 Scope

The guideline was developed in accordance with a remit originating from the Department of Health and specifying those aspects of RA care to be included and excluded.

Prior to the commencement of the guideline development, the scope was subjected to stakeholder consultation in accordance with processes established by NICE.[1,7] The full scope is shown in Appendix B.

2.3 Audience

The guideline is intended for use by the following people or organisations:

- all healthcare professionals
- people with RA and their carers
- patient support groups
- commissioning organisations
- service providers.

2.4 Involvement of people with RA

The NCC-CC was keen to ensure that the views and preferences of people with RA and their carers informed all stages of the guideline. This was achieved by:

- including two people with RA as patient representatives on the guideline development group

- consulting the Patient and Public Involvement Programme (PPIP) housed within NICE during the pre-development (scoping) and final validation stages of the guideline project
- the inclusion of patient groups as registered stakeholders for the guideline.

2.5 Guideline limitations

Guideline limitations are as follows:
- NICE clinical guidelines usually do not cover issues of service delivery, organisation or provision (unless specified in the remit from the Department of Health).
- NICE is primarily concerned with health services and so recommendations are not provided for social services and the voluntary sector. However, the guideline may address important issues in how NHS clinicians interface with these sectors.
- Generally, the guideline does not cover rare, complex, complicated or unusual conditions.
- It is not possible in the development of a clinical guideline to complete an extensive systematic literature review of all pharmacological toxicity. NICE expects the guidelines to be read alongside the summaries of product characteristics.

2.6 Other work relevant to the guideline

Related NICE technology appraisals:
- Adalimumab, etanercept and infliximab for the treatment of rheumatoid arthritis. (NICE technology appraisal guidance 130; 2007)
- Rituximab for the treatment of rheumatoid arthritis. (NICE technology appraisal guidance 126; 2007)
- Abatacept for the treatment of rheumatoid arthritis. (NICE technology appraisal guidance 141; 2008)
- Certolizumab pegol for rheumatoid arthritis. (anticipated publication date November 2009)
- Alendronate, etidronate, risedronate, raloxifene and strontium ranelate for the primary prevention of osteoporotic fragility fractures in postmenopausal women. NICE technology appraisal. (Publication date to be confirmed)

Related NICE clinical guidelines:
- Osteoarthritis: the care and management of adults with osteoarthritis. (NICE clinical guideline 59; 2008)
- Osteoporosis: assessment of fracture risk and the prevention of osteoporotic fractures in individuals at high risk (publication date to be confirmed)
- Hypertension: management of hypertension in adults in primary care (NICE clinical guideline 34 (partial upgrade of CG18); 2006)
- Lipid modification: cardiovascular risk assessment and the modification of blood lipids for the primary and secondary prevention of cardiovascular disease (NICE clinical guideline 67; 2008).

2.7 Background

The development of this evidence-based clinical guideline draws upon the methods described by the NICE Guidelines manual[1] (see www.nice.org.uk). The developers' role and remit is summarised in Table 2.1.

Table 2.1 Role and remit of the developers	
National Collaborating Centre for Chronic Conditions (NCC-CC)	The NCC-CC was set up in 2001 and is housed within the Royal College of Physicians (RCP). The NCC-CC undertakes commissions received from the National Institute for Health and Clinical Excellence (NICE). A multiprofessional Partners' Board inclusive of patient groups and NHS management governs the NCC-CC.
NCC-CC Technical Team	The technical team met approximately two weeks before each Guideline Development Group (GDG) meeting and comprised the following members: • GDG Chair • GDG Clinical Advisor • Information Scientist • Research Fellow • Health Economist • Project Manager.
Guideline Development Group (GDG)	The GDG met monthly (June 2007 to July 2008) and comprised a multidisciplinary team of health professionals and people with rheumatoid arthritis, who were supported by the technical team. The GDG membership details, including patient representation and professional groups, are detailed in the GDG membership table at the front of this guideline.
Guideline Project Executive (PE)	The PE was involved in overseeing all phases of the guideline. It also reviewed the quality of the guideline and compliance with the DH remit and NICE scope. The PE comprised of: • NCC-CC Director • NCC-CC Assistant Director • NCC-CC Manager • NICE Commissioning Manager • NCC-CC Technical Team.
Formal consensus	At the end of the guideline development process the GDG met to review and agree the guideline recommendations.

Members of the GDG declared any interests in accordance with the NICE 'Guidelines manual'.[1] A register is given in Appendix E.

2.8 The process of guideline development

The basic steps in the process of producing a guideline are:

- Developing clinical questions
- Systematically searching for the evidence
- Critically appraising the evidence

- Incorporating health economics evidence
- Distilling and synthesising the evidence and writing recommendations
- Grading the evidence statements
- Agreeing the recommendations
- Structuring and writing the guideline
- Updating the guideline.

▷ Developing evidence-based questions

The technical team drafted a series of clinical questions that covered the guideline scope. The GDG and Project Executive refined and approved these questions, which are shown in Appendix A.

▷ Searching for the evidence

The information scientist developed a search strategy for each question. Key words for the search were identified by the GDG. In addition, the health economist searched for additional papers providing economics evidence or to inform detailed health economics work (for example, modelling). Papers that were published or accepted for publication in peer-reviewed journals were considered as evidence by the GDG. Conference paper abstracts and non-English language papers were excluded from the searches.

Each clinical question dictated the appropriate study design that was prioritised in the search strategy but the strategy was not limited solely to these study types. The research fellow or health economist identified relevant titles and abstracts from the search results for each clinical question and full papers were obtained. Exclusion lists were generated for each question together with the rationale for the exclusion. The exclusion lists were presented to the GDG. Exclusion criteria used in this guideline were studies that involved a 'non-UK relevant population'. Populations considered to be 'UK-relevant' were Western Europe, North America, Canada, Australia and New Zealand. See Appendix A for literature search details.

▷ Appraising the evidence

The research fellow or health economist, as appropriate, critically appraised the full papers. In general, no formal contact was made with authors however there were *ad hoc* occasions when this was required in order to clarify specific details. Critical appraisal checklists were compiled for each full paper. One research fellow undertook the critical appraisal and data extraction. The evidence was considered carefully by the GDG for accuracy and completeness.

All procedures are fully compliant with:
- NICE methodology as detailed in the Guidelines manual[1]
- NCC-CC Quality assurance document and systematic review chart.

▷ Health economics evidence

Published economics evaluations were retrieved, assessed and reviewed for every guideline question. Full economics evaluations were included – that is those studies that compare the overall health outcomes of different interventions as well as their cost. Cost analyses and cost-consequences analysis, which do not evaluate overall health gain, were not included.

Evaluations conducted in the context of non-OECD countries were also excluded, since costs and care pathways are unlikely to be transferable to the UK NHS.

Areas for health economics modelling were agreed by the GDG after the formation of the clinical questions. The health economist reviewed the clinical questions to consider the potential application of health economics modelling, and these priorities were agreed with the GDG.

The health economist performed supplemental literature searches to obtain additional data for modelling. Assumptions, data and structures of the models were explained to and agreed by the GDG members during meetings, and they commented on subsequent revisions.

▷ Distilling and synthesising the evidence and developing recommendations

The evidence from each full paper was distilled into an evidence table and synthesised into evidence statements before being presented to the GDG. This evidence was then reviewed by the GDG and used as a basis upon which to formulate recommendations. The criteria for grading evidence are shown in Tables 2.1 and 2.2.

Evidence tables are available online at www.rcplondon.ac.uk/pubs/brochure.aspx?e=271

▷ Grading the evidence statements

Table 2.2 Levels of evidence for intervention studies[1]	
Level of evidence	**Type of evidence**
1++	High-quality meta-analyses, systematic reviews of randomised controlled trials (RCTs), or RCTs with a very low risk of bias.
1+	Well-conducted meta-analyses, systematic reviews of RCTs, or RCTs with a low risk of bias.
1–	Meta-analyses, systematic reviews of RCTs, or RCTs with a high risk of bias.*
2++	High-quality systematic reviews of case-control or cohort studies. High-quality case-control or cohort studies with a very low risk of confounding or bias and a high probability that the relationship is causal.
2+	Well-conducted case-control or cohort studies with a low risk of confounding, bias or chance and a moderate probability that the relationship is causal.
2–	Case-control or cohort studies with a high risk of confounding, bias or chance and a significant risk that the relationship is not causal.*
3	Non-analytic studies (for example case reports, case series).
4	Expert opinion, formal consensus.

*Studies with a level of evidence '–' should not used as a basis for making a recommendation.

Table 2.3 Levels of evidence for diagnostic studies[1]	
Level of evidence	Type of evidence
Ia	Systematic review (with homogeneity[a]) of level-1 studies[b]
Ib	Level-1 studies[b]
II	Level-2 studies[c] Systematic reviews of level-2 studies
III	Level-3 studies[d] Systematic reviews of level-3 studies
IV	Consensus, expert committee reports or opinions and/or clinical experience without explicit critical appraisal; or based on physiology, bench research or 'first principles'

[a] Homogeneity means there are no or minor variations in the directions and degrees of results between individual studies that are included in the systematic review.
[b] Level-1 studies are studies that use a blind comparison of the test with a validated reference standard (gold standard) in a sample of patients that reflects the population to whom the test would apply.
[c] Level-2 studies are studies that have only one of the following:
- narrow population (the sample does not reflect the population to whom the test would apply)
- a poor reference standard (defined as that where the 'test' is included in the 'reference', or where the 'testing' affects the 'reference')
- a comparison between the test and reference standard that is not blind
- case-control design.
[d] Level-3 studies are studies that have at least two of the features listed for level-2 studies.

▷ Agreeing the recommendations

The GDG employed formal consensus techniques to:
- ensure that the recommendations reflected the evidence base
- approve recommendations based on lesser evidence or extrapolations from other situations
- reach consensus recommendations where the evidence was inadequate
- debate areas of disagreement and finalise recommendations.

The GDG also reached agreement on:
- recommendations as key priorities for implementation
- five key research recommendations
- algorithms.

In prioritising key recommendations for implementation, the GDG took into account the following criteria:
- high clinical impact
- high impact on reducing variation in practice
- more efficient use of NHS resources
- allowing the patient to reach critical points in the care pathway more quickly.

Audit criteria for this guideline will be produced for NICE following publication in order to provide suggestions of areas for audit in line with the key recommendations for implementation.

▷ Structuring and writing the guideline

The guideline is divided into sections for ease of reading. For each section the layout is similar and contains:

- *Clinical introduction:* sets a succinct background and describes the current clinical context.
- *Methodological introduction:* describes any issues or limitations that were apparent when reading the evidence base. Point estimates (PE) and confidence intervals (CI) are provided for all outcomes in the evidence tables available at www.rcplondon.ac.uk/pubs/ brochure.aspx?e=271. In addition, within the guideline PE and CI are cited in summary tables for the evidence that pertains to the key priorities for implementation. In the absence of a summary table PE and CI are provided in the narrative text when the outcome adds something to the text and to make a particular point. These may be primary or secondary outcomes that were of particular importance to the GDG when discussing the recommendations. The rationale for not citing all statistical outcomes is to try to provide a 'user friendly' and readable guideline balanced with statistical evidence where this is thought to be of interest to the reader.
- *Evidence statements:* provides a synthesis of the evidence-base and usually describes what the evidence showed in relation to the outcomes of interest. Where the evidence statements are considerable the GDG have attempted to summarise these into a useful summary.
- *Health economics:* presents, where appropriate, an overview of the cost effectiveness evidence-base, or any economics modelling.
- *From evidence to recommendations:* sets out the GDG decision-making rationale providing a clear and explicit audit trail from the evidence to the evolution of the recommendations.
- *Recommendations:* provides standalone, action orientated recommendations.
- *Evidence tables:* are not published as part of the full guideline but are available online at www.rcplondon.ac.uk/pubs/brochure.aspx?e=271. These describe comprehensive details of the primary evidence that was considered during the writing of each section.

The first draft version of the guideline was drawn up by the technical team in accordance with the decisions of the GDG, incorporating contributions from individual GDG members in their expert areas and edited for consistency of style and terminology. The guideline was then submitted for a formal public and stakeholder consultation prior to publication. The registered stakeholders for this guideline are detailed on the NICE website, www.nice.org.uk. Editorial responsibility for the full guideline rests with the GDG.

The different versions of the guideline are shown in Table 2.4.

Table 2.4 Different versions of the guideline	
Full version	Details the recommendations, the supporting evidence base and the expert considerations of the GDG. Published by the NCC-CC. Available at www.rcplondon.ac.uk/pubs/brochure.aspx?e=271
NICE version	Documents the recommendations without any supporting evidence. Available at www.nice.org.uk
'Quick reference guide'	An abridged version. Available at www.nice.org.uk
'Understanding NICE guidance'	A lay version of the guideline recommendations. Available at www.nice.org.uk

▷ Updating the guideline

Literature searches were repeated for all of the evidence based questions at the end of the GDG development process, allowing any relevant papers published up until 13 June 2008 to be considered. Future guideline updates will consider evidence published after this cut-off date.

Following publication and in accordance with the technical manual, NICE will ask a National Collaborating Centre to determine whether the evidence base has progressed significantly enough to alter the guideline recommendations and warrant an update.

2.9 Disclaimer

Healthcare providers need to use clinical judgement, knowledge and expertise when deciding whether it is appropriate to apply guidelines. The recommendations cited here are a guide and may not be appropriate for use in all situations. The decision to adopt any of the recommendations cited here must be made by the practitioner in light of individual patient circumstances, the wishes of the patient, clinical expertise and resources.

The NCC-CC disclaims any responsibility for damages arising out of the use or non-use of these guidelines and the literature used in support of these guidelines.

2.10 Funding

The National Collaborating Centre for Chronic Conditions was commissioned by the National Institute for Health and Clinical Excellence to undertake the work on this guideline.

3 | Key messages of the guideline

3.1 Key priorities for implementation

Referral for specialist treatment

- Refer for specialist opinion any person with suspected persistent synovitis of undetermined cause. Refer urgently if any of the following apply:
  - the small joints of the hands or feet are affected
  - more than one joint is affected
  - there has been a delay of three months or longer between onset of symptoms and seeking medical advice.

Disease modifying and biological drugs

- In people with newly diagnosed active RA, offer a combination of DMARDs (including methotrexate and at least one other DMARD, plus short-term glucocorticoids) as first-line treatment as soon as possible, ideally within three months of the onset of persistent symptoms.
- In people with newly diagnosed RA for whom combination DMARD therapy is not appropriate,* start DMARD monotherapy, placing greater emphasis on fast escalation to a clinically effective dose rather than on the choice of DMARD.
- In people with recent-onset RA receiving combination DMARD therapy and in whom sustained and satisfactory levels of disease control have been achieved, cautiously try to reduce drug doses to levels that still maintain disease control.

Monitoring disease

- In people with recent-onset active RA, measure C-reactive protein (CRP) and key components of disease activity (using a composite score such as DAS28) monthly until treatment has controlled the disease to a level previously agreed with the person with RA.

The multidisciplinary team

People with RA should have access to a named member of the multidisciplinary team (for example, the specialist nurse) who is responsible for coordinating their care.

---

* For example, because of comorbidities or pregnancy, during which certain drugs would be contraindicated.

3.2   Algorithm

| **Person presents with musculoskeletal symptoms** |

History and examination show suspected persistent synovitis of undetermined cause

Refer for specialist opinion. Refer urgently if:
- the small joints of the hands or feet are affected, or
- more than one joint is affected, or
- there has been a delay of 3 months or longer between onset of symptoms and seeking medical advice.

INVESTIGATIONS

Consider measuring anti-CCP antibodies in those people with suspected RA who are negative for rheumatoid factor and in whom there is a need to inform decision making relating to the initiation of combination therapy. (See DMARDs recommendation.)

Offer to carry out a blood test for rheumatoid factor in people who are found to have synovitis on clinical examination and in whom RA is suspected.

X-ray the hands and feet early in the course of the disease in people with persistent synovitis in these joints.

DIAGNOSIS AND INVESTIGATIONS

TREATMENT – FOR PEOPLE WITH RA

COMMUNICATION AND EDUCATION

Explain the risks and benefits of treatment options in ways that can be easily understood. Throughout the course of their disease, offer them the opportunity to talk about and agree all aspects of their care, and respect the decisions they make.

Offer verbal and written information to improve their understanding of the condition and its management, and counter any misconceptions they may have.

People who wish to know more about their disease and its management should be offered the opportunity to take part in existing educational activities, including self-management programmes.

MULTIDISCIPLINARY TEAM

People should have ongoing access to a multidisciplinary team. This should provide the opportunity both for:
- periodic assessments of the effect of the disease on their lives
- help to manage the condition.

People should have access to a named member of the multidisciplinary team (for example, the specialist nurse) who is responsible for coordinating their care.

People should have access to specialist physiotherapy, with periodic review.

People should have access to specialist occupational therapy, with periodic review, if they have:
- difficulties with any of their everyday activities
- problems with hand function.

Offer psychological interventions to help people adjust to living with their condition.

People should have access to a podiatrist for assessment and periodic review of their foot health needs.

Functional insoles and therapeutic footwear should be made available where indicated.

SYMPTOM CONTROL

Analgesics

Offer analgesics:
- to potentially reduce the need for long-term treatment with NSAIDs or COX-2 inhibitors, when pain control is not adequate.

Oral NSAIDs/COX-2 inhibitors

Use at the lowest effective dose for the shortest possible period of time.

The first choice should be either a standard NSAID or a COX-2 inhibitor (other than etoricoxib 60 mg). These should be co-prescribed with a PPI.

When choosing the agent and dose, take into account individual patient risk factors, including age. Consider appropriate assessment and/or ongoing monitoring of these risk factors.

If a person with RA needs to take low-dose aspirin, consider other analgesics before substituting or adding an NSAID or COX-2 inhibitor (with a PPI) if pain reliefw is ineffective or insufficient.

If NSAIDs or COX-2 inhibitors are not providing satisfactory symptom control, review the disease-modifying or biological drug regimen.

GLUCOCORTICOIDS

Offer short-term treatment for managing flares in people with recent-onset or established disease, to rapidly decrease inflammation.

In people with established RA, only continue long-term treatment with glucocorticoids when:
- the long-term complications of glucocorticoid therapy have been fully discussed
- all other treatment options (including biological drugs) have been offered.

Consider offering short-term treatment with glucocorticoids to rapidly improve symptoms in peope with newly diagnosed RA if they are not already receiving glucocorticoids as part of DMARD combination therapy.

MONITORING

ANNUAL REVIEW

Offer an annual review to:
- assess disease activity and damage, and measure functional ability (eg Health Assessment Questionnaire, HAQ)
- check for the development of comorbidities, such as hypertension, ischaemic heart disease, osteoporosis and depression
- assess symptoms that suggest complications, such as vasculitis and disease of the cervical spine, lung or eyes
- organise appropriate cross referral within the multidisciplinary team
- assess the need for referral for surgery
- assess the effect the disease is having on a person's life.

ACCESS TO ONGOING SERVICE

Offer people with satisfactorily controlled established RA appointments for review at a frequency and location suitable to their needs. Make sure they:
- have access to additional visits for disease flares
- know when and how to get rapid access to specialist care, and
- have ongoing drug monitoring.

Figure 3.1 Diagnosis and treatment of rheumatoid arthritis

Do not avoid referring urgently any person with suspected persistent synovitis of undetermined cause whose blood tests show a normal acute-phase response or negative rheumatoid factor

DMARDS
Newly diagnosed RA

In people whose RA is active, offer a combination of DMARDs (including methotrexate, at least one other DMARD, plus short term glucocorticoids) as first-line treatment as soon as possible, ideally within 3 months of the onset of persistent symptoms.

In people receiving combination DMARD therapy and in whom sustained and satisfactory levels of disease control have been achieved, cautiously try to reduce drug doses to levels which still maintain disease control.

In people for whom combination therapy is not appropriate and DMARD monotherapy is started, place greater emphasis on fast escalation to a clinically effective dose rather than on the choice of DMARD.

BIOLOGICAL DRUGS

On the balance of its clinical benefits and cost effectiveness, anakinra is not recommended for the treatment of RA, except in the context of a controlled, long-term clinical study.

Patients currently receiving anakinra for RA may suffer loss of wellbeing if their treatment were discontinued at a time they did not anticipate. Therefore, patients should continue therapy with anakinra until they and their consultant consider it is appropriate to stop.

Do not offer the combination of TNF-α inhibitor therapy and anakinra to peope receiving anakinra for RA.

Other biological drugs should be used in accordance with NICE-TA guidance (see section 10 full guideline and section 2 of NICE guideline).

DIET AND COMPLEMENTARY THERAPIES

Inform people who wish to experiment with their diet that there is no strong evidence that their arthritis will benefit. However, they could be encouraged to follow the principles of a Mediterranean diet.

Inform people who wish to try complementary therapies that although some may provide short-term symptomatic benefit, there is little or no evidence for their long-term efficacy.

If a person decides to try complementary therapies, advise them:
- these approaches should not replace conventional treatment
- this should not prejudice the attitudes of members of the multidisciplinary team, or affect the care offered.

WITHDRAWING DMARDS AND BIOLOGICAL DRUGS
Established RA

In people whose disease is stable, cautiously reduce dosages of disease-modifying or biological drugs. Return promptly to disease-controlling dosages at the first sign of a flare.

When introducing new drugs to improve disease control into the treatment regimen, consider decreasing or stopping their pre-existing rheumatological drugs once the disease is controlled.

In any person in whom disease-modifying or biological drug doses are being decreased or stopped, arrangements should be in place for prompt review.

SURGERY

Offer to refer for an early specialist surgical opinion if any of the following do not respond to optimal non-surgical management:
- persistent pain due to joint damage or other identifiable soft tissue cause worsening joint function
- progressive deformity
- persistent localised synovitis.

Offer to refer people with the following complications for a specialist surgical opinion before damage or deformity becomes irreversible:
- imminent or actual tendon rupture
- nerve compression (for example, carpal tunnel syndrome)
- stress fracture.

When surgery is offered, explain that the main expected benefits are:
- pain relief
- improvement, or prevention of further deterioration of joint function
- prevention of deformity.

Offer urgent combined medical and surgical management to people who have suspected or proven septic arthritis (especially in a prosthetic joint).

If a person develops any symptoms or signs that suggest cervical myelopathy:
- request an urgent MRI scan, and
- refer for a specialist surgical opinion.

Do not let concerns about the long-term durability of prosthetic joints influence decisions to offer joint replacements to younger people.

MONITORING DISEASE

Measure C-reactive protein (CRP) and key components of disease activity (using a composite score such as DAS28) regularly to inform decision-making about:
- increasing treatment to control disease
- cautiously decreasing treatment when disease is controlled.

In people with recent-onset active RA, measure CRP and key components of disease activity (using a composite score such as DAS28) monthly until treatment has controlled the disease to a level previously agreed with the person.

Definitions: Recent-onset RA = disease duration of ≤2 years; established RA = disease duration of >2 years.

THE GUIDELINE

4 | Referral, diagnosis and investigations

4.1 Referral for specialist services

4.1.1 Clinical introduction

The key to the early identification of recent-onset RA is the identification of synovitis. This is inflammation of the membrane that lines the inside of synovial joints (most of the joints in the body). Inflammation manifests itself in pain, swelling, heat and loss of function of the affected joint. The joints will also be stiff, as if trying to move them through resistance, especially in the morning, and sometimes in the evening also. Occasionally the joints can also be red, but this is more unusual with RA, and a single red hot swollen joint should always be treated as septic until proven otherwise. Widespread synovitis may also lead to systemic symptoms of inflammation, with malaise, fever, sweats, fatigue and weight loss. All of these symptoms and signs may be present to a lesser or greater extent in a person with recent-onset RA.

The initial trigger for rheumatoid arthritis is not known. Whatever initiates the inflammation leads to a big increase in blood flow to the joint with resultant *heat* (and occasionally overlying *redness*). Subsequently the number of blood vessels in the synovial lining proliferate markedly, perpetuating the heat of the joint. The inner lining of the joint is composed of cells called synoviocytes, and these are normally only two to three cells deep. Half of these cells produce the lubricating and nutrition-giving synovial fluid, which forms a thin viscous layer in a normal joint. In inflammation, the synoviocytes increase in size and number and the production of synovial fluid increases markedly. This combination of increase in synovial fluid and proliferation of the synovial membrane causes the joint to become *swollen,* so that it has a 'boggy' feel on palpation. A number of pain receptors exist in the soft tissues and bone around the joint, and their stimulation by the swelling and other nerve irritants leads to *pain.* It is the combination of pain and swelling that results in surrounding muscle weakness and *loss of function.*

The main priority for non-specialists is to recognise synovitis as soon as possible. This means a low threshold for detecting heat, swelling, pain, loss of function, morning stiffness, and systemic features of inflammation. In the context of rheumatoid arthritis, if some of these signs and symptoms are present in small joints, then the threshold for considering RA needs to be lowered considerably. Some authorities have suggested if squeezing metacarpophalangeal or metatarsophalangeal joints is tender, this is sufficient to trigger concern.[7,14]

Colleagues in primary care face a number of challenges in recognising recent-onset RA, especially when it can initially present in such a variety of ways. Many patients present with musculoskeletal aches and pains, and even evidence of synovitis, but only a small minority will progress to rheumatoid arthritis. With the incidence of idiopathic inflammatory arthritis being around 2 per 10,000 population,[5,7] a GP with a list size of 2000 patients will see one new case of RA approximately every 2 years. Other challenges for general practitioners include:

- being asked to identify relatively rare persistent synovitis in patients that need prompt interventions, from all of the other very common causes of musculoskeletal aches and pains
- the lack of sensitive and specific diagnostic tests. Where patients develop a polyarthritis very rapidly, the clinical diagnosis and abnormal results, as well as the pain and disability, will usually result in a prompt referral to secondary care. This type of onset is in the

minority, with most patients having a much more insidious onset, or a palindromic onset where the disease might wax and wane in attacks before becoming established. The majority of patients therefore present a diagnostic dilemma in the early stages of disease.

- Laboratory results and x-rays may all be normal in the early stages, even in patients with definite RA, particularly if this is just affecting small joints. Much of the time the key skills for identification are the clinical skills of detecting synovitis, and this is not always straight forward, even for specialists.

- Some patients with a recent onset of persistent synovitis may gain useful benefit from NSAIDs or analgesics, but this may lull both the patient and general practitioner into a false sense of security with regard to the impact the drugs are having on the disease.

A further challenge in managing patients with recent onsets of synovitis is the delay in the person with the symptoms presenting to their GP in the first place. Recent studies have suggested that this accounts for a greater part of the delay in people with RA seeing a specialist for the first time, when compared with delays once the GP has seen the person.[15] People with synovitis may have accumulated damage in their joints before presenting to any member of the medical profession, and it may be that a public health awareness campaign is required to address this. However, GPs may still delay referral, because symptoms may be vague, or signs of synovitis difficult to identify, or positive responses to analgesics and NSAIDs lead to a false sense of security. Elsewhere in these guidelines, reference will be made to the need to initiate DMARDs in the 3-month window of opportunity that makes a huge difference to long-term outcomes (See section 7.3.13). This highlights the need for:

- the general public to be aware of the symptoms and signs of synovitis so that they can attend their GP early, and

- ongoing attempts to reinforce to GPs (and other doctors who might see recent-onset RA, such as casualty officers) the need for prompt referral.

These challenges lead to the following questions:

- Are there any clinical patterns of symptoms or signs of inflammatory arthritis where prognostic concerns need to register and the patient be referred to secondary services promptly?

- If such signs and symptoms are evident, is there any evidence to suggest a time-frame for such a referral?

4.1.2 Clinical methodological introduction

We looked for studies that investigated the clinical features a non-specialist should recognise in order to refer to specialist services and how quickly the referral should be made with respect to impact on symptoms, joint damage, function and quality of life in patients with a recent onset of undifferentiated inflammatory arthritis. All types of study with a UK-relevant population were selected.

Thirteen studies[15–27] were found that fulfilled the criteria. All studies were methodologically sound. Some of the studies were diagnostic studies and these had an element of prognostic design; they assessed which clinical features were able to predict patients who went on to develop RA (and fulfilled the ACR criteria) at least one year after the test was performed.

▷ Clinical features

One cohort study[16] and 12 case-series (prospective)[17–25,28,29] were found which fulfilled the criteria for which clinical features a non-specialist should recognise in order to refer. All studies were methodologically sound.

The cohort study[16] looked at the clinical features of N=474 patients with arthritic symptoms who attended an early arthritis clinic vs a routine clinic and these patients were followed for 1 year.

The 12 case-series looked at the clinical features of patients with early inflammatory arthritis, and in some studies, patients were followed up to look at the features of those that went on to develop RA. Studies differed with respect to:

- sample size (range: N=41 to N=903)
- study length (range: time not mentioned, 1–8 years).

▷ Timing of referral

Three retrospective case-series[15,26,27] were found which looked at the optimum timing of referral in patients with RA. The first case-series[26] looked at the effects of early vs late referral in N=200 patients. The second case-series[27] looked at the effects of delay in referral and starting DMARD therapy in N=198 patients. The third case-series[15] looked at delay in referral times and reasons for delay in N=169 patients.

4.1.3 Health economic methodological introduction

No health economic papers were identified.

4.1.4 Clinical evidence statements

▷ Clinical features

Table 4.1 Symptoms

Study	Patient group	Use	Clinical features
1 case-series[18] **Level Ib**	Early IA* who developed RA	Distinguish RA from other disorders (RA vs non-RA)	**Higher number of tender** (mean 9.8 vs 6.0) **and swollen joints** (mean 7.9 vs 4.4)
1 case-series[19] **Level 3**	Early IA	Referral for suspected RA	**Any joint swelling** (significant association; likelihood ratio, LR 8.2,p=0.004)
		Predictive for referral and RA diagnosis	**Morning stiffness** (not predictive)
1 case-series[20] **Level 3**	Early IA	Features present	**Clinical synovitis** (14%) **RA diagnostic criteria** (56%)
1 case-series[23] **Level II**	Very early persistent IA	Common features present	**Pain in the hand joint** (97%) **and long duration of morning stiffness** (mean 44 mins)

continued

Table 4.1 Symptoms – *continued*

Study	Patient group	Use	Clinical features
1 case-series[24] **Level II**	UPA* who developed RA	Features present	**Higher baseline joint counts** (value not given)
		Predictors of developing RA	**Pain/tenderness in small joints** (year 1: OR 0.63, 95% CI 0.27 to 1.46, p=0.0289); **swelling count in small joints** (year 1: OR 2.93, 95%CI 1.06 to 8.10, p=0.0041); NS year 3 and 5).
1 case-series[25] **Level Ib**	Early IA	Distinguish IA from non-IA conditions (features GPs and RNs* deemed most important)	**Distinguish: currently had or had a history of significant stiffness in the morning or after rest** (GPs: OR 12.7, 95% CI 3.6 to 45.8, p=0.0001 and RNs: OR 5.0, 95% CI 1.7 to 14.7, p <0.003); **observed joint swelling** (GPs: OR 39.4, 95% CI 7.4 to 208, p=0.0001 and RNs: OR 16.4, 95% CI 5.1 to 53.3, p=0.0001)
			Not distinguish: joint pain, joint swelling, joint tenderness, redness, heat
1 case-series[29] **Level II**	Suspected arthritis	Predictors of developing RA	**Morning stiffness** (significant for each of the 3 categories of VAS scale: at VAS >90 OR 9.4, 95% CI3.0 to 28.7, p <0.001); **tender joints and swollen joints** (>10 OR 2.8, 95% CI 1.1 to 7.6, p=0.038)
1 case-series[28] **Level III**	UA* who developed RA	Distinguish from those who did not develop RA	Higher % of patients had compatible with RA features: **MRI synovitis** (100% vs 40%); **MRI synovtis or MRI erosion** (100% vs 50%); **MRI synovtis and MRI erosion** (64% vs 13%); **MRI synovtis and MRI erosion and scintigraphy** (45% vs 0%)

*IA = infammatory arthritis; UPA = undifferentiated polyarthritis; UA = undifferentiated arthritis, RNs = rheumatology nurses

Table 4.2 Pattern and site of arthritis

Study	Patient group	Use	Clinical features
1 cohort study[16] **Level 2+**	Early arthritis	Common features present (early arthritis clinic vs routine outpatient group)	**Atypical presentation asymmetrical arthritis** (28% and 22%), **monoarthritis or oligoarthritis** (30% and 25%)
1 case-series[18] **Level Ib**	Early IA who developed RA	Distinguish RA from other disorders (RA vs non-RA)	**Useful:** significantly more **involvement of hands – pain or swelling of wrists or finger joints** (89.4% vs 60%, p=0.0006)
			Not useful: pain (VAS*) and pain or swelling of MTP* joints
1 case-series[19] **Level 3**	Early IA	Features present	**Swollen joints predominantly in the hands** (66%) **or knee** (18%)
		Predictive for referral and RA diagnosis	**Not predictive: restriction of swollen joints to hands or fingers**

continued

Table 4.2 Pattern and site of arthritis – *continued*

Study	Patient group	Use	Clinical features
1 case-series[20] **Level 3**	Early IA who developed RA	Features present at first visit/presentation	17% – **knee involvement** 100% – **symmetrical synovitis of the small joints of the hands and feet**
1 case-series[23] **Level II**	Very early persistent IA	Common features present	**Symmetrical arthritis** (49%)
1 case-series[25] **Level Ib**	Early IA	Distinguish IA from non-IA conditions (features GPs and RNs deemed most important)	**Not distinguish: signs of MCP*/MTP joint involvement**
1 case-series[29] **Level II**	Suspected arthritis	Predictors of developing RA	**Joint symptoms in the small joints of hand/feet** (OR 1.8, 95% CI 1.1 to 3.1, p=0.024), **asymmetric localisation of the affected joints** (data not given) and **localisation of affected joints in both upper and lower extremities** (OR 3.5, 95% CI 1.7 to 7.5, p=0.001)

* VAS = visual analogue scale; MTP = metatarsophalangeal; MCP= metacarpalphalangeal

Table 4.3 Function

Study	Patient group	Use	Clinical features
1 case-series[19] **Level 3**	Early IA	Predictive for referral and RA diagnosis	**Predictive: limitations when clenching the hands completely to a fist** (referral LR 6.1, p=0.013, diagnosis LR 10.3, p=0.001) as well as **limitations of finger flexion** (data not given) **Not predictive: general questions on every day function**
1 case-series[23] **Level II**	Very early persistent IA	Common features present	**Positive squeeze test of the MCP joints** (68%)
1 case-series[25] **Level Ib**	Early IA	Distinguish IA from non-IA conditions (features GPs and RNs* deemed most important)	**Not distinguish: loss of function and reduced range of movement**

* RNs = rheumatology nurses

Table 4.4 Joint damage

Study	Patient group	Use	Clinical features
1 cohort study[16] Level 2+	Early arthritis	Common features present (early arthritis clinic vs routine outpatient group)	**Erosions at presentation** (25% and 28%); **acute arthritis** (54% and 39%)
1 case-series[18] Level Ib	Early IA who developed RA	Distinguish RA from other disorders (RA vs non-RA)	13% **erosions**; 21% **signs of nonerosive joint involvement (mainly soft tissue swelling); Larsen score** mean 3.5; **acute onset of symptoms** (most patients)
1 case-series[28] Level III	UA who developed RA	Distinguish from those who did not develop RA	Higher % of patients had features compatible with RA: **radiographic Larsen score grade 1** (36% vs 3%); **MRI erosions** (64% vs 23%); **scintigraphy** (64% vs 26%)
			Not distinguish: RF+ (similar in both groups; 36% vs 33%)

Table 4.5 Biochemical markers

Study	Patient group	Use	Clinical features
1 case-series[18] Level Ib	Early IA who developed RA	Distinguish RA from other disorders (RA vs non-RA)	47% vs 33% were **RF+** **Not useful (NS): ESR* and CRP***
1 case-series[19] Level 3	Early IA	Predictive for RA diagnosis	**1 or more lab parameters: ESR, CRP or RF** (data not given)
1 case-series[23] Level II	Very early persistent IA	Predictors of persistent IA	**Not predictors: inflammatory markers**
1 case-series[24] Level II	UPA who developed RA	Predictors of developing RA	**Predictor: antinuclear antibodies** (year 3: OR 1.35, 95% CI 0.26 to 7.17, p=0.0059 and year 5: OR 2.1, 95% CI 0.35 to 12.34, p=0.0101); **ESR** (year 5: OR 3.55, 95% CI 1.2 to 10.5, p=0.04)
			Not predictor: RF; ESR (year 3)
1 case-series[29] Level II	Suspected arthritis	Predictors of developing RA	**CRP level**, (>50 mg/l OR 5.0, 95% CI 2.0 to 12.1, p=0.00); **RF+** (OR 2.3, 95% CI 1.2 to 4.2, p=0.009); **anti-CCP+** (OR 8.1, 95% CI 4.2 to 15.8, p <0.001)
1 case-series[28] Level III	UA who developed RA	Distinguish from those who did not develop RA	**Not distinguish: RF+** (similar in both groups; 36% vs 33%)

*ESR = erythrocyte sedimentation rate; CRP = C-reactive protein

Table 4.6 American Rheumatism Association (ARA) and New York (NY) criteria

Study	Patient group	Use	Clinical features
1 case-series[17] **Level 3**	Arthritic symptoms who developed RA	Predictors of developing RA	**Best predictors: combinations of 8th ARA criteria (swelling in 1 joint and swelling or tenderness in another 4 joints) + (symmetrical swelling or tenderness in PIP or MCP or MTP joints) or (3 swollen and tender joints):** Increase in specificities for predicting: RA with 5 erosive joints, 83% or 82%; RF+ and RF-RA both 93%; RF+ or erosive RA (both 100%)
			Not predictors: NY and ARA criteria (except 8th ARA criterion – had highest Yuden Indexes* for predicting: RA with 5 erosive joints, 53; RF+ and RF-RA 69; RF+ or erosive RA 72; specificities 75%, 86% and 98%)
1 case-series[18] **Level Ib**	Early IA who developed RA	Distinguish RA from other disorders (RA vs non-RA)	**Not distinguish: ACR criteria** (not very sensitive – value not given)
1 case-series[20] **Level 3**	Early IA who developed RA	Features present at first visit/presentation	47% had RA or fulfilled ACR criteria at follow-up
1 case-series[21] **Level II**	Early IA	Identify patients with RA diagnosis (physician diagnosis)	**Low sensitivity and specificity: ARA criteria** **List format:** sensitivity 62%, specificity 50% **Tree format:** sensitivity 78%, specificity 35%
1 case-series[22] **Level II**	Recent inflammatory joint disease	Detect RA	**Best ARA or NY classification criteria (Yuden Index): RF (73), symmetrical polyarthritis (especially the NY** clinical criterion – 48), **morning stiffness (43) and x-ray changes (38)**

*PIP = proximal interphalangeal joints; Yuden Index (sensitivity + specificity −100; maximum = 100)

▷ Timing of referral (all evidence level 3)

Table 4.7 Function

Study	Patient group	Outcome	Result (best intervention)
1 case-series[26]	Early vs late referral	NHP physical function scores and mean HAQ scores.	**Early** Mean difference: 11.0, 95% CI 3.2 to 18.8, p <0.006 and 0.34, 95% CI 0.09 to 0.58, p <0.007
		Predictor of functional disability (MAP physical function score)	**Late was a predictor of functional disability** (increase of 8 points on the score)
		HAQ score	**Late referral not a predictor** (NS)
1 case-series[27]	Early vs late referral	Rate of RF+; % patients with erosions	**RF+** (similar – 75% vs 80%) **Erosions: groups similar** (until the delay to referral was >1 year – 35% vs 73%.

One case-series[15] found that patient-dependent factors (such as delay from the onset of symptoms to the assessment in primary care), leading to a delay in consulting primary care physicians, are the principal reasons for delay in patients with RA being seen by rheumatologists.

4.1.5 Summary of evidence statements

- The ARA criteria identify patients who are likely to have persistent synovitis and a poor prognosis, but do not perform well as diagnostic criteria in recent-onset RA.[17,18,20–22] The key clinical features to facilitate identification of patients who are likely to have persistent synovitis and a poor prognosis include:
  - the number of joints affected (the more joints the worse the prognosis)[18,22]
  - the presence of both swelling and tenderness in affected joints (particularly small joints)[18,19]
  - a positive MCP squeeze test[23]
  - the involvement of PIPs and MCPs,[23] and symmetry of joints affected
- An inability to make a fist or flex the fingers was associated with an ability to identify RA from other diagnoses in one study.[19] Ever having prolonged morning stiffness is more helpful than currently having morning stiffness for early RA.[23]
- Rheumatoid factor detects less than half of eventual RA patients at presentation[18]
- Acute phase markers are no different in patients with an inflammatory arthritis that evolves in RA than those that evolve into non-RA[23]
- Delays in referral are associated with worse function at presentation[26] and if delayed by 1 year an increase in erosive changes on x-ray[27]
- The most significant factor in delaying start of DMARD was delay in referral to a rheumatologist[27]
- There is evidence that the greatest delay in patients presenting to specialist care is in the patients attending their GP with symptoms in the first place, rather than the delay in patients being referred by the GP to specialist care.[15]

4.1.6 From evidence to recommendations

The GDG felt that a diagnosis of RA should be based on clinical findings such as history and examination, with investigations sometimes being helpful. The diagnosis should not be constrained by the ACR classification criteria, which are unhelpful in recent-onset disease. The ARA criteria were considered to be better prognostic guides than diagnostic guides in early inflammatory arthritis. In other words, if a person presents with small joint disease, then this carries a poor prognosis, and should lead to urgent referral to specialist care. The same considerations apply to the number of joints affected, where evidence suggests that the greater the number, the worse the prognosis, and the greater need for early identification and referral. The most important feature of recent-onset RA is the clinical detection of synovitis. This is a clinical skill, and in early RA all blood tests may be normal despite significant disabling disease. It was therefore considered important that this message was emphasised, and that normal investigations should not put a GP off referring patients urgently to secondary care. It was acknowledged that there is evidence that much of the delay in referral to specialist care is often beyond the control of the GP, and relates to the person themselves not presenting promptly at the start of their symptoms. Given the evidence that this delay increases the risk of damage to joints, and delays introduction of DMARDs, people who present to their GP with well-established disease should be referred urgently to specialist care to try to minimise any further damage, especially if symptoms have already been present for more than three months.

RECOMMENDATIONS

R1   Refer for specialist opinion any person with suspected persistent synovitis of undetermined cause. Refer urgently if any of the following apply:
- the small joints of the hands or feet are affected
- more than one joint is affected
- there has been a delay of 3 months or longer between onset of symptoms and seeking medical advice.

R2   Do not avoid referring urgently any person with suspected persistent synovitis of undetermined cause whose blood tests show a normal acute-phase response or negative rheumatoid factor.

4.2 Presenting symptoms and signs

4.2.1 Clinical introduction

The term RA covers a very broad spectrum of disease. For recent-onset RA some patients will have rapid onset of disease, and quick evolution to a polyarthritis. Others will have an insidious onset and perhaps months of a mono- or oligoarthritis before gradually evolving into a symmetrical peripheral pattern. Patients with recent-onset and with established disease may also have extra-articular features that impact on the severity and disability of the disease, such as interstitial lung disease and vasculitis. Others may have no obvious extra-articular disease, or relatively mild but nevertheless irritating symptoms such as dry eyes. It would be useful to be able to identify patients who are likely to have a poor prognosis early in the course of the disease. These patients could then be monitored more closely so that a lower threshold could operate for intensive intervention to modify the course of their aggressive disease. Conversely, in patients lacking poor prognostic markers, or possessing good prognostic markers, a less intensive follow-up and treatment strategy might be pursued. Are there any markers that might help to make management more targeted, depending on disease prognosis?

4.2.2 Clinical methodological introduction

We looked for studies that investigated which clinical features of RA patients (recent-onset and established disease) can be used to identify those with a good or poor prognosis. Due to the large volume of evidence on prognostic features, studies were selected which were of a UK-relevant population; if the population was mixed arthritis there had to be >75% RA or RA subgroup analysis, and a sample size N>200. We also looked for studies that assessed which treatments are the best for patients with a poor prognosis; no limits were set for selection criteria except for UK-relevant population.

Thirty-three case-series were found that fulfilled the inclusion criteria. All studies were methodologically sound and assessed the clinical features of RA patients who had either a good or poor prognostic outcome (patients were either followed prospectively or data was gathered retrospectively).

▷ Recent-onset RA

23 case-series[30–52] were found which fulfilled the criteria. They differed with respect to:
- sample size (range: N=211 to N=1387)
- study length (range: 1 year to 43 years)

▷ Established RA

10 case-series [53–62] were found which fulfilled the criteria. They differed with respect to:
- sample size (range: N=263 to N=2448)
- study length (range: 6 months to 50 years)

▷ Treatment of poor prognosis patients

Three RCTs[63–65] and 1 cohort study[66,67] were found which fulfilled the criteria for which was the best treatment for RA patients with a poor prognosis. All trials were performed on patients with UA or a recent onset of RA. The cohort study[66,67] was published as two separated papers with different follow-up times and therefore the study has only been counted once. However, results from both papers are reported and referenced here.

The three RCTs[63–65] were parallel group studies. The first two RCTs[63,64] looked at DMARD treatment (single vs combination) in patients with a recent onset of RA who had a poor prognosis (N=82 and N=20 respectively). The first RCT[63] compared two different treatment arms: sulphasalazine (SSZ) 500 mg/day vs cyclosporine A (CSA) 1.5 mg/kg/day + methotrexate (MTX) 7.5 mg/week + corticosteroid (CS) methylprednisolone in a 48-week treatment phase. The second RCT[64] compared two different treatment arms: MTX 7.5 mg/week + placebo vs MTX 7.5 mg/week + infliximab (IFX) 3 mg/kg/day in a one-year treatment phase with follow-up at one year post-treatment. The third RCT[65] looked at DMARD treatment in N=110 patients with UA of which N=51 went on to develop RA. The trial compared two different treatment arms: MTX vs placebo in a 30-month treatment phase and performed a subgroup analysis of the outcome of patients in each group who had a poor prognosis (anti-CCP+ or RF+). The methodological limitations of the RCTs were as follows: those graded 1+ were either unblinded, single blind or did not have an ITT (intention to treat) analysis. The trial graded 1++ was double blinded and the authors performed an ITT analysis.

The cohort study[66,67] looked at which was the best treatment in N=206 patients with a recent onset of RA who had a poor prognosis. The trial compared two different treatment arms: early treatment (DMARDs + NSAIDs) vs delayed treatment (NSAIDs then DMARDs) in a four-year treatment phase.

4.2.3 Health economic methodological introduction

The two questions were combined as the search terms were very similar. 144 abstracts were found, of which 142 were not specific for rheumatoid arthritis. The remaining two were ordered as full papers but subsequently did not meet the inclusion criteria (they were not economic evaluations). One paper[68] was found by a GDG member which had been published online after the searches were run. It met the inclusion criteria and so it was appraised.

4.2.4   Clinical evidence statements

▷   Recent-onset RA (all Level 3 studies)

Table 4.8   Radiological damage/disease severity

Study	Prognosis	Clinical features/predictors (at presentation)
1 case-series[36]	Severity of RA (radiological erosions) at follow-up (mean 6 years)	**Combination of RF, Hb (haemoglobin) and platelet level** (54% of patients). **Best single indicator: RF titre at onset** (value not given), **but greater accuracy when combined with other variables** (value not given)
1 case-series[42]	Radiological damage (presence of erosions or not by Larsen score) at 3-year follow-up	**RF, erosion score and nodules, and 1-year ESR** **Multivariate: combination of: RF and ESR** (PPV 68%), **1st year erosion score and ESR** (PPV 84%) **Not predictors (multivariate): erosion score, swollen joint count and nodules** (82%, PPV 77%)
1 case-series[49]	Radiographic progression (modified Sharp score) at 10 years	**Predictors: HAQ score and grip strength** (many regression coefficients given)
1 case-series[52]	Greater radiological progression (greater change in Larsen score at 2 years)	**Predictors: anti-CP+** (MD 2.8, pp =0.01) **and RF+** (data not given)
1 case-series[45]	Radiological damage (Sharp van-der Heijde score) at 3-year follow-up	Predictors (univariate): Joint damage (Sharp van-der Heijde score), high ESR, high HAQ score and poor physician global assessment. **Predictors (multivariate): joint damage – Sharp van-der Heijde score** (partial R^2 0.7, p <0.0001), **RF+** (partial R^2 0.003, p=0.048), **high ESR** (partial R^2 0.03, p <0.0001), **shorter time from diagnosis** (partial R^2 0.004, p=0.03), **worse overall patient estimation of health** (partial R^2 0.02, p=0.002) **Not predictor** (univariate): **RF+**
1 case-series[33]	Radiographic progression (Sharp scores) at 19 years follow-up	Predictors (univariate): ESR, joint count and grip strength **Predictors (multivariate): ESR, RF+, joint count, disease duration and grip strength** (R^2 range 0.45 to 0.47) Not predictor (univariate): Age and gender
1 case-series[31]	Radiographic progression (modified sharp score ≤30 or >30) at 5-year follow-up	Predictors (bivariate): RF+, ESR and radiographic damage (modified sharp score) **Predictors (linear regression): ESR** (regression coefficient 0.35, p <0.001), **Sharp score** (regression coefficient 1.5, p <0.001) **and CRP** (values not given) Not predictors (bivariate): HAQ and CRP **Not predictors (linear regression): physical function and RF+**

continued

Table 4.8 Radiological damage/disease severity – *continued*

Study	Prognosis	Clinical features/predictors (at presentation)
1 case-series[47]	Radiological damage at both 3 and 6 years	**Predictors: radiologic score** (change in score not given); **anti-CCP+** (6 years but not 3 years; change in score 0.9, p <0.05); **IgM RF+** (3 years and 6 years; change in score 6 years 2.4, p <0.0001); **DAS** (3 years; change in score 0.4, p <0.01)
1 case-series[50]	Radiological progression (change in Larsen score) and new joint involvement at 5-year follow-up	**Predictors: CRP levels** (correlation 0.59) and **number of damaged joints** (which **was worse in higher CRP groups** – low CRP group and high CRP group 7.3% and 39% of joints became damaged at 5 years)
1 case-series[44]	Radiological progression (change in Larsen score) at 2 years	Predictors (univariate): Larsen score (best predictor), anti-CCP+, RF+, high ESR and high CRP. Other predictors were greater age, smoking and male gender **Predictors (multivariate): Larsen score** (OR 14.9, 95% CI 8.0 to 27.6, p=0.0005), **anti-CCP** (OR 4.7, 95% CI 2.5 to 8.7, p=0.0005) and **ESR** (OR 2.0, 95% CI 1.1 to 3.5, p=0.025)
		Not predictors (univariate): pain (VAS) and HAQ
1 case-series[41]	Radiographic severity (Increase in Larsen score) at 2-year follow-up	Predictors (univariate): High CRP level (patients in the top third), high-titer RF, presence of nodules and being in the upper third of number of swollen joints. **Predictors (multivariate): top third CRP level and high RF titre** (regression coefficients 2.8 and 1.7)
	Radiographic severity (Increase in Larsen score) at 5-year follow-up	Predictors (univariate): Larsen score at 2 years (strongest), CRP was (less strong) and similar to high RF titre and presence of nodules **Predictors (multivariate): CRP and RF** (regression coefficients 2.0 and 2.7)
1 case-series[51]	Radiographic progression at 1-year follow-up	**Foot involvement. RF+ correlated with the presence of foot erosions and worse outcome** (values not given)
1 case-series[48]	Severe disease and worse radiological joint damage at 3-year follow-up	Predictors (univariate): RF+ and anti-CCP, more swollen joints and arthritis of the shoulders, elbows, proximal interphalangeal joints, knees and ankles **Predictors (regression): presence of swollen knee (predictor of severe RA:** OR 7.0, 95% CI 1.9 to 25.9, p=0.004), **total number of swollen joints (predictor of damage** at 1-year follow-up – regression coefficients 6.1, p=0.03) **and swelling of the knee (predictors of damage** at 1, 2 and 3-year follow-up: 3 years regression coefficient 3.5, p=0.005).
		Not predictors (univariate): Prevalence of swollen MCP and MTP joints
	Joint destruction at 1-year follow-up	**Predictors: total number of swollen joints** (regression coefficient 0.9, p=0.03), **anti-CCP+** (regression coefficient 8.4, p <0.001), **CRP level** (regression coefficient 0.02, p <0.01) and **symptom duration** (regression coefficient 0.2, p <0.001).
		Not predictors: Presence of knee arthritis

continued

Table 4.8 Radiological damage/disease severity – *continued*

Study	Prognosis	Clinical features/predictors (at presentation)
1 case-series[37]	Radiographic progression at follow-up (2 years)	**Predictors: anti-CCP+** (OR 7.8, 95% CI 2.5 to 24.0, p <0.001**), anti-MCV+** (OR 3.5, 95% CI 1.5 to 8.1, p <0.01), **RF+** (values not given) and **ESR** (OR 1.0, 95% CI 1.0 to 1.04); **therapeutic response at 6, 12 or 24 months (predicted less radiological progression**; OR 0.41, 95% CI 0.2 to 0.9)
1 case-series[39]	Radiographic progression (SHS) after 10 years	**Predictors (multivariate): anti-CCP+ (strongest predictor**: OR 4.0, 95% CI 1.6 to 10.0), **female gender** (OR 3.3, 95% CI 1.3 to 7.6), **high ESR** (OR 3.2, 95% CI 1.2 to 7.6) and **IgM RF+** (OR 3.1, 95% CI 1.2 to 7.9)
		Not predictors (multivariate): IgA RF and CRP
1 case-series[46]	More rapid decrease in joint score; worse joint score at 2–3 years follow-up	**APF– * patients; RF–APF– and RF+APF– (vs RF+APF+)** values not given
	Joint involvement	**Predictor: APF better than RF** (values not given)
	More involvement of the large joints and small joints	**APF+** (MD 0.3 and 1.3, p ≤0.01), **or anti-CCP** (values not given)
	Large joints (more rapid decrease)	**APF– (vs APF+;** 42% vs 23%, p=0.01); **NS for RF+ vs RF–**
	Small joints (more affected)	**RF+ (vs RF–) but NS**
	Worse radiological damage scores at 2–3 years follow-up (APF measured by CCP or IIF tests)	**APF+ (if RF+ or RF–) vs APF negatives** (median differences 4 or 8 for CCP tests or MD 12 and 8 for IIF tests, all p <0.05); **RF+APF+ (worst score), RF+APF- (intermediate score), RF–APF– (low score)** – values not given; **NS (RF+APF– vs RF–APF+); NS (RF–APF+ vs RF+APF+); RF+APF+ worse score (vs RF–APF–)** values not given
	Obvious radiological damage in the wrist (APF measured by CCP or IIF tests)	**NS (RF+ vs RF–); APF+ worse (vs APF–)**; 55% vs 36%, p=0.02 for CCP test and 53% vs 34% for IIF test
	More often had damage in small hand and foot joints (APF measured by CCP or IIF tests)	**RF+ (vs RF–,** 89% vs 73%) and **APF+** (vs APF–, 91% vs 73% for CCP test and 90% vs 71% for IIF test)
1 case-series[39]	Odds of radiographic progression	**Increase of 1 U/ml anti-CCP** (0.8% increase); **increase of 50 U/ml** (49% increase).
	More likely to develop radiographic progression	**Low to moderate levels (25 to 200 U/ml,** OR 3.5, 95% CI 1.5 to 8.4) and **high levels (>200 U/ml,** OR 13.3, 9%% CI 4.0 to 43.8) **worse [vs anti-CCP-patients (<25 U/ml)]; high levels worse (vs low to moderate**: OR 4.8, 95% CI 1.2 to 19.2)

continued

Table 4.8 Radiological damage/disease severity – *continued*

Study	Prognosis	Clinical features/predictors (at presentation)
1 case-series of BeSt study[40]	Higher radiographic progression scores	**RF+ or ACPA+* patients treated with: sequential monotherapy** (median differences 4.8 or 5.0), **step-up combination therapy** (median differences 1.5 or 2.2) **or initial combination therapy with IFX** (median differences 1.0 or 2.0); **Groups 1,2 and 4 (vs RF– or ACPA-patients)**
		NS difference between RF+ or ACPA+ (vs RF– or ACPA–) for patients treated with initial combination therapy with CS (group 3)
	Progressive disease	**Predictors: RF** (OR 4.7, 95% CI 1.5 to 14.5) and **ACPA** (OR 12.6, 9%% CI 3.0 to 51.9) **in patients treated with sequential monotherapy, but not the other treatment groups**

* APF = antiperinuclear factor; ACPA = anti-citrullinated protein/peptides antibodies

Table 4.9 Symptoms/function/disability

Study	Prognosis	Clinical features/predictors (at presentation)
1 case-series[36]	Functional status at follow-up (mean 6 years)	**Predictors: combination of RF, Hb and platelet count** (62% of patients)
		Not predictor: RF on its own
1 case-series[31]	Functional disability (HAQ) at 5-year follow-up	Predictor (bivariate): HAQ score, ESR and radiographic damage (modified Sharp score). **Predictor (regression): HAQ and age** (regression coefficients 0.59 and 0.008, p <0.001 and p=0.01)
		Not predictor (bivariate): RF+ and CRP **Not predictor (regression): radiographic damage**
1 case-series[47]	HAQ functional disability at both 3 and 6 years (6-year values given)	**Gender** (regression coefficient –0.13, p <0.05), **disease activity** (change in HAQ –0.09, p <0.005), **IgM RF+** (regression coefficient 0.15, p <0.05), **age** (change in HAQ 0.008, p <0.0001)
1 case-series[38]	Higher disease activity (physician's assessment and DAS28 score) and more swollen and tender joints	**Anti-MCV+* (vs anti-MCV–); anti-CCP+ (vs anti-MCV+/anti-CCP–** for physician's assessment); values not given
	CRP, ESR, physicians' assessment of disease activity, number of tender and swollen joints, DAS28 score, global VAS score, pain (VAS score); HAQ at 3 years	**NS: Anti-MCV+/anti-CCP– vs anti-MCV-/anti-CCP– (but anti-MCV+/anti-CCP– worse for HAQ)**

* anti-MCV = anti-modified citrullinated vimentin

Table 4.10 Mortality/development of serious disease

Study	Prognosis	Clinical features/predictors (at presentation)
1 case-series[30]	Mortality at follow-up (mean 16 years)	**Best predictor: combination of ExRA Malmo* and RF+** (data not given) **ExRA – Malmo criteria (strongest single predictor)**: RR 4.3, CI 2.9 to 6.3), **Presence of subcutaneous rheumatoid nodules and presence of RF (moderate predictors**: RR 1.5 and 1.9 respectively).
1 case-series[32]	Increased risk of mortality and CV events at follow-up (mean range 17 to 21 years)	Predictors (univariate): male gender, higher age at disease onset, earlier progression of erosions, higher ESR, CS treatment given early in disease. DMARD treatment (>2 drugs) was associated with decreased risk **Predictors (multivariate – increased risk): male gender** (RR 2.6, 95% CI 1.33 to 4.97, p <0.01), **higher age at disease onset** (RR 1.10/year, 95% CI 1.07 to 1.15, p <0.001) and **last value ESR** (RR 1.02 mm/h, 95% CI 1.01 to 1.03, p <0.001)
		Not predictors (univariate): prolonged/extensive CS treatment
1 case-series[34]	Mortality at follow-up (up to 23 years)	Predictors (univariate): Age (strongest predictor); HAQ disability (most important, better predictor in men than women), followed by global disease severity, pain, depression, anxiety and grip strength. Laboratory variables were less important **Predictors (multivariate): HAQ** (OR 1.97, 95% CI 1.5 to 2.5, p=0.000), **RF** (OR 1.1, 95% CI 1.0 to 1.2, p=0.002), ESR (OR 1.01, 95% CI 1.00 to 1.01, p=0.008), **radiographic progression** (OR 1.03, 95% CI 1.01 to 1.05, p=0.003), **age** (OR 1.07, 95% CI 1.05 to 1.09, p=0.000) and **male gender** (OR 2.73, 95% CI 1.95 to 3.83, p=0.000). **HAQ score over the first 2 years was a better predictor than baseline HAQ score** (values not given).
		Weak predictors (univariate): RF+, nodules and radiographic progression rates

* ExRA Malmo = extra-articular disease manifestations according to the Malmö criteria

Table 4.11 Remission

Study	Prognosis	Clinical features/predictors (at presentation)
1 case-series[35]	Remission at follow-up (up to 23 years)	Predictors (univariate): RF+ (latex test) values not given **Predictors (regression): ACR criteria, latex test RF+ and lower duration of disease** (values not given)
1 case-series[43]	Remission at follow-up (3 months, 6 months, 1 year, 18 months, 2 years and 5 years)	Predictors (univariate): gender, duration of disease, anti-CCP, RF, DAS28, HAQ **Predictors (regression): Male gender** (major predictor: 5 years OR 2.8, 95% CI 1.9 to 4.2, p=0.001), **short disease duration** (5 years OR 0.93, 95% CI 0.87 to 0.98, p=0.012), **low DAS28** (DAS28 5 years OR 0.67, 95% CI 0.57 to 0.79, p=0.001), **low HAQ** (HAQ 2 years OR 0.64, 95% CI 0.48 to 0.87, p=0.004), **RF–** (RF+ 5 years OR 0.56, 95% CI 0.38 to 0.82, p=0.003)
		Not predictors (univariate): SOFI index (signals of functional impairment)

▷ Established RA (all Level 3 studies)

Table 4.12 Radiological damage/disease severity

Study	Prognosis	Clinical features/predictors (at presentation)
1 case-series[61]	TJA (total joint arthroplasty) at follow-up (up to 23 years)	**Predictors (multivariate): ESR, WBC count, Hb level, HAQ disability score, global severity score, BMI, disease duration and smoking (past or current);** values not given.
1 case-series[53]	Radiological progression (change in Larsen score) at 5-year follow-up	**Predictor: RF status** (in patients with disease duration greater than 12 years only; MD 1.4 points/year, 95% CI 0.6 to 2.1, p=0.001)
		Not predictor: AFA* status

*AFA = antifilaggrin antibodies

Table 4.13 Function/disability

Study	Prognosis	Clinical features/predictors (at presentation)
1 case-series[55]	HAQ score at 8-year follow-up	**HAQ score** (R^2 0.77), **pain scale** (R^2 0.41), **number of work hours** (R^2 −0.41) and **global health status** (R^2 0.39); all $p < 0.001$
1 case-series[56]	HAQ score at 5-year follow-up	Predictors (univariate): RAI (Ritchie articular index) and CRP levels ($p < 0.001$) **Predictors (multivariate): RAI, pain (VAS), early morning stiffness and radiographic progression (modified Larsen score);** all $p < 0.001$
1 case-series[57]	Worse disability score at follow-up (mean range 1.7 to 12 years)	**Older age** (older vs younger cumulative RR 8.6), **female gender** (20% greater disability, $p < 0.05$**), elevated ESR 30–50 mm/h** (disability increase 0.9, $p < 0.05$) and **RF (latex) titres** (RF− = disability 0.7, RF 1:160-1:320 = disability 1.0, $p < 0.05$)
1 case-series[59]	More functional disability at 13 years follow-up	Predictors (univariate): higher age, longer disease duration; higher ESR scores over time; higher RAI scores, more pain and distress and more disability over the preceding years. **Predictors (multivariate): disease duration; disability, ESR and pain and distress over the preceding years** (multiple beta values given for each step of the model)
		Not predictor (multivariate): RAI over the preceding years
	More functional disability at 21 years follow-up	Predictors (univariate): female gender, longer disease duration; higher RAI scores, more pain and distress, less social companionship and more disability over the preceding years **Predictors (multivariate): gender, disease duration; RAI, disability and pain over the preceding years** (multiple beta values given for each step of the model)
		Not predictor (multivariate): social companionship, distress and ESR over the preceding years
1 case-series[62]	Low disability score (HAQ <0.5) at 6 months follow-up	**NS difference (RF+ or RF− patients)**

Table 4.14 Mortality/development of serious disease

Study	Prognosis	Clinical features/predictors (at presentation)
1 case-series[55]	Mortality at 8 years	**Age** (accumulated R^2 0.2), **followed by prednisone use, HAQ score and male gender** (accumulated R^2 all 0.3)
1 case-series[58]	Mortality at 2 years	Predictors (univariate): RF+, high levels of anti-CCP (but not anti-CCP+ >25U) **Predictors (multivariate): age** (HR 1.09, 95% CI 1.04 to 1.09, p=0.001), **gender** (HR 2.19, 95% CI 1.56 to 3.07, p=0.001), **RF+** (HR 1.55, 95% CI 1.10 to 2.19, p=0.01), **high IgA and IgM RF** (HR 1.0 both p <0.05), **subcutaneous nodules** (HR 2.04, 95% CI 1.49 to 2.79, p=0.001), **HAQ** (HR 2.03, 95% CI 1.63 to 2.53, p=0.001),
		Not predictors (univariate): RF+ and/or anti-CCP+, pANCA+ * and high ANCA* titres **Not predictors (multivariate): IgG RF, high anti-CCP, pANCA and high ANCA titres.**
1 case-series[60]	CVD and new onset coronary artery disease (CAD) at follow-up (mean 16 years)	**Presence of ExRA (adjusted for age, sex and smoking):** HR of CVD 3.78, 95% CI 2.00 to 7.16; HR of CAD 3.16, 95% CI 1.58 to 6.33.

*p-ANCA = perinuclear antineutrophil cytoplasmic antibodies; ANCA = antineutrophil cytoplasmic antibodies

Table 4.15 Remission

Study	Prognosis	Clinical features/predictors (at presentation)
1 case-series[62]	Remission at 6 months (patients receiving anti-TNFs)	**Male gender** (values not given), **age of patient <53 years** (OR 0.6, 95% CI 0.4 to 0.9), **RF+** (OR 0.6, 95% CI 0.4 to 0.96), **HAQ score <1.63** (OR 0.6, 95% CI 0.4 to 0.8)

▷ Treatment of poor prognosis patients

Table 4.16 Symptoms

Study	Treatment	Outcomes	Follow-up	Result – best treatment
1 RCT[64] **Level 1++**	IFX + MTX vs MTX	Reduction in synovitis (MRI)	14 and 54 weeks	**Arm 1** (p <0.05)
		DAS8 score	14 weeks	**Arm 1** (p <0.05)
		ACR20, ACR50 and ACR70		**NS**
		Reduction in bone oedema (MRI); ACR50 and ACR70	54 weeks	**Arm 1** (p <0.05)
		ACR20; DAS8 score		**NS**
		ACR20, 50 and 70; DAS8 score	2-year follow-up	**NS**

continued

Table 4.16 Symptoms – *continued*

Study	Treatment	Outcomes	Follow-up	Result – best treatment
1 RCT[63] **Level 1+**	CSA + MTX + methylprednisolone vs SSZ	Swollen joint count	24 and 48 weeks	**Arm 1**
		Pain (VAS), DAS28 score		**NS**
		Tender joint count	24 weeks	**Arm 1**
		ACR20 and ACR50, tender joint count	48 weeks	**NS**
1 RCT[65] **Level 1+**	MTX vs placebo	Number of patients developing RA and DAS score	30 months	**MTX (poor prognosis patients) NS (good prognosis patients)**

Table 4.17 Function

Study	Treatment	Outcomes	Follow-up	Result – best treatment
1 RCT[64] **Level 1++**	IFX + MTX vs MTX	HAQ score	14 and 54 weeks and 2-year follow-up	**Arm 1** (p <0.05)
1 RCT[63] **Level 1+**	CSA + MTX + methylprednisolone vs SSZ	HAQ score	24 and 48 weeks	**NS**

Table 4.18 Joint damage

Study	Treatment	Outcomes	Follow-up	Result – best treatment
1 RCT[64] **Level 1++**	IFX + MTX vs MTX	New erosions (MRI)	14 and 54 weeks	**Arm 1** (p <0.05)
		Radiographic progression (SHS)	14 weeks	**NS**
1 RCT[63] **Level 1+**	CSA + MTX + methylprednisolone vs SSZ	Radiographic progression – SHS (total score, erosions and JSN)	48 weeks	**NS**
1 Cohort study[66,67] **Level 2+**	Early treatment vs delayed treatment	Change in joint damage in patients with Sharp score >0	From 0–2 and from 0–4 years	**Early**
			1–4 years	**NS**
		Change in joint damage in patients with Sharp score 0	From 0–2 and from 0–4 years and 1–4 years	**NS**

continued

Table 4.18 Joint damage – *continued*

Study	Treatment	Outcomes	Follow-up	Result – best treatment
1 RCT[65] **Level 1+**	MTX vs placebo	Slowing radiographic progression (SHS score) in poor prognosis patients (anti-CCP+ or RF+)	30 months	**Arm 1** (p <0.001 or p=0.036)
		Slowing radiographic progression (SHS score) in good prognosis patients (anti-CCP– or RF–)		**NS**

Table 4.19 Global assessment

Study	Treatment	Outcomes	Follow-up	Result – best treatment
1 RCT[63] **Level 1+**	CSA + MTX + methylprednisolone vs SSZ	Patient's global assessment	24 and 48 weeks	**NS**

Table 4.20 Quality of life

Study	Treatment	Outcomes	Follow-up	Result – best treatment
1 RCT[64] **Level 1++**	IFX + MTX vs MTX	RA QoL score	14 and 54 weeks and 2-year follow-up	**Arm 1** (p <0.05)

Table 4.21 Biochemical markers

Study	Treatment	Outcomes	Follow-up	Result – best treatment
1 RCT[64] **Level 1++**	IFX + MTX vs MTX	CRP levels (AUC)	Over the 54 weeks	**Arm 1** (p <0.05)
			54 weeks to 2-year follow-up	**NS**
1 RCT[63] **Level 1+**	CSA + MTX + methylprednisolone vs SSZ	CRP and ESR	24 and 48 weeks	**NS**
1 Cohort study[66,67] **Level 2+**	Early treatment vs delayed treatment	Change in joint damage (RF+ and RF– patients)	2 years	**Early**

Table 4.22 Remission

Study	Treatment	Outcomes	Follow-up	Result – best treatment
1 RCT[64] Level 1++	IFX + MTX vs MTX	Remission time and remission rates	Over the 2 years	**Arm 1** (p <0.05)
1 RCT[63] Level 1+	CSA + MTX + methylprednisolone vs SSZ	Remissions (% patients, ACR)	48 weeks	**NS**

Table 4.23 Adverse events

Study	Treatment	Outcomes	Follow-up	Result – best treatment
1 RCT[64] Level 1++	IFX + MTX vs MTX	AEs	Over the 2 years	**Similar**

Table 4.24 Wthdrawals

Study	Treatment	Outcomes	Follow-up	Result – best treatment
1 RCT[64] Level 1++	IFX + MTX vs MTX	Withdrawals	Over the 2 years	**Similar**
1 RCT[63] Level 1+	CSA + MTX + methylprednisolone vs SSZ	Withdrawals due to lack of efficacy	48 weeks	**Arm 1**
		Withdrawals due to AEs		**NS**

4.2.5 Health economic evidence statements

No economic evaluations of a UK population were found. Konnopka et al.[68] is a Dutch study that evaluates the use of anti-CCP antibody testing compared to diagnosing RA using the ACR criteria. The model is populated with data not sourced through any formal evidence review, and the Markov model used is generally poorly explained. The assumption of the impact of a late diagnosis on HAQ progression is uncertain, and when varied from 0.01–0.15 causes the ICER to vary from dominance to over €153k per QALY. The baseline results estimate an ICER of €930 per QALY, although the differences in costs between aCCP strategy and ACR strategy (€15,010 and €14,995 respectively), and the differences in QALYs between the aCCP strategy and ACR strategy (7.1237 QALYs and 7.1073 QALYs) are relatively small.

4.2.6 Summary of evidence statements

In recent-onset disease most of the studies looked at radiological outcomes over variable follow-up periods. The themes that emerge are as follows:

- RF titre stands out as repeatedly being a good predictor of prognosis (both for radiology and function) in most studies.[31,33,36,41–44,47,48,51,52]
- Anti-CCP positivity is a predictor of prognosis.[44,48,52] Interactions with RF occur, so that the worst prognosis is seen for patients positive for both RF and anti-CCP, the best prognosis in those patients negative for both antibodies, and intermediate prognoses for those positive for one antibody only.[46] Other variables appearing to predict prognosis in more than one study include:
  - baseline radiological score,[31,42,44,45,47] nodules[41,42]
  - acute phase markers[31,33,41,42,45,48,50]
  - HAQ score[43,45,49]
  - grip strength[33,49]
  - swollen joint count.[33,41,48]

In established disease studies looked at a mixture of functional and radiological outcomes. Recurring themes are as follows:

- Disability is predicted by:
  - baseline disability score[55,57,61]
  - older age[57–59]
  - longer disease duration.[57–59,61]
- Women tend to do worse than men.[57,58]
- No study examined whether poor prognosis patients should be treated differently.

4.2.7 From evidence to recommendations

The GDG noted that currently there is not universal availability for testing of anti-CCP antibodies. The evidence does show that anti-CCP appears to add information over and above testing for rheumatoid factor as far as prognosis is concerned, with testing positive for a combination of both rheumatoid factor and anti-CCP being associated with a particularly poor prognosis. However, until there is evidence that a poor prognosis group identified in this way might need different management, this would not justify a recommendation for the routine use of anti-CCP testing in patients who were rheumatoid factor positive. It was also noted that an anti-CCP test could be useful in people who were positive for rheumatoid factor but in whom the clinical picture was not suggestive of rheumatoid arthritis. A positive anti-CCP test in these circumstances might suggest that the individual was at risk of developing RA subsequently and therefore merited close follow-up. However, there is currently only limited data available in this group of people, and the GDG agreed that a recommendation would be premature.

The GDG agreed that the evidence suggested that the principal strength of anti-CCP testing appeared to be in people who were seronegative for rheumatoid factor and in whom intensive combination therapy would be the initial treatment (see recommendation 16). In this group of people who might be reluctant to start intensive therapy for a recent onset of persistent synovitis without further specific tests relating to diagnosis and prognosis, being positive for anti-CCP might be used to inform their decision about taking such medication. The GDG concluded that a specific consensus recommendation for this group of patients would be appropriate, but that the introduction of more widespread testing for anti-CCP in other groups would need good evidence of cost-effectiveness and that this should form the basis of a research recommendation.

RECOMMENDATION

R3　Consider measuring anti-cyclic citrullinated peptide (CCP) antibodies in people with suspected RA if:

- they are negative for rheumatoid factor, and
- there is a need to inform decision-making about starting combination therapy (see recommendation 16).

4.3　Investigations

4.3.1　Clinical introduction

The identification of persistent synovitis is largely a clinical skill. However, there are investigations that can help to demonstrate that there are abnormalities that require intervention. Some of these may be non-specific, such as evidence of inflammation taking place (eg elevated C-reactive protein (CRP), anaemia of chronic disease), whereas others may be more helpful in pointing towards a diagnosis (eg rheumatoid factor present in high titres, erosive change on x-rays). Some investigations help to rule out other causes of polyarthritis or polyarthralgias, such as thyroid function tests. Other investigations are useful baselines that help in management, such as renal and liver function tests prior to commencing NSAIDs or DMARDs. In this section the focus is on those tests that help with early recognition of the disease, but it needs to be borne in mind that these do not replace the need for a careful history and examination, and even if all tests are normal, this should not prevent appropriate interventions from taking place in a patient with persistent synovitis. Antibodies against cyclic citrullinated peptides (anti-CCP) have emerged in recent years as being as sensitive, but more specific than rheumatoid factors in the diagnosis of RA. These are covered in section 4.3 on presenting signs and symptoms. There is evidence to suggest that ultrasound and magnetic resonance imaging (MRI) scans are superior to clinical examination in the detection of synovitis, and that they are more sensitive to the presence of erosions and other early inflammatory and damage signs than conventional x-rays.[69,70] However, the long-term significance of their findings, and the limited availability to many clinicians, restricts their utility, leaving the detection of synovitis on clinician examination as the gold standard.

4.3.2　Clinical methodological introduction

We looked for studies that assessed the ability of investigative procedures to identify patients with undifferentiated inflammatory arthritis who would go on to develop RA. Due to the large volume of evidence, studies were selected which were of a UK-relevant population, patients were pre-RA/had UA, if the population was mixed arthritis there had to be >75% RA or RA subgroup analysis, and had a sample size of N>50 (except for MRI or ultrasound studies). The studies found were diagnostic studies but with an element of prognostic design; they assessed the ability of investigative tests to predict patients who went on to develop RA (fulfilled the ACR criteria) at least 1 year after the test was performed.

Two MA,[71,72] 3 case-control studies[73–76] and 12 case-series[29,35,77–86] were found that fulfilled the criteria. One of the case-control studies was published as two separate papers[74,75] reporting different outcomes and so the study has only been counted once. However results from both papers are reported and referenced here. No studies were found on ultrasound. The case-series and case-control studies were included in addition to the MAs because these studies did not appear in the MAs or were published after the MA search cut-off date. Three of these studies did appear in the MAs and were included because they reported outcomes of interest that were not included in the MAs.

▷ Meta-analyses

The first MA[71] focused on all trials looking at anti-CCP tests for the diagnosis of RA and included N=68 trials with data. Of these, N=14 trials looked at investigative procedures predicting the development of RA (N=11 involved UA patients and N=3 involved RA patients who had given blood before developing RA). The MA itself was fairly well conducted, however no tests for heterogeneity were performed. Studies included in the analysis all used the same method for detecting anti-CCP antibodies (ELISA); however, they differed with respect to:

● Type of investigative test used (N=5 studies used anti-CCP1, N=10 trials used anti-CCP2).
● Cut-off for anti-CCP+ (anti-CCP1 range 21.4 IU to 1000 IU, anti-CCP2 3.8IU to 50 IU).
● Study size (UA patients for anti-CCP1: N=1,327; UA patients for anti-CCP2: N=2,017; RA patients given blood before RA development for anti-CCP1: N=79 and for anti-CCP2: N=142)
● Study duration – length of follow-up (UA patients: range 5–36 months; RA patients given blood before RA development: range <1.5 years to 9 years).

The second MA[72] looked at the diagnostic accuracy of anti-CCP tests and RF tests in patients with a recent onset of RA (<1 year duration) and included N=86 trials. Of these, N=37 studies looked at anti-CCP tests and N=50 at RF tests. Trials differed in terms of:

● Study size (range not mentioned)
● Study design (prospective in N=18/37 anti-CCP; N=25/50 RF)
● Study quality – maximum score of 5 (N=1 very good quality; N=22, 30% reasonable quality; N=9, 10% poorer quality)
● Study duration – length of follow-up (range not mentioned)
● Comparison group (mainly patients with UA; healthy patients; other diseases; other rheumatic diseases)
● Intervention – type of anti-CCP test (anti-CCP1 N=8; anti-CCP2, N=29)
● Intervention – type of RF test (IgM, IgA, IgG)

▷ Case-control studies

The 3 case-control studies[73–76] all looked at investigative tests which could be used to predict the development of RA in pre-RA/UA patients. The first two case-control studies[73–75] looked at investigative tests (RF and antifilaggrin antibodies(AFA), anti-CCP, RF and collagen types respectively) in people who were at risk of developing RA (both N=19,072). The studies compared cases (those who went on to develop RA) with matched controls (who did not develop RA) and had follow-up times of 22 years or 12 to 16 years respectively. The third case-control study[76] looked at investigative tests (RF and AFA) in N=330 patients with UA. The study compared cases (those who went on to develop RA) with controls (patients who already had RA) and had a 1-year follow-up time.

▷ Case-series

The 12 case-series[29,35,77–86] which investigative tests and procedures could be used predict the development of RA in pre-RA/UA patients. Studies differed with respect to:

- Sample size (range: N=30 to N=1,003)
- Study length (range: 1 year to 6.9 years mean)
- Investigative procedure/test used [RF, anti-CCP, ACPA (Anti-citrullinated protein/peptide antibodies), CRP, APF (antiperinuclear factor), ESR (erythrocyte sedimentation rate), MRI, symptoms, radiographs, histopathology, ACR criteria and others)

4.3.3 Health economic methodological introduction

No health economic papers were identified.

4.3.4 Evidence statements

Table 4.25 Rheumatoid Factor (RF)

Study	Patient group	Use	Results – baseline predictors
1 case-series[77] **Level II**	Patients with various inflammatory joint disorders	RA development vs no development	**RF latex test** (high sensitivity 0.70, high specificity 0.90)
1 case-control study[74,75] **Level III**	Population at risk (no previous history of arthritis or other rheumatic disease)	Risk of RA development (cases vs controls)	**NS: RF status**
1 case-series[78] **Level II**	Patients referred to Rheumatology clinic	RA development vs no development	**RF+** (more patients; 38% vs 11%)
1 case-series[82] **Level II**	UA patients	Predictor of RA development and distinguishing from other diagnoses	**Positivity of 2 of the 3 following tests: RF; antiperinuclear factors and the HLA DR4 antigen** (Sensitivity 51%, specificity 88%)
1 case-series[83] **Level Ib**	UA patients	RA development vs no development	**NS: RF+**
1 case-control study[76] **Level II**	UA patients	RA development (cases vs controls)	**RF+** (significantly more cases – 42% vs 12%, p <0.001)

continued

Table 4.25 Rheumatoid Factor (RF) – *continued*

Study	Patient group	Use	Results – baseline predictors
1 case-series[85] **Level II**	Patients with synovitis	RA development vs no development	**GAL0*** (significantly higher levels – 77% vs 14%, p <0.001)
		Predictor of RA development	**ARA clinical criteria** (68% patients), **RF+** (83%), **GAL0 levels** 78%
1 case-series[29] **Level II**	UA patients	Predictor of RA development	**RF+** (univariate 44% vs 14% p <0.001 and multivariate OR 2.3, 95% CI 1.2 to 4.2 p=0.009)

*GAL0 = IgG that lack galactose

Table 4.26 Anti-CCP

Study	Patient group	Use	Results – baseline predictors
1 MA/SR[71] **Level III**	UA patients	Predictor of RA development	**Anti-CCP+ (anti-CCP1:**OR 20, 95% CI 14 to 31; **anti-CCP2:** OR 25, 95% CI 18 to 35)
1 MA[72] **Level III**	UA patients	RA diagnosis	**Anti-CCP better than RF** Sensitivity: a-CCP 67% (95% CI 65 to 68), RF 69% (95% CI 68 to 70) Specificity: a-CCP 95% (95% CI 95 to 96), RF 85% (95% CI 84 to 86) LR+ a-CCP 12.5 (95% CI 9.7 to 16.0), RF 4.9 (95% CI 4.0 to 6.0) LR– a-CCP0.36 (95% CI 0.3 to 0.4), RF 0.38 (95% CI 0.3 to 0.4) **IgM RF+ plus anti-CCP+ even better** LR+ 15.7 (95% CI 8.3 to 29.8) LR – 0.46 (95% CI 0.4 to 0.6)
1 case-control study[74,75] **Level III**	Population at risk (no previous history of arthritis or other rheumatic disease)	RA development (cases vs controls)	**Antibodies to CCPs** (higher mean levels: 173 vs 16.1, p=0.00008)
1 case-control study[76] **Level II**	UA patients	RA development (cases vs controls)	**NS: anti-CCP**
1 case-series[84] **Level II**	UA patients	RA development vs no development	**IgA, IgM, IgG2 and IgG3 anti-CCP (higher frequencies and levels**-data not given but **all NS); number of isotypes of anti-CCP response (higher and higher levels**-data not given, **but all NS)**
		Risk of RA development within 1 year of follow-up	**IgA anti-CCP+** (RR 1.3, 95% CI 1.0 to 1.7), **IgM anti-CCP** (RR 1.4, 95% CI 1.1 to 1.8) or **IgG anti-CCP** (RR 1.4, 95% CI 1.1 to 1.8).
1 case-series[29] **Level II**	UA patients	Predictors of RA development	**Anti-CCP+** (univariate 51% vs 11%, p <0.001 and multivariate OR 8.1, 95% CI 4.2 to 15.8, p <0.001)

- One MA/SR[71] reported three studies which looked at patients with RA who had donated blood samples before development of RA. **Level III**
  - One study found that anti-CCP2 predicted RA development with low sensitivity (4%, 25% and 52% at 9 years, >1.5 years and <1.5 years before symptoms) and had a high specificity (98%). OR 28 (95% CI 8 to 95).
  - One study did further analysis of the same patients and found that anti-CCP2 had highest predictive value compared to RF; OR 15.9 for anti-CCP2 and 6.8 for RF.
  - One study found that 5 years before symptom onset, anti-CCP1 had a low sensitivity and high specificity for predicting RA (29% and 99.5% respectively; OR 64.5 (95% CI 8.5 to 48.9).

Table 4.27 AFA (antifilaggrin antibodies)

Study	Patient group	Use	Results – baseline predictors
1 case-control study[73] **Level III**	Patients who were at risk (had history of arthritis or other rheumatic diseases)	Risk of developing RA (RF+ or RF–)	**AFA (significant for RF+ RA** – increased ORs at all quintiles of AFA level; **NS for RF– RA)** **NS: interaction RF and AFA**
		<5 years and 5 to 10 years to disease onset	**Elevated AFA** (higher risk of RF+ RA – increased ORs at all quintiles of AFA level); weak association >10 years
	RA patients and control patients		**Baseline RF and AFA associated to same extent** (ORs at all quintiles of AFA level)
1 case-series[77] **Level II**	Patients with various inflammatory joint disorders	RA development vs no development	**AFA** (moderate sensitivity 49% and high specificity 95%)

Table 4.28 APF (antiperinuclear factor)

Study	Patient group	Use	Results – baseline predictors
1 case-series[77] **Level II**	Patients with various inflammatory joint disorders	RA development vs no development	**APF** (moderate sensitivity 47% and high specificity 96%)
1 case-series[81] **Level II**	UA patients	Predictor of RA development vs no development	**APF** (fairly high sensitivity and specificity; 77% and 75%)

Table 4.29 CRP

Study	Patient group	Use	Results – baseline predictors
1 case-control study[74,75] **Level III**	Population at risk (no previous history of arthritis or other rheumatic disease)	Risk of RA development (cases vs controls)	**NS: CRP**
1 case-series[83] **Level Ib**	Polyarthritis	RA development vs no development	**NS: CRP**
1 case-control study[76] **Level II**	UA patients	Risk of RA development (cases vs controls)	**NS: CRP**
1 case-series[29] **Level II**	UA patients	Predictor of RA development	**Significant: CRP** (univariate median level 14 vs 8, p <0.001 and **multivariate 5–50 mg/titer** OR 1.6, 95% CI 0.9 to 3.0, p=0.13; **>50 mg/titer** OR 5.0, 95% CI 2.0 to 12.1, p=0.00)

Table 4.30 Radiographs and MRI

Study	Patient group	Use	Results – baseline predictors
1 case-series[79] **Level Ib**	UA patients	Predictor of RA development	**Erosions typical of RA; hand radiographs** (low sensitivity and fairly high specificity – 23% and 88%; NPV 66% and PPV 50%)
		Predictor of RA diagnosis 2 years later	**Hand radiographs** (low sensitivity, fairly high specificity – 30% and 85%; NPV 60% and PPV 58%)
1 case-series[83] **Level Ib**	Polyarthritis	Predictor of RA development	**MRI – OMERACT score for erosions in the MCP joints and the second and third MCP joints** (fairly high specificity and sensitivity – 70% and 64%)
		Distinguish RA development and other diseases	**NS: radiographs (carpus erosions and MCP erosions); MRI – OMERACT score (synovitis and tenosynovitis; carpus erosions)**
1 case-control study[76] **Level II**	UA patients	RA development (cases vs controls)	**NS: erosive disease (hands and feet) and SHS score**

Table 4.31 Other			
Study	**Patient group**	**Use**	**Results – baseline predictors**
1 case-series[77] Level II	Patients with various inflammatory joint disorders	RA development vs no development	**AKA** (low sensitivity 31%, high specificity 99%)
1 case-series[78] Level II	Patients referred to Rheumatology clinic	RA development vs no development	**Most patients: histological changes considered to be RA+** (77%), **distinctive IgM staining** (RA+, immunofluorescence, 88%); **high white cell counts** (77%)
1 case-series[80] Level Ib	Newly referred patients	RA development vs no development	**Most patients: at least 1 swollen joint** (96%); **a-pepA Abs** (best sensitivity, h specificity); **RF test + ACPA test** (increased PPV); **one serologic marker + swollen joints** (increased PPV) – data values not given
1 case-series[85] Level II	Patients with synovitis	RA development vs no development	**Significant: GAL0** (higher levels – values not given)
		Predictor of RA development	**ARA clinical criteria** (68% patients); **RF+** (83%) and **GAL0 levels** (78%); **RF+/GAL0** (high predictive ability – 91% of patients; 90% sensitivity, 95% specificity and 94% PPV)
1 case-series[86] Level Ib	UA patients	Predictor of RA development 1 year later	**No extra value: ACPA testing + HLA shared epitope** (values not given) **RF testing + ACPA testing better than RF alone** (especially for patients with at least 1 swollen joint); values not given

*AKA = antikeratin antibodies; ACPA = anti-citrullinated protein/peptide antibodies; GAL0 = IgG that lack galactose

4.3.5 Summary of evidence statements

- RF in most studies is a useful predictor of RA development.[29,76–78,82,85]
- Anti-CCP positivity is a useful predictor of RA development,[29,71,74,75,84] and in comparison to RF appears to have a higher specificity, but similar sensitivity.[71,72]
- Baseline CRP is a poor predictor of who will go on to develop RA.[74–76,83]
- AFA had a moderate sensitivity and specificity for the development of RA and was better at predicting the development of RF+ RA than RF– RA.[73,77,78,82]
- APF had a moderate sensitivity and specificity for the development of RA.[77,78,81,82]
- Baseline erosions on hand x-rays show high specificity but low sensitivity for the development of RA.[79]
- Erosions on MCP MRI scans have a fairly high sensitivity and specificity for the development of RA.[83]

4.3.6 From evidence to recommendations

Although anti-CCP antibodies are more specific than rheumatoid factor, this difference is not great, and sensitivities seem very similar. Recommendations on anti-CCP also need to be informed by health economic analysis to determine whether the extra cost and increased specificity render this test cost-effective (please refer to section 4.2.7 and 4.2.8), either for all early inflammatory arthritis, or for sub-groups (eg RA suspected, but rheumatoid factor negative). Rheumatoid factor remains a relatively cheap and useful test in undifferentiated synovitis that is helpful both diagnostically and prognostically.

After much deliberation, it was decided that x-rays of the hands and feet in early synovitis are worthwhile, because although this is a blunt instrument in detecting joint inflammation, there are occasions when erosive damage will be detected when all other tests are normal, and it also acts as a readily accessible base-line for future determinations of disease progression. As ultrasound and small joint MRI become more widely available, the long-term significance of some of the early inflammatory and erosive changes that have been described using these imaging modalities should become apparent and they may replace x-rays.

RECOMMENDATIONS

R4   Offer to carry out a blood test for rheumatoid factor in people with suspected RA who are found to have synovitis on clinical examination.

R5   X-ray the hands and feet early in the course of the disease in people with persistent synovitis in these joints.

5 | Communication and education

5.1 | Patient perceptions and beliefs

5.1.1 Clinical introduction

Guidelines are ultimately produced for the benefit of patients and it is appropriate that this guideline includes a section on the beliefs and perceptions that patients have about their disease. A paternalistic approach in which the healthcare professionals know best, and the patient is a passive recipient of care, should be a distant memory of how medicine might once have been practised. Many patients understandably desire to be active participants in their own care, and the associated decision-making process. However, even when professionals strive for patient involvement in disease management, there is still scope for disconnection between patients, their carers, and their healthcare professionals. This applies to the perception of the disease and therapeutic interventions, and the priorities for their healthcare needs.

Some pre-conceptions about RA in newly diagnosed patients may need to be addressed early in the disease course. Patients who attend their first clinic appointment may already have received a disease label diagnosis from their GP, and this may have led to their hearing a number of myths and rumours about the disease. These may have been alluded to by well-meaning but ill-informed friends and relatives, and sometimes, unfortunately, other health professionals. Some pre-conceptions about the disease may have to be addressed before appropriate perceptions and beliefs can be fostered.

For people with established RA it will be important to appreciate that their perceptions of RA and their priorities in its management might differ from those of the multidisciplinary team (MDT) managing them.

Although this is a very broad field, the two key areas that need to be addressed are:
- What patient experiences, perceptions and beliefs exert positive impacts on symptoms, joint damage, function and quality of life, and which of these can be identified, fostered and encouraged by the patient themselves and those seeking to help them?
- Conversely which patient experiences, perceptions and beliefs exert a negative impact and need to be minimised or avoided by the patient themselves and those seeking to help them?

5.1.2 Clinical methodological introduction

We looked for studies that investigated patients' experiences of RA and its treatments. Due to the large volume of evidence, studies were only included if they had been published within the last 10 years (1997 onwards); for non-qualitative studies they had to have a sample size of N>100 and a UK-relevant population, and if the population was mixed arthritis there had to be >75% RA or RA subgroup analysis.

▷ Recent-onset RA

Eight studies were found[31,87–93] that fulfilled the criteria. Studies differed with respect to the following:

- sample size (range: N=68 to N=573)
- study length – follow-up (range: immediate to five years)
- study design (N=6 observational-correlation studies; N=1 observational-longitudinal study; N=1 cross-sectional study; N=1 retrospective observational study of an RCT).

▷ Established RA

25 studies were found[94–117] that fulfilled the criteria. Two papers[94,95,98–102,104,107–109,111, 113–115,117–120] reported the same study but different outcomes. Results from both papers have been reported here but this study has been counted once. Studies differed with respect to the following:

- sample size (range: N=6 to N=7,702)
- study length – follow-up (range: immediate to five years)
- study design (N=13 observational-correlation studies; N=7 qualitative studies; N=4 cross-sectional studies; N=1 case-control study; N=1 observational study).

▷ Disease duration mixed (recent-onset and established RA) or not mentioned

Five studies were found[119,121–124] that fulfilled the criteria. Studies differed with respect to the following:

- sample size (range: N=10 to N=190)
- study length – follow-up (N=4 trials immediate, N=1 trial 1 year)
- study design (N=2 observational-correlation studies; N=2 qualitative studies; N=1 cross-sectional study).

5.1.3 Health economic methodological introduction

No health economic papers were identified for this question.

5.1.4 Clinical evidence statements

All studies were evidence grade 3, except for the qualitative studies which were given a 3+.

▷ Recent-onset RA

There were several main themes that emerged from the studies.

Areas of life worst affected and how the disease impacts patients (four studies)[87,88,90,119]

Observational studies found that pain, lack of control over pain and dissatisfaction with abilities affected psychological wellbeing, self-esteem and adjustment to disease. High levels of anxiety and depression were associated with fatigue, pain and low acceptance. Additionally,

54

patients who experienced more fatigue were more at risk of pain, were more disabled, felt more depressed, had lower self-esteem, were less satisfied with the support provided to them, showed more reduction in leisure activities, felt less independent and adjusted, and appraised their health as markedly less well.

Care – areas patients found important, areas for improvement – including information provision (one study)[119]

The observational study found that patient knowledge and the need for information was the same for patients with a recent onset of disease as for those with established RA.

Correlations between demographics, disease characteristics and disease measures (four studies)[31,89,91,92]

Observational studies found that:

- Women were significantly worse than men for many measures of symptoms, function and QoL, but not for pain, hand x-ray abnormalities or CRP level.
- Quality of life was weakly associated with clinical and laboratory variables and patients' global assessment was associated with pain, depression, disability and tender joints.
- Physical health status outcomes were predicted by baseline values of HAQ, AIMS physical, high age and AIMS psychological health status. Baseline HAQ and AIMS physical were associated with physical disability. Psychological health status was predicted by AIMS psychological dimension.
- Older, less anxious patients (STAI-SF) were significantly more likely to discontinue to take their initial DMARDs within the first year. Continuing to take DMARDs was associated with HAQ, relationship with hospital doctors (RHD), beliefs about medication questionnaire (BMQ), and significant others scale (SOS).

Attitudes to treatment (including preferences and effectiveness); one study of the BeSt trial[93]

- There was not significant (NS) difference between the four treatment groups for 'much' to 'very much' improvement of general health since start of treatment, or for current state of health with the medication they had to take (however, group 3 were less satisfied). Groups 1 and 2 had significantly less rapid relief of symptoms than groups 3 or 4 but had NS difference from each other.
- Patients' preference for a particular group before start of study: no preference (44%); only group 3 had an effect of group allocation – 22% of patients who actually received this treatment had hoped not to be assigned to group 3, whereas this percentage was much higher (>40%) in the other groups.
- Treatment patients would prefer if diagnosed with RA today: treatment with one well-known antirheumatic drug (21%); combination without prednisone (19%); combination with prednisone (12%); combination with the newest IV drug (IFX at the time) 44%.
- Patients' feelings about taking prednisone: 50% of patients assigned to group 3 disliked taking prednisone (15%, 20% and 9% in groups 1, 2 and 4 respectively).

- Patients' feelings about going to hospital for IV treatment: 8% of group 4 patients disliked having to go to hospital for IV treatment (2%, 3% and 2% in groups 1, 2 and 3 respectively).

▷ Established RA

There were several main themes that emerged from the studies.

Areas of life that patients most wanted improvement (2 studies)[97,115]

- Observational and qualitative studies found that patients most wanted improvement in pain, function (hand and fingers) and walking and bending. Patients wanting improvements in pain had a lower pain self-efficacy, greater fatigue, worse global health and used more analgesic drugs. Older people most wanted improvement in function, whereas younger patients' priorities were pain, work and mental conditions. When footwear was discussed, women wanted more information and time on which to base their choice, they wanted to voice their opinions and know that they were being listened to, and acknowledged that they understood their disease. A feeling of trust in the practitioner was seen as an important factor in the consultation. Men did not mention any aspect of their experience that needed improving.

Areas of life worst affected and how the disease impacts patients (10 studies)[94,95,98,100,104,107–109,111,114,115,118]

Observational, qualitative and case-control studies found that:
- Areas that caused major problems for patients were: their identity (private and public sphere), physical activities of daily living (ADLs) which they valued, quality of life (QoL), pain, physical and mental fatigue, decreased activity, depression, loss of confidence and motivation, frustration, self-consciousness or embarrassment at deformities, effect on relationships and family life.
- Patients were concerned about: the future (increases in pain and disability); the inefficacy of treatments, inabilities (to carry out ADLs, to be sexually active, to work – and its financial implications, to go out due to pain).
- Ongoing emotions expressed by patients were: grieving and anger due to the loss of ability to do things while making necessary changes in lifestyle, courage to confront daily pain and apparent losses, fear of the future and of medication side-effects, frustration and depression.
- A number of patients found they had to persuade themselves and others of the authenticity of their RA (the disease was 'invisible' in the early stages and people don't understand the disease). Because of negative reactions, some patients pretended to be well when they were not. Patients wanted to feel valued by society (have their difficulties appreciated and understood). They also felt an essential form of support was to receive validation and understanding from family. Family/friends often tended to overestimate the severity and characteristics of pain and to underestimate negative effects of RA on the patient's life. Physicians, on the contrary, tended to underestimate pain severity and characteristics. It is important for spouses to understand their partners' views on their control over RA and its cyclic nature, have optimistic views and not to underestimate the consequences of RA.

56

- Patients had to mastermind new 'lifeways' (find methods of disease management, adapt to changes, develop new skills and reconcile lost abilities). Accommodations were widely used to perform daily activities. These included limits and more time for more activities, assistance and devices.
- Patients' experiences of pain were described as: variable (80%), unpredictable (68%), causing major interference with paid work or domestic chores (67%), underestimation of pain by the spouse (23% patients) and by the physician (14% patients), by other family members or friends (38%).
- Women had poorer QoL outcome scores than men. QoL declined with age. The impact of RA on mental health was lower in patients <50 years old compared to other age groups.
- Women were concerned about the look of their feet and their footwear whereas none of the men talked about appearance. Men were positive about footwear and both felt it helped their mobility and reduced pain.
- RA affected patients' physical identity, social role and self-image and many changed their physical appearance to accommodate restrictions or tried to hide physical deformities.
- The importance of disease outcomes changes with time and depends on circumstances (eg at different stages of disease and during flare-ups).

Care – areas patients found important, areas for improvement – including information provision (10 studies)[94,95,98,99,101,102,113,115,117,119,120]

Observational and qualitative studies found that:
- Areas of care most important to patients were: knowledge of RA (no difference between those with recent-onset and established RA); information about concomitant medication and about medication efficacy and side-effects; communication (to be clear and effective and positive relationships with practitioners valued); access to practitioners between scheduled appointments; access to other departments; familiarity with the staff.
- Areas of care deemed inadequate were: MDT care (lack of modified toilet in the practice, having access to their file, choice of care provider, information on RA, course of symptoms, aids and home adjustments, good care coordination and being open to questions); limited contact with providers; lack of continuity of care; social support (unhappy having to rely on partners or family members); to be more involved in medical decisions (although some wanted the doctor to take more control as the disease gets worse).
- Patients wanted more information (especially women; no difference between recent-onset and established RA patients) and the content to be about: diagnosis, pathogenesis and medication; exercise; daily activities; the disease as they get sicker; purpose of lab tests; other ways to treat a problem. Many felt there was a lack of clear and unambiguous information throughout their treatment and lack of general advice on services available and claiming financial benefits. They wanted both verbal and written information.
- Satisfaction with care: somewhat satisfied or very satisfied (68%); experienced unmet healthcare needs (particularly physical symptoms, consequences of disease – body structures and function, quality of care and healthcare services, 27%). Unmet healthcare needs were associated with worse health, more comorbidities and dissatisfaction; there were concerns about communication (with healthcare professionals). Women trusted the practitioners' skills regarding footwear, but felt negatively about the way they were treated

by the assessors who often dismissed their concerns and needs. Men felt differently – they had some camaraderie with and trusted the skills of the practitioners.

- Decisions about treatment efficacy were based upon symptom reduction, 'forgetting you have RA', change in priorities for outcomes over time, magnitude of improvement/change varies with disease duration.

- Patients wanted to feel in control of their condition and tended to refuse interventions as a way of gaining control; they felt hope when medical staff searched for new treatment options. Treatments gave them improvement in symptoms, helped them get back to normal, and gave them better sleep. Biologics particularly had positive physical and emotional effects. Satisfaction with medication was significantly greater among patients taking biologics than those not taking them.

- Most patients would not want to change their therapy (including those on biologics) as long as their condition didn't get worse. Many felt their physician thought they did not need to change or there were no better medications than those they were currently taking and some did not want IV administration or injection.

- Complementary therapies: many had tried one or more for their pain including acupuncture and massage. One patient mentioned they 'can't do without…acupuncture and massage…and heat really helped'. Many were told they had no choice but to take toxic drugs to slow deterioration or alleviate their symptoms and were concerned about side-effects. Nearly all patients hoped that new research would find a cure.

- Many patients wanted better feedback from secondary care. Primary care was described in both complimentary and critical ways (delays in diagnosis and early care).

- Many patients presented themselves to healthcare staff as a 'coper' or tried to please staff 'by not being a nuisance'. They were more at ease with nurses than doctors, and only half of them were receiving treatment from other MDT members. The presence of medical or nursing students and, for female patients, seeing a male doctor, made a number of patients feel uncomfortable, especially when talking about personal issues (gynaecological/emotional).

Correlations between demographics, disease characteristics and disease measures (12 studies)[96,100–103,106,110,112,116,117,119]

Observational studies found that:

- Predictors of poorer outcomes (including disability, pain and QoL) included: pain, fatigue, RA duration disease activity, depression, radiological damage, female, older age, less favourable socioeconomic status, had paid work less often and were less often married/co-habiting, higher disease activity, more somatic/psychological comorbidity, higher number of activities affected by RA.

- Low involvement in decisions was associated with: younger age, greater satisfaction with care, living with a partner, still working, longer time in formal education, less comorbidities, lower disease activity, lower fatigue and lower levels of pain. High involvement in decisions was associated with: younger age, high levels of formal education, high levels of received patient information and high levels of patient satisfaction.

- The need for information was associated with: age and education (in women) and with fatigue, number of DMARDs taken and experience of AEs (in men). Decision-making preferences was associated with: age, education, number of DMARDs and RA knowledge (in women) and RA knowledge (in men).

- Poor function, greater impairment and disability in valued activities was associated with lower satisfaction with physical abilities, which was in turn associated with greater depression.
- High levels of anxiety and depression were predicted by higher pain, fatigue and lower acceptance.
- Passive coping was a psychological predictor of both pain and depression, and a mediator of the impact of physical disability on both pain and depression.
- Patients with RA performed significantly less non-vocational activities compared to 1 and 10 years before but were positive about their ability to perform more activities in the future.
- Performing a large number of activities was correlated with a good mental health status or psychological well-being, and the reverse was true for a low number of activities performed.
- SF-36 role physical correlated with the number of activities patients performed in past (1 year but not 10 years), at present and the number planned to pursue in the future. SF-36 physical function, however, only correlated with the number planned to pursue in the future.
- The patient's disability was a stressor for patients but not for partners. Stressors for partners and not patients were negative transactions and marital quality and the patient's disability was linked to the partner's burden. The effect of marital quality on the patient's distress depended on the partner's burden.
- Many patients with poor HAQ or PAS scores (ie poor function or disease activity levels), were satisfied with their RA control, while others with 'good' scores were dissatisfied.
- Purpose in life was associated with (multivariate): younger age, participation in leisure/social activities, better mental health and an optimistic coping style.

▷ Disease duration mixed (recent-onset and established RA) or not mentioned

Areas of life worst affected and how the disease impacts patients (2 studies)[122,123]

Observational and qualitative studies found that:
- Patients either regarded RA as a challenge for mastery in their lives and were actively trying to master it, or they adapted to their disease and felt it was 'something to get used to' and 'made the best out of a bad situation'.
- Employed patients had significantly lower depression than those not employed.

Treatment – preferences and decision-making (2 studies)[121,124]

Observational and qualitative studies found that:
- Patients' views as to who should choose medicine (patients who had not used anti-TNFs): rheumatologists (41%); decide themselves (33%); unsure (18%); joint decision (7%). Men were significantly more likely to want rheumatologists and there was NS difference between young and old patients. Some patients did not feel confident to make decisions without further support and discussion with healthcare staff and one patient felt that within internet information, 'death was quoted an awful lot'.

● Patients' views as to who should choose medicine (patients who had used anti-TNFs): all patients wanted to be involved – and those who had been involved found shared decision-making positive and beneficial.

● Four ways (themes) in which treatment decisions had been arrived at:

1. **Relinquished decision** 'leave it in the hands of the doctor' as the 'doctor knows best';

2. **Forced/informed choice** the doctor's preference maybe because he had more success with a particular drug so he 'pushed it…whereas the other drug might be the one that you really want'

3. **Shared decision** 'allowing you to come back to another consultation…[to] go away and [do some] thinking. You have to be sure it's the one *you* want'

4. **Patient choice:** patients choose for themselves, 'information should be provided in such a way as not pushed into it'.

● The majority of patients using splints for hand/wrist RA indicated that their splint use was dependent on the seriousness of the symptoms. They wore them in order to reduce symptoms and to support and immobilize the wrist. They stopped wearing the splint when they had reduced functional abilities and when performing dirty or wet activities.

Correlations between demographics, disease characteristics and disease measures (two studies)[119,123]

Observational studies found that:

● RA knowledge and the need for information was NS different between patients with long (>10 years) and short (<1 year) disease duration.

● High fatigue, pain, greater functional disability and low acceptance were predictors of high anxiety and depression and lower life satisfaction. Psychological wellbeing was correlated with optimism, pessimism and perceived stress but not with healthcare social support, active cognitive and behavioural coping, disease duration, inflammation, antidepressant use and presence of comorbidity. General social support significantly correlated with lower depression and greater life satisfaction.

● Among patients with lower stress, there was little effect of active behavioural coping on depression and life satisfaction. However, among those with higher stress, engaging in active behavioural coping was related to lower depression and greater life satisfaction.

5.15   Summary of evidence statements

Observational and qualitative studies yielded the following findings for patients with RA.

● They often experienced a lack of information (especially AEs of medication, other options for treatment, aids and devices and home adjustments);[94,95,98,99,101,102,113,115,117,119,120] wanted more involvement in decisions about their management.[101,102]

● In many cases patients still had unmet healthcare needs and wanted improvements within each area of the multidisciplinary team.[97–99,101,115] Areas of their lives most affected and where patients wanted improvement were: pain, function, ADLs and hobbies.[94,95,97–102,113,115,117,119,120]

● QoL and disease status measures were often worse in women than in men.[89,97,115] Priorities for younger patients were pain, work (see Occupational therapy section in section 6) and anxiety and depression.[97,115]

● The main priority for older patients was function.[97,115]

- Pain, fatigue, depression, loss of function, loss of valued activities, interference with ADLs and inability to work were problems for many patients with RA.[87,88,90,94–103,106,110,112,113,115–117,119,120]

- Poor psychological status was often associated with poorer outcomes of symptoms, function and QoL.[31,87–92,96,100–103,106,110,112,116,117,119]

5.1.6 From evidence to recommendations

The GDG noted that the evidence highlighted a number of problems faced by people with RA that are often not acknowledged satisfactorily by healthcare professionals. These include pain and fatigue, depression, mobility, inability to work or undertake leisure and social activities, and impact on sexual relationships. Many of these aspects and complications of their disease would best be discussed with appropriate members of the multidisciplinary team (see section 6.1), and there should also be an opportunity to raise any of these issues at annual review (see section 8.2). However, the GDG felt that it was pragmatic to have a specific recommendation for patients ensuring that periodic assessment of their disease encompassed these important factors, and this should form part of a recommendation relating to the multidisciplinary team (see section 6 on multidisciplinary teams).

The GDG also noted the evidence that patients want more involvement in the management of their disease. Because of the long-term nature of rheumatoid arthritis and (from the patient's point of view) changing priorities over time, the GDG felt that regular discussions with patients about all aspects of their treatment (including the advantages and disadvantages of different therapeutic options) was advisable. This view was strongly advocated by patient representatives, who also emphasised the crucial need to allow sufficient time for these discussions with healthcare professionals in ways that could be easily understood and acknowledged the importance of patient autonomy in decision-making.

RECOMMENDATION

R6   Explain the risks and benefits of treatment options to people with RA in ways that can be easily understood. Throughout the course of their disease, offer them the opportunity to talk about and agree all aspects of their care, and respect the decisions they make.

5.2   Patient education

5.2.1   Clinical introduction

In helping people with RA participate fully in decision making about treatment, it seems appropriate to provide information and education about their disease, treatment and how they might help themselves in managing their disease. Quality information giving is required by all health professionals, as part of their codes of conduct, to enable people to understand their condition and make decisions about treatment. This is usually provided informally on a one-to-one basis in clinic, with educational materials (eg leaflets, books, DVDs, arthritis websites). Patient education goes beyond improving knowledge and is 'a planned, organised learning experience designed to facilitate voluntary adoption of behaviours and/or beliefs conducive to health'.[125] It additionally focuses on enabling people to effectively self-manage, ie 'monitor one's condition and effect the cognitive, behavioural and emotional responses necessary to maintain a satisfactory quality of life'[126] through use of educational, motivational and behavioural techniques. This can be provided 1:1, through self-study or computer based interventions or in formal organised group sessions led by rheumatology health professionals or trained lay leaders with arthritis or other chronic conditions. Different formats may be used: an educational approach of lecture/discussion sessions to increase knowledge, satisfaction and reduce concerns; or a behavioural, also termed psychoeducational, approach, including regular skills practice, goal setting, contracting and use of home programmes to facilitate behavioural change.

Information giving and patient education programmes can be time consuming and it is therefore important to consider the benefits of such interventions. A balance needs to be struck between efforts invested by people with RA and health professionals, and the benefits gained. What is the evidence that education exerts an impact on symptoms, disease progression, function and quality of life? In particular:

- Having been provided with information, do people with RA retain the information provided and find this of benefit?
- Having undergone a patient education programme (1:1 or group) does this lead to sustained benefits or is improvement only short-term?
- Are there stages during a person's disease in which different educational interventions are more likely to be successful? Is patient education more likely to be helpful if it is provided in recent-onset than established disease?
- Are there any methods of delivering patient education that are more successful than others?

It was decided to exclude formal cognitive behavioural therapy as being beyond the scope of this question, but educational programmes using a behavioural approach are considered. Please note that NICE has published a technology appraisal on 'Computerised cognitive behaviour therapy for depression and anxiety'.[127]

5.2.2 Clinical methodological introduction

We looked for studies that investigated the benefits and harms of different patient information provision and/or educational methods and/or different patient education or self-management programmes, with respect to symptoms, joint damage, function and quality of life in patients with a recent onset of RA or in patients with established RA. Due to the large volume of evidence, only RCTs were selected which were published from 1997 onwards, had a sample size of N≥50, had a UK-relevant population and if this was mixed arthritis there had to be >75% RA or RA subgroup analysis. Trials were also selected which compared the following:

a) education/self-management vs other education/self-management methods
b) education/self-management vs usual care

NOTE: Due to the inclusion/exclusion criteria for studies set for this review, some useful evidence was excluded, namely the long-term UK Arthritis Self-management Programme.[128,129]

▷ Mixed population (recent-onset and established RA)

It was decided that for this question, due to the large amount of evidence on education and self-management programmes, it would be useful to include a published meta-analysis[130] MA even though it did not separate the RA population into recent-onset and established disease.

One Cochrane SR/MA[131] was found that fulfilled the criteria and focused on RCTs which compared patient education interventions (that included an instructional component) vs a no intervention control group in patients with recent-onset and established disease. The 'no intervention' control group did receive some intervention as they interacted with the healthcare professional making their assessments. The MA itself was well conducted; however, the 31 RCTs it included were of varying quality and differed with respect to the following:

- blinding (N=7 RCTs double blind; N=20 RCTs single blind; N=23 RCTs no blinding)
- study size (range N=18 to N=1,140)
- study quality – maximum score of 8 (N=21 studies reasonable to good quality (1+ and 1++); N=29 poor quality(1–))
- study duration – length of intervention (range: 7 hours to 15 months)
- study duration – length of follow-up (range: 8 days to 18 months).

NOTE: Because the Cochrane MA pooled together papers which had patients of both recent-onset and established RA, it was decided that duplicate papers (ie papers picked up in our search which were already included in the MA) would still be included as evidence in this section for either 'recent-onset' or 'established' RA in order to tease out any effects on these sub-populations. Results reported here from the MA, were pooled from the N=17 high quality RCTs only (data from low quality studies was excluded).

▷ Recent-onset RA

Four RCTs[132–136] were found that fulfilled the criteria. One of these RCTs was published as two separate papers[134,135] reporting different outcomes and so the trial has only been counted once, however results from both papers are reported and referenced here. The methodological limitations of the RCTs were as follows: those graded 1+ (3 RCTs) were single blind and ITT analysis was not performed. The RCT graded 1++ was blinded and ITT analysis was performed.

All four RCTs were single-blind, parallel group studies, but they differed with respect to the following:

- sample size (range: N=64 to N=326)
- trial length (range from 3 months to 4 years post-intervention)
- treatment (1 RCT[132] of education programme + DMARDs vs education leaflet + DMARDs; 1 RCT[133] of standard education programme vs cognitive-behavioural education programme; 1 RCT[134,135] of a standard education programme vs a joint protection education programme; 1 RCT[136] of a self-management occupational therapy (OT) programme vs usual care).

▷ Established RA

Nine RCTs[137–145] were found that fulfilled the criteria. Three of these RCTs[137,140,142] were excluded as evidence due to methodological limitations (not blinded and ITT analysis was not performed). The methodological limitations of the remaining included RCTs were as follows: those graded 1+ were either single blind (3 RCTs) and/or ITT analysis was not performed (2 RCTs). The remaining RCT was graded 1++ as it was both single blind and ITT analysis was performed.

The 6 included RCTs[138,139,141,143–145] were all parallel group studies, but they differed with respect to the following:

- sample size (range: N=59 to N=363)
- blinding (4 RCTs single blind, 2 RCTs unblinded/blinding not mentioned)
- trial length (range: 4 weeks to 1-year intervention; follow-up ranged from immediate to 9 months post-intervention)
- treatment (1 RCT[137] included a standard education programme vs standard care; 1 RCT[138] of an education programme + leaflet vs standard care + leaflet; 1 RCT[140] of group education with significant other vs patient only group education vs control self-help guide; 1 RCT[142] of spouse-included self-management programme + usual care vs patient only education programme + usual care; 1 RCT[143] of ACR RA leaflets + mind map vs ARC RA leaflets; and 1 RCT[145] of an education programme + information leaflet vs usual medical care + information leaflet).

5.2.3 Health economic methodological introduction

No health economic studies were appraised.

5.2.4 Evidence statements

Table 5.1 Mixed population (recent-onset and established RA)				
Study	Treatment	Follow-up	Outcomes	Result – best treatment
Cochrane MA[131] **Level 1++**	Patient education vs no intervention	1st and final follow-up	Joint counts, anxiety, ESR, CRP	**NS**
		1st follow-up	Disability, patient global assessment, psychological status and depression	**Education** (p=0.01, p=0.03, p=0.01, p <0.001)
		Final follow-up	Disability, patient global assessment, psychological status and depression	**NS**

▷ Recent-onset RA

Education/self-management vs usual care

- One RCT[136] found that the self-management/occupational therapy (OT) programme was significantly better than the control (no intervention) groups for: use of some self-management methods (particularly hand and arm exercises, joint protection and rest); receipt of a working splint and a resting splint; owning and use of assistive devices. However there was NS difference for: DAS28, HAQ, AIMS2 scores and for self-efficacy (ASES) score. **Level 1++**

Table 5.2 Special education (CBT or joint protection) vs standard education programmes

Study	Treatment	Outcomes	Follow-up	Result – best treatment
1 RCT[133] **Level 1+**	CBT education programme vs standard education programme	Morning stiffness; pain (VAS); tender and swollen joints; ESR	3 months post intervention	**NS**
		AIMS2 physical function and effect; RAI arthritis helplessness subscale	3 months post-intervention	**CBT** ($p=0.009$ and $p=0.01$; $p=0.003$)
			6 months post-intervention	**NS**
		AIMS2 subscales of current health and symptoms); RAI arthritis internality subscale; total self-efficacy scale	6 months post-intervention	**NS**
1 RCT[134,135] **Level 1+**	Joint protection education programme vs standard education programme	Pain (VAS); tender and swollen joints; joint damage (numbers of deformities); grip strength; hand joint alignment and motion; AIMS2 scores; ASE dimensions; number of patients taking RA medication and participating in OT; RAI (Rheumatoid helplessness index) measure of helplessness	12 months and 4 years post-intervention	**NS**
		Early morning stiffness; AIMS2 dimension of ADLs; joint protection behaviour assessment; number of visits to doctor in previous 6 months		**Joint protection** ($p=0.01$ and $p<0.05$; both: $p=0.04$; $p=0.001$; $p<0.01$)
		Hand Pain (VAS); assessor's and patient's global disease status; number of disease flare-ups; number of patients participating in physiotherapy	12 months	**Joint protection** ($p=0.02$; $p=0.003$ and $p=0.03$; $p=0.004$; $p=0.005$)
			4 years post-intervention	**NS**

Education programme vs education leaflet

- One RCT[132] found that there was NS difference between education programme + DMARD and the education leaflet + DMARD for DAS score, M-HAQ score and range of motion – shoulders, elbows and knees, AIMS subscales, CRP, compliance with activities and joint protection (but education significantly better for compliance with energy conservation). **Level 1+**

▷ Established RA

Table 5.3 Education programme vs standard care

Study	Treatment	Follow-up	Outcomes	Result – best treatment
1 RCT[139] Level 1+	Education programme vs standard care	24 weeks	Total number of withdrawals pain scores; joint inflammation (articular Index); morning stiffness; CRP	Similar NS
1 RCT[145] Level 1++	Education programme + leaflet and usual medical care + leaflet	1 year	Morning stiffness; DAS28	NS
1 RCT[146] Level 1+	Education programme (joint protection) + drug treatment (IFX) vs drug treatment (IFX)	8 months	Pain (VAS) and HAQ; AIMS 2 dimensions of physical, symptoms and social interaction	Education (p <0.001; p <0.05)
			RAI, AIMS 2 dimensions of psychological and work	NS
1 RCT[138] Level 1++	Education programme vs standard care	1 year	PKQ – patient knowledge, p=0.0002	Education
			Improvements in Larsen scores, HAQ, SF-36 dimensions of social functioning and general health perception, RAI, compliance	NS
1 RCT[145] Level 1++	Education programme + leaflet and the usual medical care + leaflet	1 year	Coping; QoL (EMIR) symptomatic dimension; patient satisfaction; knowledge	Education (p=0.03; p <0.0001; p=0.02)
			Physical activity (Baecke questionnaire – sports activity and hobbies), behavioural changes, nocturnal awakening, HAQ (QoL), HADS anxiety and depression, QoL (EMIR dimensions); fatigue (FACIT-F)	NS

- One RCT[146] found that 75% of patients found the education programme very useful and only 8% found it not useful at all for ADLs.

Table 5.4 Education/self-management programme (patient + significant other) vs education programme (patient only)

Study	Treatment	Follow-up	Outcomes	Result – best treatment
1 RCT[143] **Level 1+**	Spouse Included self-management programme + usual treatment vs the Patient only education programme + usual treatment	2 weeks and 6 months post-intervention	Increased communication	**Spouse + patient education** (p <0.001)
			Disease activity; DAS28 score; DAS score; IRGL dimensions (mobility, dexterity and pain); psychological functioning (IRGL dimensions); disease stressors: pain, limitations and dependence (CORS); coping – decreasing activity; marital satisfaction (MMQ); social support (IRGL dimensions); spousal criticism; total number of withdrawals	**NS or similar**
1 RCT[141] **Level 1++**	Patient + significant other education programme vs patient only education programme	12 months (3 months post-intervention)	Fatigue	**Education for patients only** (p=0.001)
			Disease activity; DAS28 score; DAS score; all Self-efficacy and health behaviour measures; effects on social interactions; use of self-management activities and active coping strategies	**NS**

Education programme vs education leaflet

- One RCT[141] found that there was NS difference between patient + significant other education programme and education leaflet for DAS28 score, self-efficacy measures, all health behaviour measures; Use of self-management activities; degree to which people use active coping strategies – Dutch Coping with Rheumatoid Stressors). However education programme with significant other programme was significantly worse for fatigue p=0.04). **Level 1++**

ARC booklet + mind map vs ARC booklet

- One RCT[144] found that there was NS difference between the ARC booklet + mind map vs ARC booklet groups for: Increase in knowledge.
  The same RCT[144] found that poor reading ability leads to poor knowledge which is associated with more anxiety and depression. **Level 1+**

5.2.5 Summary of evidence statements

The Cochrane meta-analysis[131] showed patient education had small, short-term effects on disability, joint counts, patient global assessment, psychological status and depression. There was no evidence of long-term benefits. Education groups generally do not show benefit compared with controls. One RCT showed no difference between an education programme and education leaflets for a range of outcomes.[132] Another RCT showed that a one-to-one education programme compared with standard care only resulted in improved patient knowledge and adherence to treatment, but no difference for a range of other outcomes.[138,139] There was some evidence of short-term benefits in hand pain, number of disease flare-ups and global assessments, joint protection behaviour and a long-term (4 years) decrease in morning stiffness, and decreased visits to the GP, though there was no change in use of conventional drugs.[134,135] The same studies showed less development of some hand deformities, and although there was no functional hand improvement,[134,135] some short and long-term improvements in aspects of activities of daily living were seen.[133–135] One RCT[136] found that the self-management/OT programme was significantly better than the control (no intervention) groups for use of some self-management methods and for receipt and use of splints and other assistive devices.

Cognitive behavioural approaches seemed to have short-term benefits for mood and decreased a sense of helplessness,[133] but other trials showed no improvement.[134,135] Attending a programme with a carer or 'significant other' did not improve outcomes on the whole.[141,143]

5.2.6   From evidence to recommendations

The GDG noted that there was an enormous amount of information from which it was difficult to tease out precisely what was, and what was not, effective. The GDG noted that there were many potential confounding factors. There was no doubt that patients want to be given clear explanations during the course of their disease, and that they wish to receive this in both written and verbal forms. Although there was some evidence that in established disease written information can improve some outcomes, no studies were identified which evaluated written information in recent-onset disease. There have been very few evaluations of structured 1:1 patient education programmes, and the GDG felt that this was one of a number of areas where further studies were needed. Nevertheless, in view of the clear wishes of patients to receive both written and verbal information about their condition, the GDG felt that it was appropriate to make a recommendation to this effect.

A recurring feature of many studies was the demonstration of short-term, but not long-term, benefits. The GDG felt that this was an area where it would be sensible to make a research recommendation about the provision of refresher courses which might overcome this problem; these would also enable patients who do not wish to receive information early on, the opportunity to obtain this at a later date.

The GDG noted that the provision of programmes for patients that encourage self-management is now considered a fundamental aspect of care for all long-term conditions, and that there was evidence that group education, led by healthcare professionals using a behavioural approach, was effective in this regard for people with RA. Most studies of group programmes led by trained lay people using a behavioural approach, such as the Arthritis Self Management Programme and Chronic Disease Self Management Programme have been with community-based volunteers with a range of rheumatological diagnoses. The GDG felt that there was currently insufficient evidence to justify these programmes specifically for RA (although an appropriate research recommendation was made), but the generic concept of attending lay-led self management programmes was supported.

In summary, the GDG noted the lack of clearcut evidence in many areas, the need for further research, and the clear desire of patients to have access to a wide range of educational activities.

It was accordingly felt appropriate to make a rather general recommendation supporting a range of activities that might already be available until such time as further studies (including cost effectiveness data) have identified the most appropriate educational methods.

RECOMMENDATIONS

R7   Offer verbal and written information to people with RA to:

- improve their understanding of the condition and its management, and
- counter any misconceptions they may have.

R8   People with RA who wish to know more about their disease and its management should be offered the opportunity to take part in existing educational activities, including self-management programmes.

6 The multidisciplinary team

6.1 The multidisciplinary team

6.1.1 Clinical introduction

A multidisciplinary team approach (incorporating various healthcare professions such as specialist nurses, physiotherapists, occupational therapists and podiatrists) is often used in the management of patients with rheumatoid arthritis. The composition of the team in any individual centre will vary, but emphasis should be placed on the tasks required to care for the individual patient's needs, with the aim of minimising the impact of the disease. This combined approach brings together the skills and knowledge of all team members, for both the assessment and management of disease but requires a high level of communication and cooperation. The patient can often be an active member of the team, in order to address and manage all aspects of care.

This chapter of the guideline assesses the evidence for the effectiveness of all of the interventions traditionally delivered by individual members of the multidisciplinary team. Details of the specific interventions offered by physiotherapists, occupational therapists, and podiatrists are summarised in the relevant sections. The role of the rheumatology nurse specialist is summarised below.

▷ The rheumatology nurse specialist

The rheumatology nurse specialist is an integral part of the multidisciplinary team caring for patients with rheumatoid arthritis. Although the role may vary depending on the needs of the service, most nurses will have clinical, educational and advisory aspects as part of their work. Rheumatology nurse specialists may also be involved in research, management and strategic development. However the key feature of these posts is to ensure the physical, emotional and social wellbeing of people with rheumatoid arthritis using a patient centred approach.

▷ Clinical

Most rheumatology nurse specialists will run nurse-led clinics where they assess and treat patients working in close collaboration with the consultant rheumatologist. This will usually involve examination of the joints, assessment of the patient's overall condition and wellbeing, monitoring blood results of patients on immunosuppressive drug treatments and requesting and reviewing investigations. Some rheumatology nurse specialists will perform joint injections, prescribe and alter treatments and carry out other therapies such as infusions. The rheumatology nurse specialist is usually the professional who is the main co-ordinator of care within the multidisciplinary team, referring to team members and other agencies as required.

▷ Education, support and advice

The diagnosis of rheumatoid arthritis can be devastating and in conjunction with the team members the rheumatology nurse specialist will be able to offer support and advice to help reduce the fear and anxiety such a diagnosis can bring. Detailed explanations of diagnosis, drug therapies and other managerial strategies and therapies can be provided by the rheumatology nurse specialist at the onset and throughout the course of the condition. Due to the impact of the disease process and concerns over therapies instigated, a key element of the rheumatology nurse specialist role is to provide an easily accessible point of contact for patients and their carers. Most rheumatology nurse specialists will provide this service through a telephone helpline. In collaboration with the multidisciplinary team many rheumatology nurse specialists have developed or assist with patient self management groups in order to empower patients and help them develop coping strategies.

Education is an important element of the role and most rheumatology nurse specialists act as a resource for their colleagues and the wider healthcare community. Some will be involved in the development and running of rheumatology educational programmes for healthcare professionals. These may range from study days to formal diploma, degree and MSc courses in association with a university in order to increase knowledge and expertise in caring for patients with rheumatoid arthritis.

Although the entire GDG (and most especially the patient representatives) acknowledged the role of the rheumatoid nurse specialist as described above, it was felt inappropriate to look for evidence around the role of just this one profession and hence the role of the multidisciplinary team (MDT) was addressed in its entirety.

6.1.2 Clinical methodological introduction

We looked for studies that investigated the benefits and harms of multidisciplinary teams on patients with RA (recent-onset and established disease). Selected studies were of a UK-relevant population and if this was of mixed arthritis there had to be >75% RA or RA subgroup analysis.

Five RCTs[147–152] and three case-series[153–155] were found that fulfilled the inclusion criteria. One of the RCTs was published as two separate papers[148,149] reporting different follow-up times and so the trial has only been counted once. However, results from both papers are reported and referenced here. Two of the RCTs[151,152] were excluded as evidence due to methodological limitations (unblinded and ITT analysis was not performed). The methodological limitations of the remaining included RCTs were as follows: they were all graded 1+ as they were either single blind or ITT analysis was not performed.

▷ Recent-onset RA

Two case-series[154,155] of N=110 and N=70 patients respectively, evaluated the effects of a multidisciplinary team (MDT) care programme on patients with recent-onset RA. Prier et al.[154] had a 3-month treatment phase whilst Nordmark et al.[155] had a 2-year treatment phase.

▷ Established RA

Three RCTs[147–150] and one case-series[153] were found for patients with established RA.

The three RCTs compared MDT care to either non team care (N=59) (Ahlmen),[147] routine out-patient care (N=68) (Vliet Vlieland, Vljeland)[148,149] or waiting list control (N=68) (Scholten).[150] All had a 1-year treatment phase with follow-up at 2 years (Vlijeland) and 5 years (Scholten).

The case-series[153] looked at the effects of a MDT care programme on N=92 patients and had a 3-week treatment phase with follow-up at 3 months.

6.1.3 Health economic methodological introduction

One study was identified and appraised. Van den Hout et al.[156] is a Dutch cost-utility study comparing clinical nurse specialist care, inpatient multidisciplinary team care and day patient multidisciplinary team care. Two papers[157,158] were excluded for not being specific to a multidisciplinary team.

6.1.4 Clinical evidence statements

▷ Recent-onset RA

Symptoms, function and quality of life

- One case-series[154] found that the MDT care programme led to a NS change in QoL (AIMS) at 3 months follow-up. **Level 3**
- One case-series[155] found that after 2 years of MDT care, all patients experienced significant decreases in pain (mean change in VAS: range –16 to –24, all p <0.05) except for those who stopped working and were receiving sickness benefit. **Level 3**

Knowledge and satisfaction

- One case-series[154] found that patients who attended the MDT care programme had a significant increase in knowledge of RA at the 3-month follow-up (mean increase test score 6.2, p <0.0001). **Level 3**

Use of RA treatments

- One case-series[155] found that for patients who attended the MDT care programme there was: no change in the number of patients receiving DMARDs; and the number of patients receiving MTX or combination therapy with MTX increased from 8% to 41% at 2-year follow-up (end of team treatment programme) as did the number receiving corticosteroids (increase from 11% to 15%). **Level 3**

▷ Established RA

Symptoms

- Two RCTs[147–149] found that there was NS difference for RAI at 12 weeks,[147] 52 weeks and 104 weeks.[148,149] Also NS difference was found for self-rated physical discomforts (body symptoms scale, BSS), and LAI (Lansbury articular index – joints painful on pressure or motion) at 12 weeks[147] and pain (VAS), number of swollen joints, fatigue and grip strength at 12 weeks, 52 weeks, 104 weeks;[148,149] ACR20 at 104 weeks.[148,149] **Level 1+**
- One RCT[148,149] found that inpatient MDT care was significantly better than routine outpatient care for: morning stiffness at 12 weeks (MD 2.62, p <0.05) and ACR20 at 12 weeks (MD 10.0, p <0.05) and 52 weeks (MD 18, p <0.05). **Level 1+**

- One case-series[153] found that patients who attended the MDT care programme had significant improvements in: DAS (mean change –0.59, 95% CI –0.8 to –0.38, p <0.001), pain, VAS (mean change –12, 95% CI –17 to –7, p <0.05), swollen joints (mean change –3.3, 95% CI –5.2 to –1.4, p <0.05), and RAI (mean change –1.6, 95% CI –2.5 to –0.7, p <0.05) at 3 months follow-up and 26% and 52% of patients fulfilled the ACR20 and EULAR response criteria. **Level 3**

Function

- One RCT[148,149] found that there was NS difference between inpatient MDT and routine outpatient care for: HAQ at 12 weeks, 52 weeks and 104 weeks. **Level 1+**
- However, another RCT[150] found that MDT care programme significantly improved HAQ disability score (0–5 scale) at 52 weeks (mean change –0.4, p <0.001) and at 5 years (mean change 0.9, p <0.0001). **Level 1+**
- One case-series[153] found that patients who attended the MDT care programme had significant improvements in: HAQ (mean change –0.16, 95% CI –0.24 to –0.08, p <0.05) and SOFI (mean change –2.6, 95% CI –3.5 to –1.7, p <0.05) at 3 months and 26% and 52% of patients fulfilled the ACR20 and EULAR response criteria respectively. **Level 3**

Global assessment

- One RCT[148,149] found that inpatient MDT treatment was significantly better for patient's global assessment of disease activity (VAS) at 4 weeks (MD 3.9, p <0.05), 12 weeks (MD 3.3, p <0.05) and 52 weeks (MD2.8, p <0.05) at 4 weeks, 12 weeks and 52 weeks, however there was NS difference at 104 weeks. **Level 1+**
- One case-series[153] found that patients who attended the multidisciplinary care programme had significant improvements in: patient's and physician's global assessment of disease activity (VAS mean change –13, 95% CI –18 to –8, p <0.05) at 3 months follow-up. **Level 3**

Quality of life

- One RCT[147] found that the MDT care group was significantly better for: overall health (Sickness Impact Profile – SIP; MD 3.5, p <0.05) but NS for MACL (mood) scores at 12 weeks. **Level 1+**
- One RCT[148,149] found that inpatient MDT treatment was significantly better than routine outpatient care for: anxiety (scale 0–10) at 12 weeks (MD 3.3, p <0.05), but NS 52 weeks and 104 weeks; depression (scale 0–10) at 12 weeks (MD 2.4, p <0.05), but NS at 52 weeks and 104 weeks. **Level 1+**
- One RCT[150] found that at 52 weeks, MDT care programme significantly improved coping with illness (FQCI scale 5 to 25), (mean change –1.9, p <0.01) and Beck depression score (scale 0–63), (mean change 2.5, p <0.001). **Level 1+**

Biochemical markers

- Two RCTs[147–149] found that there was NS difference between the two groups for CRP at 12 weeks[147] and ESR and CRP at 12 weeks, 52 weeks and 104 weeks.[148,149] **Level 1+**

- One case-series[153] found that patients who attended the MDT care programme had significant improvements in ESR (mean change −6, 95% CI −10 to −3, p <0.05) at 3 months follow-up. **Level 3**

Use of medication/treatment

- One RCT[147] found that there was NS difference between the two groups for: use of medication (DMARDs, NSAIDs and corticosteroids) at 12 weeks. **Level 1+**
- One RCT[150] found that at 52 weeks, MDT care programme significantly improved the use of joint protection devices (mean change 68.5%, p <0.001), regular relaxation exercises (mean change 60.5%, p <0.001) and regular remedial gymnastics (mean change 26.3, p <0.001). **Level 1+**

6.1.5 Summary of evidence statements

In recent-onset RA the roles for the multidisciplinary team include:

- recognising the importance and efficacy of work and social roles and ensuring that patient can fulfil these[155]
- usually being responsible for patient education[154]
- ensuring that patients have access to a wide range of professionals with different knowledge and skills[154]
- monitoring the disease and appropriate alteration of DMARD therapy in order to maintain good control.[155]

In established RA the multidisciplinary team may:

- be helpful in monitoring and ensuring good disease control,[148,149,153] and also in aiding improvement in patient's mood and coping with the disease in the short-term.[147–150] However, there is a lack of evidence to show whether or not there is any benefit in the long-term[148,149]
- influence patient function,[150,153] however it should be noted that the evidence is contradictory.[148,149]

6.1.6 From evidence to recommendations

Despite the lack of demonstrated benefit, the consensus opinion of the GDG recognised the importance of the multidisciplinary team, and that it could provide a variety of services to the patient with RA using knowledge and skills that complemented those of the rheumatologist, addressing issues above and beyond the purely medical problems in both recent-onset and established RA. It was also noted that the opportunity for patients to raise any issues about their disease (a need identified in the patient perceptions and beliefs section – see section 6.3) could be most appropriately addressed by ensuring that patients were offered ongoing access to the MDT.

Despite the paucity of evidence, the GDG supported the view of the patient perspective that non medically qualified members of the MDT (eg specialist nurses) seemed to have more time with patients in assessing disease activity and monitoring the impact of drugs in treating their disease. Multidisciplinary team partnership working is a core element to the seamless delivery of good patient care as highlighted by the Quality for All Darzi report of June 2008. There is a concern that in the absence of a multidisciplinary team approach, individuals may work in isolation, care may either be fragmented or duplicated and this will in turn affect the quality of care received by the patient. Therefore the GDG consensus view was that it is important to have one nominated member of MDT team nominated named as the person responsible for coordinating their patient care.

RECOMMENDATIONS

R9   People with RA should have ongoing access to a multidisciplinary team. This should provide the opportunity for periodic assessments (see recommendations 36 and 37) of the effect of the disease on their lives (such as pain, fatigue, everyday activities, mobility, ability to work or take part in social or leisure activities, quality of life, mood, impact on sexual relationships) and help to manage the condition.

R10   People with RA should have access to a named member of the multidisciplinary team (for example, the specialist nurse) who is responsible for coordinating their care.

6.2   Physiotherapy

6.2.1   Clinical introduction

Despite the pharmacological advances for the treatment of RA many patients still present with functional deficits which physiotherapy seeks to address.

Physiotherapy aims to reduce pain and stiffness, prevent deformity and maximise function, independence and quality of life. These aims are supported by a variety of interventions which may be conveniently grouped under active and passive headings. In the former, education and exercise are the key components and until recently, the fear of accelerating joint damage has limited activities to range of movement and isometric exercises. However, the past couple of decades has seen a paradigm shift towards dynamic conditioning exercise, fuelled, in part, by studies which show that patients with RA are inactive[159] and at higher risk of cardiovascular disease and osteoporotic fractures than the non-RA population.[160]

According to the World Confederation of Physical Therapists, physiotherapy is 'concerned with identifying and maximizing movement potential, within the spheres of promotion, prevention, treatment and rehabilitation, in partnership with their clients'.[161] The components of physiotherapy interventions include:

- Exercise therapy – on land and in water (hydrotherapy/aquatic physiotherapy) and includes aerobic activities, flexibility and muscle-strengthening exercises, core stability exercise, balance rehabilitation, promotion of lifestyle physical activity.
- Patient education and self-management – joint protection strategies, energy conservation/fatigue management, sleep hygiene training, management of flare, pain-relief strategies, relaxation training, exercise and physical activity recommendations.
- Thermotherapy – hot/cold packs, paraffin/wax baths and infrared.
- Electrotherapy – Transcutaneous Electrical Nerve Stimulation (TENS), Ultrasound, Pulsed Electromagnetic Energy (PEME), Interferential therapy (IFT) and Laser.

- Provision and education of use of assistive devices – walking aids, splints, orthoses, insoles.
- Manual therapy – includes mobilisation, manipulation, myofascial release, trigger point therapy, acupuncture and massage.

A threefold increased risk of hip fractures with rheumatoid arthritis has been reported in Central Finland.[162] In part this may be due to patients with RA who have reduced physical capacity which occurs early in the course of disease.[163] Intuitively it would seem that exercise strategies that aim to improve or maintain health-related fitness may enhance biomechanical efficiency. The benefits of physical activity and exercise strategies may only be apparent if the stimulus is sufficient, regular and sustained, hence issues of concordance could be as important as the activity itself.

Passive treatments, success of which depends less on patient concordance, include manual therapy techniques and the application of electrophysical agents. These are used for specific clinical impairments on a time limited basis and aim to enhance the ability to exercise or increase physical activity. Manual therapy is 'a clinical approach utilising skilled, specific hands-on techniques....' which includes joint and soft tissue mobilization and manipulation.[164] Electrophysical agents represent both thermotherapy (superficial heat/cold) and electrotherapy (see examples above) and are used to reduce pain and improve function.

Physiotherapy management of RA uses a multi-modal or comprehensive approach which consists of a combination of education, exercise and pain relief agents, with the emphasis varying depending on clinical need and the goals agreed between therapist and patient. Encouraging self-management strategies and self-efficacy for sustained regular physical activity is an overarching theme and demands supportive and reinforcing health education and promotion.

In considering the effectiveness of physiotherapy, there is a need to evaluate the evidence for physiotherapy in minimising the impact of disease on symptoms, joint damage, function and quality of life across the RA life span. In particular:

1. Which exercise strategies, if any, offer the greatest benefit in respect of symptoms, joint damage, function and quality of life?
2. Which of the various manual therapy strategies could provide superior symptomatic relief and functional gain and for what duration?
3. Which of the electrophysical agents could offer the greatest therapeutic effects in terms of symptomatic relief and functional gain and for what duration?

6.2.2 Clinical methodological introduction

We looked for studies that investigated the efficacy of different aspects of physiotherapy (PT) with respect to symptoms, joint damage, function and quality of life in patients with RA (recent-onset and established disease). Due to the large volume of evidence, only MA and RCTs were selected which were of a UK-relevant population and intervention; if the population was mixed arthritis there had to be >75% RA or RA subgroup analysis; and for trials looking at TENS and exercise, the sample size had to be N ≥50 (and for strengthening exercises, N >70).

Five SRs/MAs[165–169] and 17 RCTs[170–191] were found that fulfilled the inclusion criteria. Three of these RCTs were published as multiple papers, reporting different outcomes or time-points and so these trials have only been counted once, however results from all the papers are reported and referenced here. Three RCTs[172,185–188,192,193] were excluded as evidence due to methodological limitations (lack of blinding and ITT analysis was not performed). The methodological limitations of the remaining included RCTs were as follows: they were all graded 1+ due to being single blind and ITT analysis was not performed (6 RCTs), or unblinded and ITT analysis was performed (1 RCT), or single blind and ITT analysis was performed but had high drop-out rates (2 RCTs). One of the RCTs[190] on exercise was included even though it had a sample size <70, because it was the only trial of exercise looking at patients who had active RA.

All trials except one[191] (patients with recent-onset RA), were conducted using patients with established RA, and the MAs used trials which were of a mixed population (recent-onset and established RA).

▷ Mixed population (recent-onset and established RA)

Five SRs/MAs[165–169] were found that fulfilled the criteria. All MAs were well-conducted, however, the RCTs included in the analysis were of varying quality.

The first SR/MA[165] looked at hot and cold therapy and included 7 RCTs in the analysis, which were all of poor to moderate quality. However, the RCTs differed with respect to:
- patients (N=4 hospitalised, N=7 outpatients)
- disease duration (ranging from duration 5 years or less to mean 14 years)
- intervention (1 RCT each on ice therapy, paraffin bath plus exercise, three different thermotherapy modalities (paraffin wax bath, faradic bath and ultrasound), different temperatures of heat, 2 RCTs heat)
- comparison group (control, exercise, cryotherapy)
- study size (range: N=14 to N=90).

The second SR/MA[166] looked at laser therapy and included 6 RCTs in the analysis which differed with respect to:
- intervention – wavelength (1 RCT 633 nm, 1 RCT 850 nm, 1 RCT 820 nm, 1 RCT 830 nm, 1 RCT 820 nm, 1RCT 632.5 nm)
- intervention – Output power (1 RCT 10mW, 1 RCT 940 mW,, 1 RCT 40mW, 1 RCT 21 mW, 1 RCT 15 mW, 1RCT 1mW)
- comparison (5 RCTs placebo and 1 RCT contralateral joint)
- study size (range: N=17 to N=72)
- blinding (4 RCTs double blind, 1 RCT triple blind, 1 RCT partial blinding).

The third SR/MA[167] looked at TENS therapy and included 3 RCTs (which were all of reasonable to good quality) in the analysis but differed with respect to:
- intervention (1 RCT 15 mins of 70 Hz, 1 RCT 20 mins of 100 Hz, 1 RCT 5 mins of 70 Hz)
- comparison group (2 RCTs placebo, 1 RCT AL-TENS)
- study size (range: N=19 to N=33)
- blinding (1 RCT double blind, 1 RCT single blind, 1 RCT unblinded)
- follow-up (1 RCT 15 days, 2 RCTs not specified).

The fourth SR/MA[168] looked at ultrasound therapy and included 2 RCTs (which were of poor to moderate quality) in the analysis and had a 3-week treatment phase. However, the RCTs differed with respect to:

- intervention (1 RCT ultrasound combined with either exercises, electric current, wax baths or electric current and exercises; 1 RCT ultrasound alone)
- comparison group (placebo ultrasound)
- study size (1 RCT N=30, 1 RCT N=50)
- blinding (1 double blind, 1 unblinded).

The fifth SR/MA[169] looked at tai-chi exercise therapy and included 4 RCTs (which were of poor quality and unblinded) in the analysis, but differed with respect to:
- intervention (1 RCT health education + range of motion (ROM) dance and relaxation; 1 RCT oral Chinese herbs + education + exercise + massage + hot compress; 2 RCTs tai chi exercises)
- comparison group (2 RCTs oral Chinese herbs; 2 RCTs no exercise)
- study size (range N=28 to N=100)
- study duration – length of intervention (range: 8 weeks to 10 weeks)

▷ Recent-onset RA

The included RCT[191] was a methodologically sound randomised, parallel group study in N=228 patients. The trial compared two different treatment arms: exercise programme (healthy physical activity) vs usual care in a 1-year treatment phase.

▷ Established RA

The 13 included RCTs differed with respect to the following:
- sample size (range: N=57 to N=310)
- blinding (12 RCTs single blind, 1 RCT unblinded)
- trial length (range: 3 weeks to 2 years; follow-up 1 RCT 6 months)
- treatment (2 RCTs general PT; 11 RCTs exercise)

6.2.3 Health economic methodological introduction

One study was identified and appraised. Van den Hout et al.[194] is a Dutch cost-utility analysis comparing a long-term high intensity exercise program (RAPIT program) to usual individual physical therapy.

6.2.4 Clinical evidence statements

▷ Mixed population (recent-onset and established RA)

Table 6.1 Hot and cold therapy

Study	Treatment	Follow-up	Outcomes	Result – best treatment
1 MA[165] **Level 1++**	Knee: heat therapy (50°F vs 60°F and 50°F vs 70°F)	**72 h (end of treatment)**	Pain measurement (amount of morphine).	**NS**
1 MA[165] **Level 1++**	Knee: ice packs vs hot packs	5 days (end of treatment)	Thermographic Index, joint circumference, number of patients preferring ice, number of patients with improved pain and stiffness grading	**NS**
	Shoulder: ice packs vs hot packs	3 weeks (end of treatment)	McGill pain questionnaire, Flexion and Abduction ROM	**NS**
	Hand: wax bath vs control	4 weeks (end of treatment)	Change in: flexion and extension of the dominant hand, pinch function, grip strength, pain on resisted and non-resisted motion, stiffness (both hands)	**Wax bath** (all p=0.04)
			Grip function	**NS**
	Hand: wax bath + exercises vs exercises	4 weeks (end of treatment)	Change in flexion and extension of the dominant hand; change in grip strength and function; change in pain on resisted and non-resisted motion and for change in stiffness (both hands)	**Wax bath** (all p=0.04)
			Pinch function	**NS**
	Hand: wax bath vs exercises	4 weeks (end of treatment)	Change in: flexion and extension of the dominant hand, grip strength, grip and pinch function, stiffness (both hands) and pain on resisted and non-resisted motion	**Wax bath** (all p=0.04 except grip strength p=0.008)
	Hand: wax therapy vs ultrasound	End of treatment: 1, 2 and 3 weeks	Hand grip; PIP circumference; articular index; timed task; activity score; ROM (3 wks only)	**NS**
	Wax bath vs faradic bath + ultrasound	End of treatment: 1, 2 and 3 weeks	Hand grip, PIP circumference, articular Index, timed task	**NS**
		1 and 2 weeks 3 weeks	Activity score	**NS**
	Cryotherapy vs control	End of treatment: 2, 3 and 4 days	Change in post-surgery oedema	**NS**

Table 6.2 Laser

Study	Treatment	Follow-up	Outcomes	Result – best treatment
1 MA[166] **Level 1++**	Laser vs placebo	End of treatment (10 and 20 weeks)	Change in pain (VAS); pain, 0 to 12 scale; knee ROM (left and overall); morning stiffness duration; grip strength (mmHg –10 weeks, NS 20 weeks) and ESR	**Laser** (most p <0.01)
			Pain (McGill); RAI; HAQ; ROM (PIP, MCP, right knee and ankle); morning stiffness; RF+; grip strength (kg); swelling (right and left suprapatellar, MCP and PIP); walking speed and CRP	**NS**

- The same MA[166] also found that there were no significant differences between laser and placebo according to: methodological quality; treatment duration (pain); joint compared with nerve application (pain); and wavelength (pain). However, there was a significant difference in favour of dose: low dose laser therapy (≤ 3 J/cm^2) compared with placebo but not high dose laser therapy compared with placebo (for change in pain (VAS) but NS dose effect for grip strength). **Level 1++**

Table 6.3 Ultrasound

Study	Treatment	Follow-up	Outcomes	Result – best treatment
1 MA[168] **Level 1++**	Ultrasound vs placebo	10 weeks (end of treatment)	Change in: number of painful articulations and swollen articulations; dorsal flexion of the wrist and grip strength	**Ultrasound** (p <0.001)
			Change in: circumference of PIP joints and duration of morning stiffness	**NS**
	Hand: ultrasound vs wax	End of treatment (1, 2 and 3 weeks)	Hand grip; PIP circumference; articular index; timed task and activity score	**NS**
	Hand: ultrasound vs faradic bath + ultrasound	End of treatment (1, 2 and 3 weeks)	Activity score	**Ultrasound** (p <0.05)
		3 weeks	Hand grip; PIP circumference; articular Index; timed task; ROM	**NS**
	Hand: ultrasound + faradic bath vs wax bath	End of treatment (1, 2 and 3 weeks)	Activity score	**US + faradic bath** (p <0.05)
		3 weeks	Hand grip; PIP circumference; articular Index; timed task; ROM	**NS**

Table 6.4 TENS

Study	Treatment	Follow-up	Outcomes	Result – best treatment
1 MA[167] Level 1++	Hand: TENS vs placebo	3 weeks (end of treatment)	Change in resting pain (VAS)	**TENS** (p <0.00001)
			Change in grip pain	**NS**
	Hand: C-TENS vs placebo	End of treatment (same day)	Change in joint tenderness	**C-TENS** (p=0.004)
			Resting pain (VAS); grip pain (VAS) and tender joints	**NS**
	Hand: C-TENS vs AL-TENS	End of treatment (15 days)	Number of patients improved	**NS**

Table 6.5 Exercise

Study	Treatment	Follow-up	Outcomes	Result – best treatment
1 MA[165] Level 1++	Hand: exercise vs control	End of treatment (4 weeks)	Change in: flexion and extension of the dominant hand, grip strength, grip and pinch function, stiffness (both hands), pain on resisted and non-resisted motion	**Exercise** (all p=0.04 except flexion/ extension p=0.004)
1 MA[169] Level 1++	Tai Chi exercises vs control	Range: 8 to 10 weeks	ROM – ankle plantar flexion; lower extremity flexion; withdrawals	**Tai-chi** (p=0.02; p=0.004; p=0.003)
			Functional Assessment; RAI; swollen joints; 50-foot walk; grip strength; patient global: number rated 'recovery' at 2 months and 3 months; ROM – shoulder flexion, shoulder internal and external rotation and total upper extremity combined; self-reported enjoyment – benefit and frequency	**NS**

▷ Recent-onset RA

Physical exercise programme vs control group (usual care)

- One RCT[191] found that physical exercise programme was significantly better than control group (usual care) at 1 year for: EuroQoL EQ-5D (VAS); timed stands test and grip strength (both p <0.01). However, there was NS difference for: ROM; pain (VAS); HAQ-DI; DAS28; percentages of patients taking different types of medication and percentage of patients reaching healthy physical activity. **Level 1++**

▷ Established RA

Table 6.6 General physiotherapy

Study	Treatment	Follow-up	Outcomes	Result – best treatment
1 RCT[173,174] Level 1++	PT vs Control (waiting list)	6 weeks (end of treatment)	Morning stiffness Pain (VAS), grip strength, tender joints, Stanford self-efficacy scale	**PT** (p <0.036) **NS**
		52 weeks	Pain (VAS); morning stiffness; grip strength; tender joint count (all p <0.001) and Stanford self-efficacy scale and ADLs	**PT** (all p <0.001 except ADLs p <0.05)
1 RCT[175] Level 1+		3 weeks	RAI, pain (VAS), ROM and ADL	**PT** (all p <0.005)
			ESR and joint size	**NS**

Exercise

Table 6.7 Strengthening/mobilisation

Study	Treatment	Follow-up	Outcomes	Result – best treatment
1 RCT[176] Level 1++	Joint protection + strengthening/ mobilisation exercise vs joint protection	6 months	**Dominant key grip; AIMS2 upper limb function, was worse for number of drop-outs**	**Joint protect + exerc** (p <0.01)
			AIMS (hand and finger function); Jebsen-Taylor function score; right index finger flexion; dominant gross grip; tender and swollen joint counts and patient's global assessment of disease activity	**NS**
1 RCT[170] Level 1+	Strengthening exercise (rehabilitation) vs Control (waiting list)	5 weeks (end of treatment)	Quadriceps strength	**Exercise** (p <0.05)
		5 weeks; 6 months follow-up	HAQ score	**NS;** **Exercise** (p <0.05)
		5 weeks and 6 months follow-up	Morning stiffness, pain (VAS), patient's and assessor's global assessment and swollen and tender joints	**NS**
1 RCT[190] Level 1+	Intensive exercise (rehabilitation) vs Conservative exercises	24 weeks	ACR responders; muscle strength (isometric extension)	**Intensive exercise** (p <0.05)
			Swollen joints, ESR, pain (VAS), DAS, joint mobility, HAQ, 50 foot walk time, joint mobility (EPM-ROM).	**NS**

Table 6.8 Hydrotherapy

Study	Treatment	Follow-up	Outcomes	Result – best treatment
1 RCT[177] **Level 1+**	Hydrotherapy vs land exercise	3 months	Self-rated overall effect of treatment	**Hydrotherapy** (p <0.001)
			EQ-5D utility and VAS; HAQ; pain (VAS) and 10 m walk time	NS
1 RCT[171] **Level 1+**	Hydrotherapy vs land exercise vs seated immersion vs progressive relaxation	4 weeks (end of treatment)	RAI (joint tenderness) and AIMS2 (mood and tension)	**Hydrotherapy** (all p=0.03)
			Knee and wrist ROM; morning stiffness; grip strength; AIMS 2 (physical capacity, pain, social, work and affect) and pain (McGill)	NS

Table 6.9 Range of motion and resistance

Study	Treatment	Follow-up	Outcomes	Result – best treatment
1 RCT[178] **Level 1+**	ROM exercise vs Control (active lifestyle)	12 weeks	Painful joints in the left hand	Exercise (p <0.05)
			Painful joints in the right hand; MCP and PIP extension, dexterity and grip strength (all in the left and right hands)	NS
	Resistance + ROM exercise vs Control (active lifestyle)		Dexterity in the left hand	**Exercise** (p <0.05)
			Painful joints, MCP and PIP extension and grip strength in the left and right hands; dexterity in the right hand	NS

Table 6.10 Aerobic

Study	Treatment	Follow-up	Outcomes	Result – best treatment
1 RCT[179,180] **Level 1++**	High intensity aerobic exercise (RAPIT) vs control group (usual care)	Over the 2 years	Radiographic damage (Larsen score for all small joints – hands and feet; and for small joints of the feet only – all p=0.047) and bone mineral density of the hip	**Exercise** (all p <0.05)
			Radiographic damage (Larsen score for small joints of the hands only) and bone mineral density of the spine	NS
		1 and 2 years	MACTAR score and muscle strength	**Exercise** (all p <0.05)
			HAQ score; DAS4 score and radiographic damage (Larsen score for large joints)	NS

continued

Table 6.10 Aerobic – *continued*

Study	Treatment	Follow-up	Outcomes	Result – best treatment
1 RCT[183] Level 1+	Aerobic exercises (Self-training vs self-training + PT training vs group training vs group training and pool) vs Control (no training)	2 years	ESR, number of swollen joints, pain (VAS), morning stiffness, HAQ, Larsen score, functional score and Isometric muscle strength of knee extensors; dropouts	**All NS except dropouts worse for Aerobic**
1 RCT[182] Level 1+	Class aerobic exercise vs Control (usual exercise)	Over the 12 weeks	Overall symptoms; walk time and grip strength	**Aerobic** (p=0.04; both p <0.005)
	Home aerobic exercise vs Control (usual exercise)		Walk time and grip strength	**Aerobic** (both p <0.005)
			Overall symptoms	**NS**
1 RCT[184] Level 1+	Individualised aerobic exercise vs General exercise	12 months	MACTAR score; HAQ score; DAS28 and QoL (RAQoL and RAND-36 mental and physical)	**NS**

6.2.5 Health economic evidence statements

The average annual medical cost per patient for the RAPIT program was 2,115 euros, compared to 1683 euros for usual care. The RAPIT group showed no significant different in QALY using SF-6D, and using EQ-5D and VAS the usual care program showed greater QALY gains. The study reports ICERs for total societal cost (but not direct medical costs), concluding that using EQ-5D and VAS, the UC has better cost-utility, and using the SF-6D the ICER is 67,000 euros per QALY, but with no significant difference in the net benefit. Therefore this paper does not provided convincing cost-effectiveness evidence in support of a high intensity exercise program.[194]

6.2.6 Summary of evidence statements

In general, exercise provokes a favourable response in terms of physical and psychological benefits.[149,169,171,177,181–183] Aerobic (dynamic) exercise programmes improve the components of health-related fitness, enhance psychological status, reduce pain and fatigue and have a positive effect on functional capacity without exacerbating disease activity or accelerating joint damage.[180–183] Specific exercise, aimed at enhancing joint range of motion (joint flexibility) or muscle strength (resistance training) results in some specific improvements.[171,181] The majority of evidence comes from patients with chronic, stable RA in functional class I/III.[181,183] Exercise in water provides similar physical benefits to exercise on land but may have additional and important psychological effects (which positively impact on concordance).[171,177] Adoption of regular physical activity and exercise strategies is more successful if personalised contact with a health professional occurs in which the benefits and barriers to exercise are discussed and there is opportunity for group contact.[182,184] The different modes of exercise and their method of delivery affect outcome directly[184] and indirectly via issues of concordance.[179,180,182]

There is some evidence that a comprehensive package of care, delivered in the community and addressing patient specific needs through education, exercise and pain relief modalities has long-term benefits on self-efficacy, disease management knowledge and some measures of disease activity and function.[173,174]

The data for clear benefit for the use of electrophysical agents in the management of RA is lacking. The present data set highlights conflicting results in, mainly poor quality studies in which multiple interventions and outcomes confuse synthesis; therefore little confidence can be attached to the findings. However, some agents, eg TENS, wax baths, suggest that short-term symptomatic relief may occur.[165,167]

The therapeutic effect of manual therapy cannot be determined for RA due to the dearth of literature in this area.

6.2.7 From evidence to recommendations

Exercise, whether on land or in water is beneficial for most people with RA.

The GDG felt that it was necessary for all people with RA to have access, with periodic review, to physiotherapy for advice about incorporating an appropriately tailored exercise programme aimed at improving both general health related fitness and specific locomotor and balance problems into their lives.

Concordance with exercise was highlighted as a particular problem. The GDG consensus was that it is important that all members of the MDT provide people with RA with consistent and supportive messages regarding its benefits.

The GDG noted that the provision of electrophysical agents such as wax baths and TENS were akin to the provision of analgesics, in that although there is no evidence of long-term effect on disease progression many patients find that they provide short-term symptomatic relief. The GDG consensus was that it would be premature to discard these treatments which may be favoured by patients for their palliative effect.

In reviewing the evidence for comprehensive physiotherapy the GDG noted that the results, whilst promising, would benefit from additional research.

RECOMMENDATION

R11   People with RA should have access to specialist physiotherapy, with periodic review (see recommendations 36 and 37), to:
- improve general fitness and encourage regular exercise
- learn exercises for enhancing joint flexibility, muscle strength and managing other functional impairments
- learn about the short-term pain relief provided by methods such as transcutaneous electrical nerve stimulators [TENS] and wax baths.

6.3 Occupational therapy

6.3.1 Clinical introduction

Occupational therapy (OT) aims to improve a person's ability to perform daily activities and participate in valued life activities and roles at work, in the home, leisure and socially; facilitate successful adaptations in lifestyle; and to prevent or minimise functional and psychological problems. Comprehensive OT programmes can include a wide range of interventions (see Table 6.11 below). Enabling self-management using strategies such as joint protection and fatigue management is a central part of treatment. Enhancing concordance is essential and so OTs frequently offer cognitive-behavioural approaches. There is a particular focus in OT on maintaining hand function in RA. 'We use our hands for almost everything we do, so keeping them going is really important for me.' Work rehabilitation is provided both for those still in work at risk of job loss, as well as those unemployed. 'Working has helped boost my self esteem. I truly believe that if I wasn't working, my RA would have progressed faster and I would be in a worse state than I am now.' 'The visit [OT work assessment] was a turning point in my life…with the adjustments that followed I could continue to support my family…and achieve a measure of success in the workplace' (National Rheumatoid Arthritis Society, NRAS booklet: *I want to work: a self-help guide for people with RA* (2007).[13]

Table 6.11 Comprehensive occupational therapy interventions	
Occupational interventions	**Therapies include**
Activities of daily living (ADL) rehabilitation	Self-management education (group and individual)
Work rehabilitation: including on-site work assessment, ergonomics/ adaptations, employer liaison, work environment adaptation, functional capacity evaluation and work hardening	Joint protection training; energy conservation/ fatigue management and sleep hygiene training Assistive devices
Exploring voluntary work & adult education; leisure rehabilitation	Orthoses
Stress and pain management	Hand and upper limb therapy & exercise
Relaxation training	Therapeutic activities
Communication and assertiveness training	Home assessment, recommending environmental modifications and housing adaptations
Counselling (may also provide cognitive-behavioural therapy with post graduate training)	Mobility aids prescription (including wheelchair/powered aids)
Family/carer liaison and support	Foot care advice
Advice on social security benefits and community resources	Exercise for health and wellbeing

All OTs have dual training in physical and mental health rehabilitation. Many people with RA discuss the 'frustration' caused by multiple functional difficulties, pain, fatigue and at times feelings of stress or low mood. Thus psychological interventions are often used to help people in adjusting to living with their disease.

Data suggest[195–199] that from an early stage some 60% of people have problems that could potentially benefit from OT for the hand (joint protection, hand exercises, orthoses) and ADL training. Over a third of people with RA could benefit from work rehabilitation. At a later disease stage, this figure could be higher. What is the evidence that OT interventions have an impact on symptoms, disease progression, function and quality of life in either recent-onset or established RA? In particular:

- Does OT help to maintain functional ability and/or slow its deterioration?
- Does hand therapy (ie joint protection, hand exercises, hand splints) have any impact on maintaining hand function?
- Does OT help maintain or improve participation in social roles, in particular work?
- Does OT have any impact on psychological status?

6.3.2 Clinical methodological introduction

We looked for studies that investigated the efficacy of different aspects of occupational therapy (OT) with respect to symptoms, joint damage, function and quality of life in patients with RA (recent-onset and established disease). Due to the large volume of evidence, only MAs and RCTs were selected which were of a UK-relevant population; if the population was mixed arthritis there had to be >75% RA or RA subgroup analysis and for trials looking at splints, orthoses or CBT the sample size had to be N ≥30.

Two MAs[200,201] and eight RCTs[136,202–209] were found that fulfilled the inclusion criteria. One of the RCTs[207,208] was published as two separate papers and reported the 18-month and 5-year follow-up results of an RCT already included in the MA on psychological interventions.[200] Two RCTs[136,207] were found looking at patients with a recent onset of RA, all the other RCTs were conducted involving patients with established RA, and the two MAs used trials which were of a mixed population (recent-onset and established RA). The methodological limitations of the RCTs were as follows: those graded 1+ were either single blind and ITT analysis was not performed (three RCTs) or unblinded and ITT analysis was performed (two RCTs). The trial graded 1++ was both single blind and the authors performed ITT analysis.

Note: studies on joint protection have been covered in the education section.

▷   Mixed population (recent-onset and established RA)

Two MAs[200,201] were found and focused on RCTs which compared either psychological interventions[200] or splints and orthoses.[201] Both MAs were well-conducted, however the RCTs included in the analysis were of varying quality.

The first SR/MA[200] included 25 RCTs in the analysis which differed with respect to:

- study size (range N=8 to N=141)
- study quality – maximum score of 10 (some poor and some reasonable–good quality)
- study duration – length of intervention (range 3 days to 9 months with follow-up range from 2–18 months)

- comparison group (placebo; usual care; waiting list)
- intervention (N=13 multimodal cognitive-behavioural interventions; N=5 included biofeedback; N=5 more traditional psychotherapeutic interventions; N=2 intervention involved patients expressing difficult emotions or stressful experiences).

The second SR/MA[201] included 7 RCTs in the analysis, all looking at working wrist splints (the RCTs on foot orthoses have been covered in the podiatry question). However, the RCTs differed with respect to:

- comparison group (3 RCTs no splint, 2 RCTs other splints)
- study size (range N=10 to N=110 for wrist splints)
- study quality – maximum score of 5 (some poor and some reasonable-good quality for wrist splints)
- study duration – length of intervention (range: 1 week to 6 months for wrist splints)

▷ Recent-onset RA

The two included RCTs[136,207] compared OT vs usual care and had sample sizes of N=326 and N=53 respectively. One RCT[136] had a treatment phases of 6 to 8 weeks with 6-month follow-up and the other RCT[207] was an 18-month follow-up of a trial included in the MA[200] on psychological interventions.

▷ Established RA

The 7 included RCTs[136,202–206] differed with respect to the following:

- sample size (range: N=47 to N=144)
- blinding (1 RCT double blind, 4 RCTs single blind, 2 RCTs unblinded)
- trial length (range: 4 weeks to 6 months; follow-up ranged from 6 months to 5 years)
- treatment (4 RCTs CBT vs standard care or attention-placebo; 1 RCT customised splint vs two commercial splints; 1 RCT OT vs no treatment; 1 RCT CBT for pain vs mindfulness-based emotion regulation therapy vs education control group)

6.3.3 Health economic methodological introduction

Two studies were identified and appraised. Li et al.[158] is a Canadian cost-utility analysis comparing a primary therapist model (PTM) to a traditional therapy model (TTM). Van den Hout et al.[194] is a cost-utility analysis of a multidisciplinary job retention and rehabilitation program compared to usual care in patients at risk of job loss.

6.3.4 Clinical evidence statements

Table 6.12 Mixed population (recent-onset and established RA)

Study	Treatment	Outcomes	Follow-up	Result – best treatment
1 MA[200] **Level 1++**	Psychological interventions vs control	Pain	Treatment end	**Psych** (13 RCTs, effect size 0.22, 95% CI 0.07 to 0.37, p=0.003)
			Follow-up end	**NS**
		Disability	Treatment end	**Psych** (5 RCTs: effect size 0.30, 95% CI 0.12 to 0.42, p=0.00001).
			Follow-up end	**NS**
		Self-efficacy	Treatment end	**Psych** (5 RCTs: effect size 0.35, 95% CI 0.11 to 0.59, p=0.017).
			Follow-up end	**NS**
		Tender joints	Treatment end	**NS**
			Follow-up end	**Psych** (5 RCTs: effect size 0.30, 95% CI 0.04 to 0.56, p=0.005)
		Psychological status and coping	Treatment end and follow-up end	**Psych** (p=0.007 and p=0.04)
1 MA[201] **Level 1++**	Working wrist gauntlet vs no splint	Grip strength of non-dominant hand (palmar splint and elastic with metal stay ready made gauntlet)	Immediate	**Gauntlet** (1 RCT, N=38; p <0.05)
		Grip strength of dominant hand and non-dominant hand (working splint, plastazote and polythene sheeting custom-made gauntlet)		**NS**

continued

Table 6.12 Mixed population (recent-onset and established RA) – *continued*

Study	Treatment	Follow-up	Outcomes	Result – best treatment
	Working wrist gauntlet (elastic with metal insert)	Passive joint motion	1 week	**Gauntlet** (1 RCT, N=55; p <0.05)
	vs no splint	Work performance and pain using screwdriver or shears; dexterity; Pain on motion, activity or at rest; grip strength; morning stiffness; active joint motion, pronation and supination; pinch grip; joint and forearm circumference; HAQ		NS
	Futuro wrist gauntlets and Thermolyn custom-made wrist gauntlets	Wrist pain; tender and swollen joints; passive wrist ROM; grip strength with & without orthoses	2 weeks	NS
	Futuro wrist gauntlets, Alimed wrist gauntlets and Roylan wrist gauntlets	Dexterity and grip strength without orthoses	1 week	NS
	Resting hand and wrist splints were significantly better than no splints	Patient preference	1–6 months	**Splints** (1 RCT, N=78; p <0.001)
		Grip strength; swollen joints and RAI		NS
	Circumferential cotton-padded splint and pan-type hard thermo-plastic splint	Patient preference	1 month	NS

▷ Recent-onset RA

- One RCT[136] found that OT was significantly better than the control (no intervention) groups for: use of some self-management methods (particularly hand and arm exercises, joint protection and rest); receipt of a working splint and a resting splint; owning and use of assistive devices. However, there was NS difference for: HAQ; DAS28 score; AIMS2 scores; self-efficacy (ASES) score. **Level 1++**

Table 6.13 Established RA

Study	Treatment	Outcomes	Follow-up	Result – best treatment
1 RCT[202] **Level 1++**	OT vs control (no treatment)	Functional score (AIMS); Pooled index (symptoms and function)	6 weeks	**OT** (p=0.006; p=0.04)
		Pain (VAS), HAQ and Beck depression scale		**NS**
1 RCT[204] **Level 1+**	CBT vs control (routine care)	Physical functioning (functional disability, pain, fatigue) and psychological functioning (depression, negative mood, anxiety)	6 months treatment and 1-year follow-up	**CBT** (all p <0.05)
		Illness cognition, Coping with stress and coping with pain; Disease Activity and Social functioning		**Similar; NS**
1 RCT[207] **Level 1++**	CBT vs control (standard care)	HAD depression and anxiety and for HAQ	18 months	**CBT** (p <0.05)
		Pain (11-point scale), RAI, ESR and Coping strategies Questionnaire (CSQ).		**NS**
		Lower use of healthcare resources overall; number of: inpatient nights, physiotherapy referrals, injections and total occasions of care	5 years	**CBT** (p <0.05)
		Number of: Rheumatology consultations, psychiatric referrals, patients discharged as improved, orthopaedic referrals and surgeries		**NS**
1 RCT[205] **Level 1+**	CBT vs control (routine care) vs control (attention-placebo)	Coping strategies questionnaire	6 months and 12 months	**CBT** (p=0.0017 and p=0.0001)
		Pain (VAS and McGill); AIMS, ways of coping scale, AHI and Beck depression scale		**NS**
1 RCT[206] **Level 1+**	Mindfulness-based stress reduction programme (MBSR) vs control (waiting list)	Psychological distress (p=0.04) and Well-being	2 months (end of treatment)	**NS**
		Depressive symptoms and DAS28	2 months and 6 months	**NS**
		Psychological distress and well-being	6 months	**MBSR** (p=0.04; p=0.03)

continued

Table 6.13 Established RA – *continued*

Study	Treatment	Outcomes	Follow-up	Result – best treatment
1 RCT[203] **Level 1+**	Customised leather wrist splint (LWS) and the commercially available wrist splints (RWS and AWS)	Pain (VAS, AHFT – arthritis hand function test – all items); MACTAR score	4 weeks (end of treatment)	NS
	Commercially available wrist splints (RWS vs AWS)	Grip	4 weeks (end of treatment)	RWS (p=0.03)
		Pain (VAS), AHFT – all items and MACTAR score		NS
		Dexterity		AWS (p=0.04)
1 RCT[209] **Level 1++**	Treatment (mindfulness vs CBT for pain) vs control (education)	Positive affect, coping efficacy for pain and catastrophizing	30 days	**Mindfulness and CBT** (p <0.01)
		Change in: daily pain, negative affect and daily depression symptoms		NS
		Pain control		**Mindfulness**

6.3.5 Health economic evidence statements

The Li et al. study[158] showed no statistically significant differences in either QALY or societal cost, but suggests that a primary therapy model has the potential to be a cost-effective alternative to the traditional occupational and physical therapist roles. The trial was only a 6-month study and so long-term analysis of the costs and benefits could help. The van den Hout et al. study[194] concluded that there was no significant difference in either costs or QALYs. The variability of costs in this study means that impact of the job retention program are unclear and the lack of any significant difference of costs or QALYs means conclusions on the cost-effectiveness cannot be made. The applicability of this Dutch care program may be limited in a UK setting.

6.3.6 Summary of evidence statements

- A programme of comprehensive occupational therapy (see Table 6.11 for description) improved short-term functional ability in established RA.[202] In recent-onset RA, comprehensive OT significantly improved use of self-management strategies[136] but not symptoms or functional ability (most participants' RA was well controlled by DMARDs).
- Hand therapy can impact on hand function. Several studies (reviewed under section 5.2) in recent-onset RA patients have evaluated joint protection and energy conservation training using a group educational-behavioural approach. One study[134,135] found that the joint protection group had significant reductions in some symptoms compared to controls at 1 year (morning stiffness and hand pain) and 4 years (morning stiffness).

- Another RCT in patients with established RA receiving anti-TNF therapy[146] found that joint protection, energy conservation and hand/upper limb exercise training, was significantly better than a control group for reductions in pain, physical symptoms and improved functional ability at 8-months follow-up. Most studies of working wrist orthoses[201] were generally comparisons of splint designs and had short-term follow-ups. These identified little difference between splint designs, indicating splint choice should suit patients' preferences. In the short–term (ie immediately or 1–2 weeks) and the longer-term (only one study in the MA looked at longer term – 6 months)[210] the studies found that there were no differences between splint and control groups. However, the splint group had significant improvements in pain, pinch and grip strength when wearing the splint as compared to not-wearing and there was a significant preference for splint use.[210]

- Hand exercises are provided by both occupational therapy and physiotherapy. There is moderate evidence that a combination of range of movement and resistive/strengthening hand exercises can significantly improve dexterity, key grip and self-reported upper limb function.[176,178] This is more effective than range of movement exercise alone.

- There was a lack of evidence that work rehabilitation for people with RA still in work at risk of job loss is effective.

- Psychological interventions commonly used by OTs (relaxation, imagery, stress management and teaching cognitive coping skills) were found in a systematic review[200] to significantly reduce pain and improve functional ability and psychological status at the end of treatment and follow-up. However, effectiveness varied depending upon the nature of the intervention and was less in studies with comparison groups of education, attention or placebo control. Stress reduction techniques and CBT were also found to be significantly better at improving some aspects of psychological status (eg coping, psychological distress).[205,206] One study[207] also identified changes in functional ability. Studies have not identified changes in pain. Outcomes may be dependent on the nature and duration of the therapy.

6.3.7 From evidence to recommendations

The GDG noted that comprehensive occupational therapy programmes help to improve functional ability in people with established RA and increase use of self-management in recent-onset RA. Additionally it was felt it was important for all people with RA to have access, with periodic review, to occupational therapy for assessment and provision of tailored comprehensive programmes. The GDG considered that the evidence supported joint protection training and hand exercises (strength and flexibility) for people with hand function difficulties. To be effective this should be provided by health professionals using an educational-behavioural approach and not just simple advice.

The GDG noted that the limited evidence for resting splints indicated that these do not have a significant effect on symptoms, although it was accepted that patients commonly express a preference for wearing these, particularly during active periods of hand pain and inflammation. Although there is no overall evidence of the long-term benefit from hand splints, the GDG noted that the provision of such splints would be similar to the provision of analgesics in that many patients find them symptomatically beneficial.

The GDG were disappointed with the lack of evidence that work rehabilitation can minimise the impact of disease on symptoms, joint damage, function and quality of life, as working people with RA report finding work assessment and interventions particularly beneficial.

The GDG noted there was good evidence that psychological interventions (eg relaxation, stress management and cognitive coping skills) have a beneficial impact on the reduction of pain and improved functional ability in both recent-onset and established disease, and that stress reduction techniques and cognitive behavioural therapy could improve some aspects of psychological status. Although the management of depression was beyond the scope of this guideline,* the GDG felt that it was appropriate to make a recommendation offering these psychological interventions to those patients who needed help in coping with the consequences of their disease. These could be provided either by an occupational therapist or any other member of the MDT who had appropriate training, or by specialist referral if deemed necessary.

In view of the limited evidence for many specific OT interventions the GDG felt that there should be a research recommendation to assess the effectiveness of both comprehensive and specific OT interventions.

RECOMMENDATIONS

R12   People with RA should have access to specialist occupational therapy, with periodic review (see recommendations 36 and 37), if they have:
- difficulties with any of their everyday activities, or
- problems with hand function.

R13   Offer psychological interventions (for example, relaxation, stress management and cognitive coping skills**) to help people with RA adjust to living with their condition.

6.4   Podiatry

6.4.1   Clinical introduction

Feet are a part of the musculoskeletal system that many of us take for granted, but the large number of bones and synovially-lined structures mean that the vast majority of people with RA will experience significant problems, usually in a symmetrical pattern. For many this will be a part of their initial presenting complaint, although the increasing prevalence of foot problems is strongly related to disease duration.[212]

Involvement of the feet, even to a mild degree, is a significant cause of impaired mobility and functional capacity in RA.[213] In about three quarters of people with RA, the foot contributes to difficulty with walking and is the main or only cause of walking impairment in one quarter.[214] Involvement of the feet in people with RA is not confined to joint damage and structural change but may extend to impaired vascular supply, neurological deficit, soft tissue pathology, impaired tissue viability and problems arising from an inability to maintain basic foot care because of the proximal and systemic effects of RA.

Although foot problems are almost universal for people with RA, this area of care is often neglected, and the provision of podiatry services is often inadequate.[215] Because feet are complicated yet vital, experts are needed who can assist people with RA with their foot-related

---

* For management of depression, see NICE guideline.[211]
** Such as managing negative thinking.

disease and disability. In the UK, foot health services can be provided by a range of professions although podiatry/chiropody is recognised as the profession primarily providing foot care. Podiatrists/chiropodists working in or for the NHS must be HPC registered and will usually have undertaken pre-registration training at degree level.

The basic foot care needs of people with RA can usually be addressed adequately by all HPC registered podiatrists, working in primary care settings as well as in specialist rheumatology units. Some patients with more complex foot health needs (eg complex orthosis provision, high risk care, need for joint injection or surgical assessment) may however require assessment and treatment by a podiatrist with more specialist training or experience in the field of rheumatology, and better integration with a multidisciplinary rheumatology team.

6.4.2 Clinical methodological introduction

We looked for studies that investigated the efficacy of different aspects of podiatry with respect to symptoms, joint damage, function and quality of life on patients with RA (recent-onset and established disease). Studies were selected which were of a UK-relevant population and if the population was mixed arthritis there had to be >75% RA or RA subgroup analysis.

One MA,[201] 3 RCTs[216–219] and one case-series[220] were found that fulfilled the inclusion criteria. One of the RCTs was published as two separate papers[217,219] reporting different outcomes and so the trial has only been counted once. However results from both papers are reported and referenced here. One of the RCTs[218] was excluded as evidence due to methodological limitations (high drop-out rate especially in one arm and ITT analysis was not performed). All other trials were methodologically sound (blinded and the authors performed ITT analysis). No papers were found looking at patients with a recent-onset of RA.

▷ Mixed population (recent-onset and established RA)

One Cochrane SR/MA[201] was found and focused on RCTs which compared all types of orthoses vs placebo, active intervention or regular treatment. Only the results for trials on foot orthoses have been reported here. The MA itself was well conducted; however, the three RCTs it included were of varying quality. Studies included in the analysis differed with respect to:

- intervention (supporting insoles, extra depth shoes and insoles in extra depth shoes)
- comparison group (regular footwear, extra depth shoes, placebo insoles)
- study size (range N=28 to N=102 for foot orthosis)
- study quality – maximum score of 5 (all studies reasonable to good quality for foot orthoses)
- study duration – length of intervention (2 months to 3 years for foot orthoses).

▷ Established RA

Two RCTs[216,217,219] and one case-series[220] were found which looked at aspects of podiatry in patients with established RA.

The two RCTs[216,217,219] were both single-blind, parallel group studies. The first RCT[216] looked at callus treatment in N=38 patients and compared two different treatment arms: normal callus treatment vs sham callus treatment, with a 5-week follow-up. The second RCT[217,219] looked at foot orthoses in N=101 patients and compared 2 different treatment arms: rigid foot orthoses vs control (no orthoses) in a 30-month treatment phase.

The case-series[220] looked at the effects of heat-mouldable shoes on N=25 patients with RA (disease duration not mentioned) in a 3-month treatment phase.

6.4.3 Health economic methodological introduction

Three papers were found and two did not meet the inclusion criteria.[221,222] The third paper, Clark et al.[223] was a critical review of foot orthoses in patients with RA. Two papers reviewed[217,224] considered the cost of orthoses, but neither contained any form of cost-comparison or health economic evaluation.

6.4.4 Clinical evidence statements

▷ Mixed population (recent-onset and established RA)

Extra depth shoes vs regular footwear (2 months)

- One MA[201] found that extra depth shoes were significantly better than regular footwear at 2 months for: HAQ (1 RCT, N=30; effect size WMD −0.20, 95% CI −0.35 to −0.05; p=0.01); pain on walking (1 RCT, N=30; effect size WMD −18.7, 95% CI −28.5 to −8.9; p=0.0002); pain on climbing stairs (1 RCT, N=30; effect size WMD −27.0, 95% CI −37.8 to −16.2; p <0.00001)and pain-free walking time (1 RCT, N=30; effect size WMD 18.2, 95% CI 8.2 to 28.2; p=0.0004). However, there was NS difference for: fatigue and subjective well-being. **Level 1++**

Semi-rigid insoles vs extra-depth shoes (12 weeks)

- One MA[201] found that semi-rigid insoles were significantly better than extra-depth shoes at 12 weeks for: pain, VAS (1 RCT, N=48; effect size WMD −1.9, 95% CI −3.3 to −0.51; p=0.007). However, there was NS difference for: RB walking, RB stairs, RB stand, Toronto ADL – walking and stairs dimensions, Toronto ADL – stairs dimension, walking, lower extremity joint counts and MTP joint count (number of painful joints). **Level 1++**

Soft insoles vs extra-depth shoes (12 weeks)

- One MA[201] found that there was NS difference between soft insoles and extra depth shoes at 12 weeks for: pain (VAS); RB walking, RB stairs, RB stand, Toronto ADL – walking and stairs dimensions, 50 foot walk time, lower extremity joint counts and MTP joint count (number of painful joints). **Level 1++**

Semi-rigid insoles vs placebo (12 weeks)

- One MA[201] found that supporting insoles (Rohadar posted foot orthoses) were significantly better than placebo insoles at 3 years for: hallux abductus angle remained <21 degrees (1 RCT, N=98; effect size WMD RR 3.6, 95% CI 2.2 to 5.9; p <0.00001). However there was NS difference for: painful foot joint count, foot function index and foot pain. **Level 1++**

▷ Established RA

Normal callus debridement vs sham callus debridement

- One RCT[216] found that there was NS difference between normal callus debridement and sham callus debridement for: forefoot pain (VAS), Plantar pressure measures and spatial temporal gait measures at 4 weeks post-intervention. **Level 1++**

Heat-mouldable shoes (Level 3)

- One case-series[220] found that for heat mouldable shoes:
  - 80% wore their shoes all the time during the day and 20% sometimes
  - 72% wore their custom-made semi-rigid foot orthoses in their shoes and 28% did not
  - 20% had their shoes modified to control hindfoot vagus
  - 50% of those who had foot orthoses stated that they always wore their inserts in their shoes
  - 80% of patients felt they walked better with the heat-mouldable shoes; 20% were not walking better
  - significantly more patients found that they walked better with the heat-mouldable shoes compared to previous shoes
  - patients found that their heat-mouldable shoes were significantly better than previous shoes and were significantly more comfortable.

Customised foot orthosis vs control (no orthosis)

- One RCT[217,219] found that the customised foot orthosis was significantly better than the control group (no orthosis) for: foot function index (total, pain and disability – all p <0.05) and for dorsi-flexion/plantar flexion motion, inversion/eversion motion, internal/external ankle joint complex (AJC) rotation and internal rotation at 30 weeks (all p <0.01). However there was NS difference between customised foot orthosis and the control group (no orthosis) for: foot function index (functional limitation), global pain, DAS score, HAQ and Larsen score (hands and feet) at 30 weeks. **Level 1++**

6.4.5 Summary of evidence statements

- The following interventions have evidence for efficacy: extra-depth shoes compared with regular footwear,[201] semi-rigid insoles compared with extra-depth shoes (pain and toe deformity),[201] heat-mouldable shoes (according to consumer feedback),[220] and customised orthoses compared with no orthoses (function, pain and disability).[217,219] There was no evidence to support callus debridement.[216] There was no difference between soft insoles and extra-depth shoes.[201]
- Most trials were conducted over relatively short time periods (5 weeks to 30 weeks)[201,216,217,219] with one exception (3 years for supporting insoles versus placebo insoles).[201]

6.4.6 From evidence to recommendations

There is evidence that insoles and footwear have a positive impact on symptoms, function and quality of life for people with RA. There is a hierarchy of strength of evidence affect, with the most robust evidence being for custom-built shoes, tailored to the patient's own feet, and the least evidence for soft insoles.

The GDG felt that it was necessary for all patients to have access to a podiatrist. Basic assessments and interventions can be conducted by all HPC registered podiatrists, and an assessment of foot health needs followed by appropriate intervention or referral appears warranted in all cases. The GDG also agreed that access to more skilled 'specialist' podiatrists may be required for more complex assessments and interventions.

Simple interventions such as mass-produced insoles are not well evidenced, whereas for more complex interventions, such as provision of customised insoles and therapeutic footwear, the evidence was stronger. The GDG felt that simple insoles were suitable for general use because of their low cost, while provision of more complex insoles and footwear may require specialist podiatric involvement.

RECOMMENDATIONS

R14   All people with RA and foot problems should have access to a podiatrist for assessment and periodic review of their foot health needs (see recommendations 36 and 37).

R15   Functional insoles and therapeutic footwear should be available for all people with RA if indicated.

7 | Pharmacological management

7.1 Disease modifying antirheumatic drugs (DMARDs)

7.1 A Introducing disease modifying drugs (DMARDs)

7.1.1 Clinical introduction (introducing DMARDs)

In previous decades, DMARDs were introduced when patients fulfilled the ARA classification criteria for RA,[2] or when there were radiological erosions. It is now recognised that the ARA classification criteria are not designed to identify recent-onset RA (see section 4), and that persistent synovitis needs an appropriate disease modifying drug intervention irrespective of the distribution of joints affected, and the results of investigations. Consequently, the early introduction of DMARDs has been advocated for any persistent idiopathic synovitis. This decision is not always straightforward, because of diagnostic and prognostic difficulties, and also concerns over toxicity associated with DMARDs. There are also practical difficulties, with delays from symptom onset, to presentation to GP, to referral to secondary care, averaging 9 months in total in the UK. Irrespective of these diagnostic, prognostic and practical difficulties, a concept of a 'window of opportunity' has emerged in the RA literature, expressing the belief that the earlier the introduction of DMARDs, the greater the impact on long-term outcomes. Is there any evidence to support this?

Having decided to start a DMARD, the rheumatologist is then faced with the problem of determining which DMARD should be used, and whether a monotherapy or combination of DMARDs should be employed. Given appropriate information, people with RA may prefer one drug over another, because of mode or frequency of administration, lifestyle and perceived side effect profiles, and other considerations (eg comorbidities, pregnancy). The clinician will also bring their own clinical experience to these decisions, based on their interpretation of the evidence, and personal experience of efficacy and toxicity with different drug regimens. On occasions, the choice will be determined by DMARD toxicity profiles and patient co-morbidities. A large number of trials of a variety of monotherapies and combination therapies have now been published. It should be possible to determine whether there are drug approaches that have greater efficacy and tolerability than others, and all other considerations being equal, should be used in preference to other regimens for patients with a recent onset of RA. It should also be possible to address the cost-effectiveness of different treatment strategies to determine whether some should take priority over others. The sequential use of adalimumab, etanercept and infliximab for the treatment of RA was not covered in this guideline as it is the subject of a NICE technology appraisal (publication date to be confirmed). Please see the NICE website www.nice.org.uk for further details.

7.1.2 Clinical methodological introduction (introducing DMARDs)

We looked for studies that investigated the efficacy and safety of early introduction of DMARDs with respect to symptoms, joint damage, function and quality of life in patients with a recent onset of RA. Due to the large volume of evidence, only Level 1 and 2 studies (MA, RCT, cohort and case-control studies) were selected which were of a UK-relevant population.

Ten studies were found that fulfilled the criteria. These consisted of 1 MA,[225] 6 RCTs,[226–234] and 3 cohort studies.[66,67,235,236] Three of the RCTs (1 RCT;[228,229] 1 RCT;[226,227] 1 RCT[231,232]) and one of the cohort studies[66,67] were each published as 2 separate papers reporting different outcomes or follow-up times, so these studies have only been counted once, however results from both papers are reported and referenced here. Two of the RCTs[233,234] were excluded as evidence due to methodological limitations (1 RCT was unblinded and ITT analysis was not performed, the second had a high rate of withdrawals, 79%). The methodological limitations of the remaining included RCTs were as follows: those graded 1+ were either double blind and ITT analysis was not performed (1 RCT) or unblinded but did have ITT analysis (2 RCTs). The trial graded 1++ was both blinded and ITT analysis was performed.

▷ SR/MAs

The SR/MA[225] focused on 12 studies (6 follow-up studies of RCTs and 6 cohort studies) which compared early vs delayed treatment with DMARDs in patients with a recent onset of RA (<2 years). The MA itself was well conducted, however, the 12 studies it included were of varying quality. Studies included in the analysis differed with respect to:

- Study size (range N=23 to N=189)
- Study quality (maximum score of 6) – (N=6 studies poor or reasonable quality – score of 2 or 3 (1– or 1+); N=6 good quality – score of 4 or 5 (1++))
- Delay in DMARD initiation (difference in months in mean disease duration at DMARD initiation between the two treatment arms) – 6 to 14 months
- Study duration – length of follow-up (1 to 5.6 yrs)

▷ RCTs

All 4 included RCTs [1 RCT;[231,232] 1 RCT;[228,229] 1 RCT;[226,227] 1 RCT[230]) had variable inclusion criteria and differed with respect to the following:

- Sample size (range: N=120 to N=238)
- Blinding (2 RCTs double blind, 2 RCTs single blind/unblinded for some outcomes)
- Trial length and follow-up (range: 36 weeks to 5 years)
- Treatment – type of DMARDs used (1 RCT HCQ, 1 RCT auranofin, 1 RCT SAARD vs delayed pyramid, 1 RCT 3 DMARDs –SSZ+MTX+HCQ + CS vs 1 DMARD SSZ ± CS)*
- Treatment regimen – single drugs and combinations compared
- Treatment regimen – dose.

▷ Cohort studies

The first cohort study[66,67] included N=206 patients with a recent onset of RA who were either a) promptly treated with DMARDs and NSAIDs or b) had delayed treatment with DMARDs + NSAIDs. The mean delay to treatment was approximately 4 months in the delayed treatment group and patients were followed prospectively for 4 years. The second cohort study[235] included N=149 patients with a recent onset of RA who were treated with DMARDs when they

---

* HCQ = hydroxychloroquine, SAARD = slow acting antirheumatic drugs, SSZ= sulphasalazine, MTX = methotrexate, CS = corticosteroid.

had either a) very early RA (mean duration 3.1 months) or b) early RA (mean duration 9.2 months). The patients were followed prospectively for 3 years. The third cohort study[236] included N=40 patients with a recent onset of RA who were either a) promptly treated with DMARDs or b) had delayed treatment with DMARDs. The mean delay to treatment in the delayed group was approximately 9 months after the early treatment group and patients were followed prospectively for 3 years.

7.1.3 Health economic methodological introduction (introducing DMARDs)

Seven papers were identified and four were excluded for not being a cost-effectiveness analysis[237–239] or not being an early RA population.[240] The remaining three studies[241–243] met the inclusion criteria and were appraised.

7.1.4 Clinical evidence statements (introducing DMARDs)

▷ Recent onset of RA

Table 7.1 Symptoms/quality of life (early vs delayed treatment)

Study	Outcomes	Follow-up	Result – best treatment
One RCT[228,229] Level 1+	Number of swollen joints and Beck depression score; RAI (AUC over 5 years); 5 years: values not given	2 years and 5 years	**Early** (p <0.05)
	Pain (VAS); morning stiffness and general health (5 years)	2 years and 5 years	**NS**
One RCT[231,232] Level 1+	Pain (MD 10, 95% CI 1 to 19), joint score (tender and swollen joints – MD39, 95% CI 4 to 74), percentage of patients showing clinical improvement (joint score – 67% vs 51%), wellbeing VAS (MD 9, 95% CI –1 to 18) and morning stiffness (MD 29 mins, 95% CI –13 to 72)	6 months and 1 year	**Early** (values for 1 year, p <0.05)
	Joint score, pain (VAS), general wellbeing (VAS) and morning stiffness (mins)	Over 5 years (AUC)	**NS**
	Number of patients showing clinically relevant improvement (≥20%)	3, 6, 9, 12 and 21 months	**NS**
One RCT[226,227] Level 1++	Composite scores of both joint index and pain index (MD 0.33 and 0.55) and for clinically significant improvement (≥20% – values not given)	36 weeks (and mean over all assessment times)	**Early** (all p <0.05)
	Pain index clinically significant improvement (≥20%): values not given	3-year follow-up	**Early** (p <0.05)
	AIMS psychological scale	36 weeks (and mean over all assessment times)	**NS**

continued

Table 7.1 Symptoms/quality of life (early vs delayed treatment) – *continued*

Study	Outcomes	Follow-up	Result – best treatment
One cohort study[66,67] **Level 2+**	DAS score (values not given); DAS –AUC (median difference 64 units, 95% CI 59 to 69, p=0.002)	1 year, 2 years and over the 2 years	**Early** (p <0.05)
One cohort study[235] **Level 2+**	RAI and number of swollen joints (values not given)	Over the 3 years	**Early** (p <0.05)
One cohort study[236] **Level 2+**	VAS pain (MD –28%); ACR20 (MD 30%), ACR50 (MD 35%) and ACR70 (MD 15%)	3 months and 3 years	**Early** (3 year values given p <0.05)
	Tender joints (MD 19%); EULAR good responders (80% vs 65%); DAS28 ≤3.2 (75% vs 35%)	3 years	**Early** (3 year values given p <0.05)
	Swollen joints; EULAR response rates	3 months and 3 years	**NS**

Table 7.2 Function (early vs delayed treatment)

Study	Outcomes	Follow-up	Result – best treatment
One RCT[228,229] **Level 1+**	Kietel functional score (5 years values not given)	2 years and 5 years	**Early** (p <0.05)
	HAQ (5 years values not given)	2 years	**Early** (p <0.05)
	HAQ and grip strength	5 years	**NS**
One RCT[231,232] **Level 1+**	HAQ (MD 0.3, 95% CI 0.2 to 0.6); HAQ clinical improvement (67% vs 51%); grip strength (MD –7, 95% CI –12 to –2 kpa)	6 months and 1 year	**Early** (1 year values given, p <0.05)
	HAQ and grip strength	Over 5 years (AUC)	**NS**
1 RCT[226,227] **Level 1++**	HAQ (MD 0.23)	36 weeks (and mean over all assessment times)	**Early** (p=0.004)
	Physical function index (clinically significant improvement – values not given)	3-year follow-up	**Early** (better)
One cohort study[66,67] **Level 2+**	HAQ score and HAQ score (AUC)	1 year, 2 years and over the 2 years	**NS**
One cohort study[236] **Level 2+**	HAQ (3 years: MD 0.4)	3 months and 3 years	**Early** (p <0.05)

Table 7.3 Joint damage (early vs delayed treatment)

Study	Outcomes	Follow-up	Result – best treatment
One MA[225] Level 1++	Radiographic progression rate	Median follow-up 3 years	**Early** (SMD –0.19, 95% CI –0.34 to –0.04)
One RCT[228,229] Level 1+	Larsen Score; erosion score, number of eroded joints and number of engaged joints (5 years values not given)	5 years	**Early** (p <0.05)
One RCT[231,232] Level 1+	Increase in radiographic damage (JSN, erosion and total radiographic damage score)	1 year and 5 years	**NS**
One RCT[230] Level 1+	Increase in Larsen score	2 years	**NS**
One cohort study[66,67] Level 2+	Progressive joint destruction – Sharp score >5 (2 years: 38% vs 58%)	1 and 2 years	**Early** (p=0.01)
	Rate of progression (3 years: median difference 1.3 points/year, p=0.032)	1, 2 and 3 years	**Early** (significantly better)
		4 years Years 1–4 and 2–4	**NS** **NS**
One cohort study[235] Level 2+	Erosive disease and Larsen scores	Over the 3 years	**NS**
One cohort study[236] Level 2+	Larsen score (3 years: MD 11.1)	1, 2 and 3 years	**Early** (p <0.05)
	Patients with erosions – Larsen score ≥2 (MD 3)	3 years	**Early** (p <0.05)

Table 7.4 Global assessment (early vs delayed treatment)

Study	Outcomes	Follow-up	Result – best treatment
One RCT[226,227] Level 1++	Patient's and physician's global assessment of therapeutic benefit (MD 0.67 and 0.57)	36 weeks	**Early** (p=0.01 and 0.032)
		3-year follow-up	**NS**
One cohort study[236] Level 2+	Patient's and physician's global assessment (3 years: MD 29% and 32%)	3 months and 3 years	**Early** (p <0.05)

Table 7.5 Biochemical markers (early vs delayed treatment)

Study	Outcomes	Follow-up	Result – best treatment
One RCT[231,232] Level 1+	ESR (1 year: MD 11, 95% CI –2 to 28 mm/h)	1 year	**Early** (p <0.05)
	ESR (AUC)	Over 5 years (AUC)	**NS**
	CRP (1 year: MD 18, 95% CI 3 to 32 mg/L)	6 months and 1 year	**Early** (p <0.05)
One RCT[226,227] Level 1++	ESR	36 weeks	**NS**
One cohort study[66,67] Level 2+	CRP (values not given)	3 months	**Early** (p <0.05)
	CRP	1 year and 2 years	**NS**
	CRP – AUC (median difference 9 units)	Over the 2 years	**Early** (p=0.04)
One cohort study[235] Level 2+	CRP (values not given)	Over the 3 years	**Early** (p <0.05)
	ESR	Over the 3 years	**NS**
One cohort study[236] Level 2+	CRP levels and ESR	3 months and 3 years	**NS**

Table 7.6 Adverse events (AEs) (early vs delayed treatment)

Study	Outcomes	Follow-up	Result – best treatment
One RCT[231,232] Level 1+	GI AEs	1 year	**NS**
One RCT[226,227] Level 1++	Clinically significant AEs	36 weeks	**NS**
	Total number of AEs (N=39 vs N=38)	36 weeks	**Similar**

Table 7.7 Withdrawals (early vs delayed treatment)

Study	Outcomes	Follow-up	Result – best treatment
One RCT[228,229] **Level 1+**	Withdrawals due to lack of response (19% vs 49%), patients still continuing on the original treatment (37% vs 52%)	2 years	**Early** (p <0.001)
	Withdrawals due to AEs (28% vs 3%)	2 years	**Delayed** (p <0.01)
One RCT[231,232] **Level 1+**	Total number of withdrawals (mainly due to lack of efficacy) and due to AEs: 20% and 21%	2 years	**Early** (p <0.05)
One RCT[226,227] **Level 1++**	Withdrawals due to lack of efficacy (7% vs 17%)	36 weeks	**Early** (better)
	Withdrawals due to AEs	36 weeks	**NS**
One cohort study[66,67] **Level 2+**	Number of withdrawals (4% vs 15%)	2 years	**Early** (better)
	Change in initial DMARD therapy due to: AEs (12% vs 3%), lack of efficacy (22% vs 9%)	Over 2 years	**Delayed** (better)
One cohort study[236] **Level 2+**	DMARD switching due to AEs or lack of efficacy (3 times more frequent in early group)	Over 3 years	**Delayed** (p <0.05)

Table 7.8 Remission (early vs delayed treatment)

Study	Outcomes	Follow-up	Result – best treatment
One RCT[231,232] **Level 1+**	Median lag time until first complete response (remission): 12 months vs 20 months at 5 years	1 year and 5 years	**Early** (p <0.05)
	Number of patients achieving complete response (remission) over 5 years	Over 5 years	**NS**
One RCT[230] **Level 1+**	Frequency of patients with remission: both 42%	2 years	**Early** (p=0.021).
	Frequency of patients with remission (in combination treatment group)	2 years	**NS**
One cohort study[235] **Level 2+**	Number of patients in remission	Over the 3 years	**NS**

7.1.5 Health economic evidence statements (introducing DMARDs)

Grigor et al.[242] was the only study of a UK population; Verhoeven et al.[241] and Korthals et al.[243] were Dutch and Belgian respectively, and so their relevance to a UK population is limited. Grigor et al. has a high inclusion criteria for recent-onset RA (<5 years) although the mean disease duration of the trial was 19 months. Grigor et al. estimates that the intensive step-up TICORA strategy dominates the routine step-up strategy (sulfasalazine monotherapy with a DMARD added if initially failed). Verhoeven et al. and Korthals et al. are both based on the COBRA trial, and they estimate that combined step-down therapy or prednisolone, methotrexate and sulphasalazine dominate sulphasalazine monotherapy.

7.1.6 Summary of evidence statements (introducing DMARDs)

- For symptoms, joint damage, function and quality of life, delay in introducing DMARDs is inferior to early commencement.[66,67,225–229,231,232,235,236]
- Prompt introduction of DMARDs can lead to benefits up to 5 years after the drugs are introduced when compared with a delayed start.[228,229]
- Early introduction of drugs also results in fewer adverse reactions and withdrawals.[66,67,226–229,231,232,236]
- There was some evidence that combination therapies could extend the window of opportunity for DMARDs to be effective when compared with monotherapies.[230]
- But the key message to emerge was to start effective DMARD therapy as soon as possible.

7.1 B Optimal sequencing of disease modifying drugs (DMARDs)

7.1.7 Clinical methodological introduction (optimal sequencing of DMARDs)

We looked for studies that investigated the efficacy and safety of different sequences of DMARDs with respect to symptoms, joint damage, function and quality of life in patients with a recent onset of RA. Due to the large volume of evidence, only Level 1 and 2 studies (MA, RCT, Cohort and Case-control studies) were selected which were of a UK-relevant population and had a sample size of N≥100.

Twelve studies were found that fulfilled the criteria. This consisted of 2 MA,[244,245] 9 RCTs,[242,246–262] and 1 cohort study (prospective).[263] Two of the RCTs (1 RCT – the CIMESTRA study;[246,247] 1 RCT – the COBRA trial[253,254] were each published as 2 separate papers. 2 RCTs (1 RCT – the FINRACO study;[248–251] 1 RCT – the BeSt study[256–259] were each published as 4 separate papers. These all reported different outcomes or follow-up times, so these trials have only been counted once, however results from all papers are reported and referenced here. The MA[245] and one of the RCTs[252] were excluded as evidence due to methodological limitations (the MA had limitations to the search methodology, and the authors did not perform quality assessment or tests for heterogeneity. The RCT was open label and ITT analysis was not performed). The methodological limitations of the remaining included RCTs were as follows: those graded 1+ were either double blind and an ITT analysis was not performed (1 RCT) or unblinded and ITT analysis was not performed (2 RCTs). The RCTs graded 1++ were both blinded and the authors performed ITT analysis (5 RCTs) and the MA graded 1++ tested for heterogeneity and assessed the quality of the included trials).

The included studies were separated into two different groups in order to analyse and compare the data: 1) aggressive vs non-aggressive sequences of DMARD treatment and 2) general sequences of DMARDs.

NOTE: For many of the trials, the sequences of the DMARDs may have differed for patients even within the same arm of a trial, because often doses and DMARDs used were adjusted or changed for individual patients during the study depending upon whether they developed AEs or showed lack of clinical efficacy. This was done to reflect clinical practice.

▷ Aggressive vs non-aggressive DMARD treatment

Three RCTs (1 RCT – the COBRA trial;[253,254] 1 RCT – the CIMESTRA study;[246,247] 1 RCT – the FINRACO study[248–251]) all addressed aggressive vs non-aggressive DMARD therapy.

The first RCT – the COBRA trial[253,254] compared 2 different treatment arms. Group 1 (aggressive): patients were given SSZ, then CS and MTX were added. These drugs were then tapered and withdrawn; Group 2 (non-aggressive): patients were given SSZ and continued on SSZ. The second RCT – the CIMESTRA trial[246,247] included N=163 patients with a recent onset of RA. The trial had 2 arms in which patients were given either 1) aggressive DMARD treatment (SSZ given, then MTX + prednisolone added) or 2) non-aggressive DMARD treatment (SSZ given and continued on this drug) in a 2-year treatment phase. The third RCT – the FINRACO trial[248–251] included N=199 patients with a recent onset of RA. The trial had 2 arms in which patients were given either 1) aggressive DMARD treatment (3 DMARDs + prednisolone) or 2) Non-aggressive DMARD treatment (Single DMARD ± prednisolone) in a 5-year treatment phase.

▷ General sequences of DMARDs

One MA[244], 6 RCTs (1 RCT – the BeSt study;[256–259] 1 RCT – the MASCOT study;[255] 1 RCT – Feraccioli et al.;[260] 1 RCT – the TICORA study;[242] 2 other RCTs – Choy et al. and Braun et al.[261,262]) and one prospective cohort study (Hider et al.)[263] all addressed sequences of DMARDs.

The MA[244] focused on RCTs and quasi-randomised RCTs which compared DMARD monotherapy vs DMARD combination therapy, in patients with both a recent onset (<3 years) and established RA (>3 years). The MA itself was well conducted and was methodologically sound. However, the 36 RCTs it included were of varying quality. Studies included in the analysis were similar with respect to:
- Study design (All RCTs/quasi-randomised controlled trials)
- Intervention (DMARD)
- Comparison group (combination therapy with 2 or more DMARDs or 1 DMARD + 1 biological agent)
- Blinding (double blind assessment was performed)
- Allocation concealment
- ITT analysis was performed
- Study size (all fairly small, N <100)

However, they differed with respect to:
- Study size (range N=11 to N=89)

- Study quality – maximum Jadad score of 5 (N=30 studies good quality; N=6 poor quality)
- Study duration – variable, (exact lengths not mentioned).

NOTE: Because the MA pooled together papers which had patients of both recent-onset and established RA, it was decided that duplicate papers (ie papers picked up in our search which were already included in the MA) would still be included as evidence in this section for 'recent-onset' RA in order to explore any effects within these sub-populations.

The 6 included RCTs[242,255–262] all assessed sequences of DMARDs but had variable inclusion criteria. The trials differed with respect to the following:

- Sample size (range: N=111 to N=508)
- Blinding (1 RCT triple blind, 2 RCTs double blind, 2 RCTs single blind, 1 RCT unblinded)
- Trial length (1 RCT 6 months, 3 RCTs 18 months, 2 RCTs 2 years)
- Treatment – type and sequences of DMARDs used and compared
- Treatment regimen – doses of DMARDs

Treatments used

1. The first RCT – the BeSt study[256–259], compared 4 different treatment arms. Group 1: sequential monotherapy; Group 2: step-up combination therapy; Group 3: initial combination therapy with CS; and Group 4: initial combination therapy with infliximab. Therapies were changed depending on DAS score.

2. The second RCT, the MASCOT study[255] compared 3 different treatment arms. Group 1: patients were given SSZ then SSZ + MTX; Group 2 patients were given SSZ and continued on SSZ; Group 3: patients were given SSZ then MTX.

3. The third RCT (Feraccioli et al.)[260] compared 3 different treatment arms. Group 1: patients were on DMARD then MTX was added; Group 2: patients were on DMARD then CsA (cyclosporin A) was added; Group 3: patients were on DMARD then SSZ was added.

4. The fourth RCT – the TICORA study[242] compared 2 different treatment arms. Group 1 (Intensive): initial monotherapy with SSZ (escalating dose) then triple therapy; Group 2 (Routine): initial monotherapy with SSZ then alternative monotherapy or step-up combination therapy. Therapies were changed depending on DAS score.

5. The fifth RCT (Braun et al.)[262] compared 2 different treatment arms in patients who had not previously been treated with DMARDs. Group 1: SC (subcutaneous) MTX; Group 2: Oral MTX.

6. The sixth RCT (Choy et al.)[261] compared 4 different treatment arms. Group 1: MTX (starting 7.5 mg/week increasing incrementally to 15 mg/week). Group 2: Step-down prednisolone started with MTX (60 mg/day initially, reduced to 7.5 mg at 6 weeks, 7.5 mg/day from 6–8 weeks, stopped by 34 weeks). Group 3: ciclosporin started 3 months after MTX (initial dose 100 mg/day, increased gradually to target dose of 3 mg/kg daily). Group 4: all treatments

The prospective cohort study (Hider et al.)[263] included N=439 patients who were taken from NOAR (The Norfolk Arthritis Register) and had been treated with either MTX or SSZ as first-line therapy and were followed prospectively for 2 years.

7.1.8 Health economic methodological introduction (optimal sequencing of DMARDs and biologics)

The search terms for the DMARDs and biologic questions were combined in order to look at the cost-effectiveness evidence of the optimal sequencing of biologics and traditional DMARDs in early RA. To identify evidence related to biologics, the HTA review by Chen et al.[237] was reviewed. No studies addressed early RA, although this was addressed by the BRAM model in the HTA report itself. One other study[239] was also identified.

7.1.9 Clinical evidence statements (optimal sequencing of DMARDs)

▷ Recent-onset RA

Aggressive vs non-aggressive treatment

Table 7.9 Symptoms/quality of life

Study	Outcomes	Follow-up	Result – best treatment
COBRA study[253,254] **Level 1++**	Pooled index (MD 0.6, 95% CI 0.4 to 0.8), tender joints (MD 8, 95% CI 4 to 13), swollen joints (MD 5, 95% CI 2 to 7), VAS pain (MD 14, 95% CI 5 to 23), MACTAR score (MD 3, 95% CI 1 to 5)	28 weeks	**Aggressive** (all p ≤0.001 except pain p=0.002)
		56 weeks	**NS**
	DAS28 score reduction over time (change 0.1/year)	Change from 1–5 years	**Aggressive**
CIMESTRA study[246,247] **Level 1++**	ACR-N	1 year and 2 years	**Aggressive** (p <0.05)
	ACR20 (1 year MD 17; 2 years MD 15)	1 year and 2 years	**Aggressive** (p <0.05)
	ACR50 (2 years MD 17)	1 year	**NS**
		2 years	**Aggressive** (p <0.05)
	ACR 70	1 year and 2 years	**NS**
	DAS28	2 years	**NS**
	Tender and swollen joints, ACR70 and pain (VAS)	1 and 2 years	**NS**
FINRACO study[248–251] **Level 1+**	ACR50 (values not given) and swollen joint count (values not given)	2 years	**Aggressive** (p <0.05)
	DAS 28 (median difference 0.52), DAS28 AUC (mean difference 0.70), work disability (median difference 19.8 days)	5 years	**Aggressive** (p <0.05, p <0.001, p <0.01)

MD = mean difference

Table 7.10 Functions

Study	Outcomes	Follow-up	Result – best treatment
COBRA study[253,254] **Level 1++**	HAQ score (MD 0.5, 95% CI 0.3 to 0.7), grip strength (MD 14, 95% CI 9 to 19)	28 weeks	**Aggressive** (both p <0.0001)
		56 weeks	**NS**
CIMESTRA study[246,247] **Level 1++**	HAQ score; patients with HAQ score ≤0.25	1 year (and 2 years HAQ score)	**NS**
FINRACO study[248–251] **Level 1+**	Physical function	2 years	**NS**

Table 7.11 Joint damage

Study	Outcomes	Follow-up	Result – best treatment
COBRA study[253,254] **Level 1++**	Erosion score (Median difference 3.0); total radiographic damage –SHS score (median difference 8.0)	28, 56 and 80 weeks	**Aggressive** (all p ≤0.01; values at 80 weeks given)
	JSN (median difference 28 weeks: 1.0)	28 weeks and over time (mean change from 1–5 years)	**Aggressive** (p <0.05)
		56 and 80 weeks	**NS**
CIMESTRA study[246,247] **Level 1++**	Larsen score, Rate of radiographic progression and development of bone erosions	1 year	**NS**
	Total Sharp score, erosion score, JSN and progression since baseline	2 years	**NS**
FINRACO study[248-251] **Level 1+**	Eroded joints (5 years: median difference 3.0), joint damage – Larsen score (5 years: median difference 6.0), increase in Larsen score (5 years: MD 33%, 95% CI 15 to 50)	2 years and 5 years	**Aggressive** (all p <0.01)

Table 7.12 Global assessment

Study	Outcomes	Follow-up	Result – best treatment
COBRA study[253,254] **Level 1++**	Assessor's global assessment (MD 16, 95% CI 8 to 24)	28 weeks	**Aggressive** (p=0.0001)
		56 weeks	**NS**
	Patient's global assessment	28 weeks and 56 weeks	**NS**
CIMESTRA study[246,247] **Level 1++**	Patient's and physician's global assessment	2 years	**NS**
FINRACO study[248–251] **Level 1+**	Patient's and physician's overall assessments	2 years	**NS**

Table 7.13 Biochemical markers

Study	Outcomes	Follow-up	Result – best treatment
COBRA study[253,254] **Level 1++**	ESR (MD 13, 95% CI 5 to 22)	28 weeks	**Aggressive** (p=0.002)
		56 weeks	**NS**
CIMESTRA study[246,247] **Level 1++**	ESR and CRP	2 years	**NS**
FINRACO study[248–251] **Level 1+**	ESR (values not given)	2 years	**Aggressive** (p <0.05)

Table 7.14 Adverse events

Study	Outcomes	Follow-up	Result – best treatment
CIMESTRA study[246,247] **Level 1++**	AEs in >10% of patients (N=63 vs N=89).	1 year	**Non-aggressive (better)**
	Number or type of AEs	2 years	**NS**
FINRACO study[248–251] **Level 1+**	Number of patients with AEs; SAEs or GI AEs	2 years	**NS**

Table 7.15 Withdrawals

Study	Outcomes	Follow-up	Result – best treatment
COBRA study[253,254] **Level 1++**	Total number of withdrawals (8% vs 29%), withdrawals due to AEs (3% vs 8%) and due to lack of efficacy (5% vs 15%)	56 weeks	**Aggressive (better)**
CIMESTRA study[246,247] **Level 1++**	Withdrawals due to SAEs (N=1, 1% vs N=3, 4%)	2 years	**Similar**

Table 7.16 Remission

Study	Outcomes	Follow-up	Result – best treatment
COBRA study[253,254] **Level 1++**	Remission (ACR and DAS)	48 weeks, 1 year and 2 years	**NS**
	Remission (EULAR)	2 years	**NS**
FINRACO study[248–251] **Level 1+**	Patients with sustained remission (ACR)	Over the 2 years	**Aggressive (p=0.013 – OR 4.6, 95% CI 1.2 to 17.0)**
	Patients with sustained remission (DAS28)	Over the 2 years	**Aggressive (p <0.001– OR 5.6, 95% CI 2.6 to 11.6)**
	Patients with sustained remission (EULAR)	Over the 2 years	**Aggressive (p <0.001 – OR 5.4, 95% CI 2.7 to 10.6).**

- One RCT, the FINRACO study[248–251] found that sustained remission protects against radiographic joint damage – patients in sustained remission had less radiographic progression over 2 years compared with patients who were in remission at 6 months and lost it later (MD 3 points, p <0.001). **Level 1+**

General sequences

Table 7.17 Symptoms/quality of life

Study	Sequence	Outcomes	Follow-up	Result – best treatment
1 MA[244] **Level 1++**	MTX + α-TNF inhibitors vs MTX	Overall efficacy (RR 0.22, 95% CI 0.14 to 0.32)	End of follow-up	**MTX + α-TNF** (p=0.00001)
	MTX + SSZ and/or anti-malarials vs monotherapy	Overall efficacy (8 studies: RR 0.41, 95% CI 0.24 to 0.7)		**Arm 1** (p=0.00001)
	CS added to single DMARD as bridging therapy vs monotherapy	Overall efficacy		**NS**
	Other non-biological DMARD combinations vs monotherapy	Overall efficacy (RR 0.37, 95% CI 0.25 to 0.5)		**Arm 1** (p=0.00001)
	Combination therapy vs monotherapy	ACR20 (RR 1.5, 95% CI 1.3 to 1.9); joint counts (31% benefit); major clinical improvement (RR 2.1, 95% CI 1.6 to 2.7)		**Arm 1** (all p <0.00001)
MASCOT study [255] **Level 1++**	SSZ then SSZ + MTX vs SSZ continuous	DAS score (median difference 0.37)	Change from 6–18 months	**Arm 1** (p=0.039)
		Pain (VAS), swollen joint count, RAI, ACR20, ACR50 and ACR70	Change from 6–18 months	**NS**
	SSZ then SSZ + MTX vs SSZ then MTX	DAS score (median difference 0.41) and RAI (median difference 4.0)	Change from 6–18 months	**Arm 1** (both p <0.05)
		HAQ, pain (VAS), swollen joint count, ACR20, ACR50 and ACR70	Change from 6–18 months	**NS**
	SSZ then MTX vs SSZ continuous	DAS score, RAI, swollen joint count, pain (VAS), ACR20, ACR50 and ACR70	Change from 6–18 months	**NS**
1 RCT (Ferraccioli et al.)[260] **Level 1+**	DMARD then DMARD + MTX vs DMARD then DMARD + SSZ	Swollen joints (MD 2.6), VAS pain (MD 1.9)	18 months	**Arm 1** (all p <0.05)
		Swollen joints	Between 18–36 months	**NS**
		Tender joints (18 months: MD 3.6, 18–36 months MD 1.1)	18 months and between 18–36 months	**Arm 1** (p <0.05)
	DMARD then DMARD + CsA vs DMARD then DMARD + SSZ	VAS pain (MD 2.1), tender joint count (3.5)	18 months Between 18–36 months	**Arm 1** (both p=0.001) **NS**
		Swollen joints	18 months and Between 18–36 months	**NS**

continued

Table 7.17 Symptoms/quality of life – *continued*

Study	Sequence	Outcomes	Follow-up	Result – best treatment
BeSt study[256–259] **Level 1+**	Step-up combination vs sequential monotherapy or initial combination with IFX	DAS44 of ≤2.4	1 year and 2 years	**NS**
	Sequential monotherapy vs initial combination with CS or IFX	DAS44 of ≤2.4 (53% vs 71% or 74%)	1 year 2 years	**Arm 1** (p=0.004 and p=0.001) **NS**
	Initial combination with CS vs step-up combination or initial combination with IFX	DAS44 of ≤2.4	1 year and 2 years	**NS**
	Initial combination with IFX vs step-up combination	DAS44 of ≤2.4	1 year and 2 years	**NS**
1 RCT (Braun et al.)[262] **Level 1++**	SC MTX vs Oral MTX	ACR20 (78% vs 70%), ACR70 (41% vs 33%), swollen joints (MD 1.0)	24 weeks	**SC** (all p <0.05)
		ACR50, tender joints, DAS28	24 weeks	**NS**
1 RCT (Choy et al.)[261] **Level 1++**	MTX increasing dose vs MTX + prednisolone (decrease dose)	SF-36 (MD 2.4), DAS28 score (MD 0.05)	2 years	**Arm 1 (better)**
	MTX increasing dose vs MTX then add ciclosporin	SF-36 (MD 1.9), DAS28 score (MD 0.08)	2 years	**Arm 1 (better)**
	MTX + prednisolone (decrease dose) vs MTX then add ciclosporin	SF-36 (MD 0.4), DAS28 score (MD 0.03)	2 years	**Arm 2 (better)**
	MTX + prednisolone + ciclosporin vs all other arms	SF-36 (MD 2.2 and 4.1 and 4.5), DAS28 score (MD 0.25 and 0.33 and 0.30)	2 years	**Arm 1 (better)**
TICORA study [242] **Level 1++**	Intensive vs routine	VAS pain (MD 25, 95% CI 14 to 36), ACR20 (OR 5.7, 95% CI 1.9 to 16.7), ACR50 (OR 6.1, 95% CI 2.5 to 14.9), ACR70 (OR 11, 95% CI 4.5 to 27), disease activity score (MD 1.6, 95% CI 1.1 to 2.1); joint swelling (MD 3, 95% CI 1 to 5); joint tenderness (MD 8, 95% CI 4 to 12); SF-12 physical domain (MD 5.3, 95% CI 0.8 to 9.8).	18 months	**Arm 1** (p <0.0001; p=0.0028; p=0.0003; p=0.021)
		SF-12 mental domain	18 months	**NS**

continued

Table 7.17 Symptoms/quality of life – *continued*

Study	Sequence	Outcomes	Follow-up	Result – best treatment
1 cohort study (Hider et al.)[263] **Level 2+**	Starting on SSZ vs starting on MTX	Swollen and tender joints	2 years	**NS**
		Swollen and tender joints (median difference 2 and 3)	5 years	**Arm 1** (p=0.01, p=0.02)
		DAS28	5 years	**NS**

Table 7.18 Function

Study	Sequence	Outcomes	Follow-up	Result – best treatment
MASCOT study[255] **Level 1++**	SSZ then SSZ + MTX vs SSZ continuous or SSZ then MTX	HAQ score	Change from 6–18 months	**NS**
	SSZ then MTX vs SSZ continuous	HAQ score	Change from 6–18 months	**NS**
BeSt study[256–259] **Level 1+**	Step-up combination vs sequential monotherapy	D-HAQ	1 and 2 years and over time (2 years)	**NS**
	Sequential monotherapy vs initial combination with CS or IFX	D-HAQ (values not given)	1 year and Over time (2 years)	**Arm 2** (all p <0.001)
			2 years	**NS**
	Initial combination with CS vs step-up combination or initial combination with IFX	D-HAQ (values not given)	1 and 2 years	**NS**
			Over time (2 years)	**Arm 1** (all p <0.001)
	Initial combination with IFX vs step-up combination	D-HAQ (values not given)	1 and 2 years	**NS**
			Over time (2 years)	**Arm 1** (all p <0.001)
1 RCT (Braun et al.)[262] **Level 1++**	SC MTX vs oral MTX	HAQ	24 weeks	**NS**
1 RCT (Choy et al.)[261] **Level 1++**	MTX increasing dose vs MTX + prednisolone (decrease dose)	HAQ (MD 0.01)	2 years	**Arm 1 (better)**
	MTX increasing dose vs MTX then add ciclosporin	HAQ (MD 0.09)	2 years	**Both similar**
	MTX + prednisolone (decrease dose) vs MTX then add ciclosporin	HAQ (MD 0.08)	2 years	**Arm 2 (better)**
	MTX + prednisolone + ciclosporin vs all other arms	HAQ (MD 0.21 and 0.30 and 0.22)	2 years	**Arm 1 (better)**

continued

Table 7.18 Function – *continued*

Study	Sequence	Outcomes	Follow-up	Result – best treatment
TICORA study [242] **Level 1++**	Intensive vs routine	HAQ (MD 0.5, 95% CI 0.2 to 0.8)	18 months	**Arm 1** (p=0.0025)
1 cohort study (Hider et al.)[263] **Level 2+**	Starting on SSZ vs starting on MTX	HAQ	2 and 5 years	**NS**

Table 7.19 Joint damage

Study	Sequence	Outcomes	Follow-up	Result – best treatment
MASCOT study[255] **Level 1++**	SSZ then SSZ + MTX vs SSZ continuous or SSZ then MTX	Total Sharp score, total erosions (hands and feet), JSN	Change from 6–18 months	**NS**
	SSZ then MTX vs SSZ continuous	Total Sharp score, total erosions (hands and feet), JSN	Change from 6–18 months	**NS**
BeSt study[256–259] **Level 1+**	Step-up combination vs Sequential monotherapy	SHS score – radiographic progression (values not given)	Over the 2 years	**Arm 1** (p=0.044)
		Number of patients with no progression of total SHS (> SDD)	1 year	**NS**
		Total SHS	1 and 2 years	**NS**
		Total SHS, erosion score and JSN score	2 years	**NS**
	Sequential monotherapy vs Initial combination with CS or IFX	Total SHS (>SDD)	1 year	**NS**
		Total SHS (2 years: median difference 6.4 or 6.5), erosion score (2 years: median difference both 1.0)	1 and 2 years	**Arm 2** (all p <0.05, all p <0.001)
		JSN score (MD both 1.0)	1 year 2 years	**Arm 2** (all p <0.05) **NS**
		SHS score (radiographic progression)	Over the 2 years	**Arm 2** (all p <0.001)

continued

Table 7.19 Joint damage – *continued*

Study	Sequence	Outcomes	Follow-up	Result – best treatment
	Initial combination with CS vs Step-up combination	Total SHS (>SDD)	1 year	**NS**
		Total SHS (2 years: median difference 1.0), erosion score (2 years: median difference 0.5)	1 and 2 years	**Arm 1** (all p <0.05, all p <0.001)
		JSN score	1 and 2 years	**NS**
		SHS score – radiographic progression (values not given),	Over the 2 years	**Arm 1** (all p <0.001)
	Initial combination with CS vs Initial combination with IFX	Total SHS (>SDD)	1 year	**NS**
		Total SHS, erosion score, JSN score	1 and 2 years	**NS**
		SHS score – radiographic progression (values not given)	Over the 2 years	**Similar**
	Initial combination with IFX vs Step-up combination	JSN (MD 0), total SHS (>SDD: 93% vs 73%)	1 year	**Arm 1** (p <0.05, p <0.001)
		Total SHS (2 years: median difference 1.0), erosion score (2 years: median difference 0.5)	1 and 2 years	**Arm 1** (all p <0.05, all p <0.001)
		JSN	2 years	**NS**
		SHS score – radiographic progression (values not given)	Over the 2 years	**Arm 1** (all p <0.001)
1 RCT (Choy et al)[261] **Level 1++**	MTX increasing dose vs MTX + prednisolone (decrease dose)	Cases of new erosions (28% vs 16%), change in Larsen score (MD 3.71)	2 years	**Arm 2 (better)**
	MTX increasing dose vs MTX then add ciclosporin	Cases with erosions (28% vs 17%), Change in Larsen score (MD 2.88)	2 years	**Arm 1 (better)**
	MTX + prednisolone (decrease dose) vs MTX then add ciclosporin	Cases of new erosions Change in Larsen score (MD 0.17)	2 years	**NS** **Arm 1 (better)**
	MTX + prednisolone + ciclosporin vs all other arms	Cases of new erosions (13% vs 28% and 17% and, change in Larsen score (MD 4.42 and 1.54 and 1.71)	2 years	**Arm 1 (better)**

continued

Table 7.19 Joint damage – *continued*

Study	Sequence	Outcomes	Follow-up	Result – best treatment
TICORA study[242] **Level 1++**	Intensive vs routine	Erosion score (MD 2.5), TSS (MD 4.0)	18 months	**Arm 1** (p=0.002, p=0.02)
		JSN	18 months	**NS**
1 cohort study (Hider et al.)[263] **Level 2+**	Starting on SSZ vs starting on MTX	Larsen score, percentage of patients with erosions	5 years	**NS**
		Percentage of patients with erosions (propensity adjusted)	5 years	**NS**

One RCT – the BeSt study[256–259] found that patients who do not achieve and maintain DAS ≤ 2.4 with MTX, regardless of the success of consecutive treatment steps, develop significantly more radiographic joint damage compared to patients with DAS ≤ 2.4 on initial MTX (MD 6 units of TSS, p=0.007). After failure on initial MTX, treatment with subsequent conventional DMARDs is unlikely to result in a DAS ≤ 2.4 and allows progression of joint damage. **Level 1+**

Table 7.20 Global assessment

Study	Sequence	Outcomes	Follow-up	Result – best treatment
MASCOT study[255] **Level 1++**	SSZ then SSZ + MTX vs SSZ continuous	Patient's and physician's global assessment	Change from 6–18 months	**NS**
	SSZ then SSZ + MTX vs SSZ then MTX	Patient's and physician's global assessment	Change from 6–18 months	**NS**
	SSZ then MTX vs SSZ continuous	Patient's and physician's global assessment	Change from 6–18 months	**NS**
1 RCT (Ferraccioli et al.)[260] **Level 1+**	DMARD then DMARD + MTX vs DMARD then DMARD + SSZ	Patient's and physician's global assessment (MD2.9 and 2.8)	18 months	**Arm 1** (p <0.05)
			18–36 months	**NS**
	DMARD then DMARD + CsA vs DMARD then DMARD + SSZ	Patient's and physician's global assessment (MD 1.5 and 2.7)	18 months	**Arm 1** (p <0.05)
			18–36 months	**NS**
TICORA study[242] **Level 1++**	Intensive vs routine	Patient's and assessor's global assessment of disease activity (MD 30, 95% CI 17 to 42 and MD 24, 95% CI 14 to 34)	18 months	**Arm 1** (p <0.0001)

Table 7.21 Biochemical markers

Study	Sequence	Outcomes	Follow-up	Result – best treatment
MASCOT study[255] **Level 1++**	SSZ then SSZ + MTX vs SSZ continuous	ESR, CRP	Change from 6–18 months	**NS**
	SSZ then SSZ + MTX vs SSZ then MTX	ESR (Median difference 1.0) CRP	Change from 6–18 months	**Arm 1** (p=0.033) **NS**
	SSZ then MTX vs SSZ continuous	ESR, CRP	Change from 6–18 months	**NS**
1 RCT (Ferraccioli et al.)[260] **Level 1+**	DMARD then DMARD + MTX vs DMARD then DMARD + SSZ	ESR (18 months MD 30.2, 36 months MD 5.5); CRP (18 months MD 11.2, 36 months MD 0.9)	18 months and 18–36 months	**Arm 1** (p=0.01, p=0.001; both p=0.001)
	DMARD then DMARD + CsA vs DMARD then DMARD + SSZ	ESR	18 months and 18–36 months	**NS**
		CRP (18–36 months MD 8.1)	18 months	**NS**
			18–36 months	**Arm 1** (p=0.03)
TICORA study[242] **Level 1++**	Intensive vs routine	ESR (MD 18, 95% CI 8 to 28) CRP	18 months	**Arm 1** (p=0.0007) **NS**
1 cohort study (Hider et al.)[263] **Level 2+**	Starting on SSZ vs starting on MTX	CRP	5 years	**NS**

Table 7.22 Adverse events

Study	Sequence	Outcomes	Follow-up	Result – best treatment
1 RCT (Ferraccioli et al.)[260] **Level 1+**	DMARD then DMARD + MTX vs DMARD then DMARD + SSZ	Number of patients with AEs (88% vs 47%)	18 months	**NS**
			36 months	**Arm 2 (better)**
	DMARD then DMARD + CsA vs DMARD then DMARD + SSZ	Number of patients with AEs (95% vs 45%)	18 months	**NS**
			36 months	**Arm 2 (better)**
BeSt study[256–259] **Level 1+**	Step-up combination vs sequential monotherapy	Number of patients with AEs and SAEs	1 year, 2 years and over time (2 years)	**NS**
	Sequential monotherapy vs initial combination with CS or IFX	Number of patients with AEs and SAEs	1 year and 2 years	**NS**

continued

Table 7.22 Adverse events – *continued*

Study	Sequence	Outcomes	Follow-up	Result – best treatment
	Initial combination with CS vs step-up combination	Number of patients with AEs and SAEs	1 year and 2 years	NS
	Initial combination with CS vs initial combination with IFX	Number of patients with AEs and SAEs	1 year and 2 years	NS
	Initial combination with IFX vs step-up combination	Number of patients with AEs and SAEs	1 year and 2 years	NS
TICORA study [242] Level 1++	Intensive vs routine	Number of AEs (N=46 vs N=85)	18 months	Arm 1 (better)
1 RCT (Braun et al.)[262] Level 1++	SC MTX vs oral MTX	Percentage of patients with at least 1 moderate AE	24 weeks	NS
		Percentage of patients with SAEs (5.7% vs 4.3%)	24 weeks	Similar

Table 7.23 Withdrawals

Study	Sequence	Outcomes	Follow-up	Result – best treatment
1 MA[244] Level 1++	Combination therapy vs monotherapy	Withdrawals (RR 0.4, 95% CI 0.3 to 0.5), withdrawals due to toxicity (RR 1.37, 95% CI 1.16 to 1.62), withdrawals due to lack of efficacy (RR 0.89, 95% CI 0.80 to 0.99)	End of follow-up	Arm 1 (p <0.0001; p=0.033)
MASCOT study[255] Level 1++	SSZ then SSZ + MTX vs SSZ continuous and vs SSZ then MTX	Total number of withdrawals (17% vs 14% and 16%), withdrawals due to AEs (21% vs 18% and 26%) and due to lack of efficacy (4% vs 7% and 4%)	18 months	Similar
	SSZ then MTX vs SSZ continuous	Total number of withdrawals (16% vs 14%), withdrawals due to AEs (26% vs 18%) and due to lack of efficacy (4% vs 7%)		Similar

continued

Table 7.23 Withdrawals – *continued*

Study	Sequence	Outcomes	Follow-up	Result – best treatment
BeSt study[256–259] **Level 1+**	Step-up combination vs Sequential monotherapy	Number of withdrawals (7% vs 5%)	2 years	**Similar**
	Sequential monotherapy vs Initial combination with CS or IFX	Number of withdrawals (5% vs 6% and 3%)	2 years	**Similar**
	Initial combination with CS vs Step-up combination	Number of withdrawals (6% vs 7%)	2 years	**Similar**
	Initial combination with CS vs Initial combination with IFX	Number of withdrawals (6% vs 3%)	2 years	**Similar**
1 RCT (Ferraccioli et al.)[260] **Level 1+**	DMARD then DMARD + MTX vs DMARD then DMARD + SSZ	Number of withdrawals (18 and 36 months: 12% vs 48%) Withdrawals due to toxicity (18 and 36 months: 7% vs 48%)	18 months and 36 months	**Arm 1 (better)** **Arm 1** (p=0.0001)
	DMARD then DMARD + CsA vs DMARD then DMARD + SSZ	Number of withdrawals (18 and 36 months: 17% vs 48%) Withdrawals due to toxicity (18 and 36 months: 12% vs 48%)	18 months and 36 months	**Arm 1 (better)** **Arm 1** (p=0.0001)
1 cohort study (Hider et al.)[263] **Level 2+**	Starting on SSZ vs starting on MTX	Proportion of patients with no change in treatment (50% vs 56%)	Over the 2 years	**Arm 2 (better)**

Table 7.24 Remission

Study	Sequence	Outcomes	Follow-up	Result – best treatment
MASCOT study[255] **Level 1++**	SSZ then SSZ + MTX vs SSZ continuous	Percentage of patients with EULAR good response (18% vs 7%) and percentage in remission (10% vs 5%)	18 months	**Arm 1 (better)**
	SSZ then SSZ + MTX vs SSZ then MTX	Percentage of patients with EULAR good response (18% vs 5%) and percentage in remission (10% vs 3%)	18 months	**Similar**
	SSZ then MTX vs SSZ continuous	Percentage of patients with EULAR good response (5% vs 7%) and percentage in remission (3% vs 5%)	18 months	**Similar**

continued

Table 7.24 Remission – *continued*

Study	Sequence	Outcomes	Follow-up	Result – best treatment
1 RCT (Ferraccioli et al.)[260] **Level 1+**	DMARD then DMARD + MTX vs DMARD then DMARD + SSZ	Magnusson criteria (full response): 40% vs 21%	3 years	**Arm 1 (better)**
		Number of patients in full remission (ACR): 9% vs 7%	3 years	**Similar**
	DMARD then DMARD + CsA vs DMARD then DMARD + SSZ	Magnusson criteria (full response): 40% vs 21%	3 years	**Arm 1 (better)**
		Number of patients in full remission (ACR) 9% vs 7%	3 years	**Similar**
TICORA study[242] **Level 1++**	Intensive vs routine	EULAR good response (OR 5.8, 95% CI 2.4 to 13.9), EULAR remission (OR 9.7, 95% CI 3.9 to 23.9)	Over the 2 years	**Arm 1 (both p <0.0001)**
1 cohort study (Hider et al.)[263] **Level 2+**	Starting on SSZ vs starting on MTX	Percentage of patients in remission	2 and 5 years	**NS**

7.1.10 Health economics evidence statements (optimal sequencing of DMARDs and biologics)

Only two studies were identified and only one of these relates to the UK (Chen et al.).[237] The other is US based (Spalding et al.)[239] and therefore of questionable relevance, given the different drug prices and healthcare systems.

The model was a patient level simulation and considered adalimumab, etanercept, infliximab + MTX, adalimumab + MTX, etanercept + MTX against a sequence of DMARDs. Spalding et al. developed a Markov model considering adalimumab, etanercept, infliximab + MTX, adalimumab + MTX against MTX.

For first line use of biologics, with or without MTX, Chen et al.[237] estimate ICERs well in excess of the usual NICE threshold. First line use of infliximab is associated with extremely high ICERs in both studies. Adalimumab and etanercept without MTX generate lower ICERs in both studies but these are still unlikely to be considered cost effective. Third line use of each of the three anti-TNFs is considered cost-effective as reflected in current NICE guidance.[130]

Table 7.25 Summary of published econmic analyses

Study	Country (sponsor)	TNF inhibitors considered	Form of economic evaluation	Disease duration (years)	Model used and time horizon
Spalding et al.[239]	USA Astellas Pharma	Adalimumab, etanercept, infliximab + MTX, adalimumab + MTX	Cost Utility	3 months	Markov, Lifetime
Chen et al.[237]	UK NHS-HTA	Adalimumab, etanercept, infliximab + MTX, adalimumab + MTX, etanercept+ MTX	Cost Utility	Various (even within 'early' RA)	Patient Level Simulation, Lifetime

Table 7.26 Summary of published ICERs for TNF-inhibitors

Drug	Comparator	Study	ICER	
Adalimumab	DMARD sequence	Chen	Adalimumab (no MTX)	£35k per QALY
			Adalimumab (+ MTX)	£30k per QALY
			3rd Line Early RA Data	
			Adalimumab (no MTX)	£53k per QALY
			Adalimumab (+ MTX)	£171k per QALY
			1st Line Early RA Data	
	MTX	Spalding	Adalimumab (no MTX)	$64k per QALY
			Adalimumab (+ MTX)	$195k per QALY
Etanercept	DMARD sequence	Chen	Etanercept (no MTX)	£30k per QALY
			Etanercept (+ MTX)	£29k per QALY
			3rd Line Early RA Data	
			Etanercept (no MTX)	£49k per QALY
			Etanercept (+ MTX)	£78k per QALY
			1st Line Early RA Data	
	MTX	Spalding	Etanercept (no MTX)	$90k per QALY
Infliximab	DMARD sequence	Chen	Infliximab (with MTX)	£30k per QALY
			3rd Line Early RA Data	
			Infliximab (with MTX)	£654k per QALY
			1st Line Early RA Data	
	MTX	Spalding	Infliximab (with MTX)	$410k per QALY

In England and Wales, the usual incremental cost-effectiveness threshold is considered to be in the region of £20,000 to £30,000 per QALY gained for NICE. The typically quoted acceptable ICER in the US is $50,000 per QALY gained although caution must be used in translating this or dollar values to England and Wales.

7.1.11 Summary of evidence statements (optimal sequencing of DMARDs)

- For many patients, monotherapies such as methotrexate work well.[256–259]

- Sequential monotherapies comparing methotrexate and sulphasalazine do not show any obvious differences between the drugs,[255,263] although other studies comparing sulphasalazine with methotrexate and cyclosporin in combination therapies suggest that the latter two are superior for some outcomes to the former.[260]

- If a patient fails on methotrexate monotherapy, the chances they will have a good response to other conventional DMARDs are less.[259]

- For symptoms, quality of life, ability to achieve remission, and slowing joint damage, a variety of combination therapies appear to be superior to monotherapy.[244,246–251,253–259,264]

- For other outcomes such as function there is less evidence of a difference.[246–251,253–258,259]

- There is no difference in tolerability between monotherapies and combination therapies.[244,246–251,253,254,256–259,264]

- One study compared oral with subcutaneous methotrexate, but failed to find any substantial difference between the two, and did not include a health economic analysis.[308]

- Some studies show a convergence of outcomes between the arms of the trial over time.[246,247,253,254]

- Many of the studies showed similar improvements with a variety of monotherapies and combination therapies, and suggested that the type and combination of drug used was less important than the speed and intensity of the DMARD introduction.[244,246–251,253–259,264,] Intensity refers to the rapid escalation of DMARD to therapeutic doses.

7.1.12 From evidence to recommendations (early introduction and optimal sequencing of DMARDs)

The GDG noted that there was overwhelming evidence to support the strategy of early introduction of DMARDs. However, the GDG were mindful that all trials had been conducted in patients with active inflammatory joint disease, and there is currently no evidence to support the approach that must be taken in mild synovitis, or palindromic arthritis where the disease activity waxes and wanes with periods of activity and inactivity. It was therefore felt that the early introduction of DMARDs in RA needed to relate specifically to active RA, and the treatment of mild disease needed to be considered as a research recommendation.

The key area that had been agreed for health economic modelling (see section 2.8) was an assessment of the cost effectiveness of various DMARD strategies in patients with recent-onset RA, including the initiation therapy with combinations of disease modifying drugs. The results of this analysis (see Appendix C) demonstrated clear benefits of a combination strategy, compared with monotherapy, and demonstrated that step-down combinations of DMARDs are likely to be very cost-effective or even cost-saving, and other DMARD combinations are very likely to be cost-effective. The GDG felt that the opportunity should be taken of now recommending this approach as first line treatment unless specifically contraindicated.

There is evidence that methotrexate is at least as efficacious as other DMARD monotherapies, if not more so in some studies. Rapid acceleration of the drug can achieve excellent response in most patients. The NICE TA on anti-TNFs recommends that methotrexate to be tried before anti-TNF therapies can be considered.[130] The GDG was also mindful of emerging evidence to suggest that if a patient fails on methotrexate, they are unlikely to respond to other conventional DMARDs, and consideration should be given to anti-TNF therapies once a patient has failed on a trial of at least two conventional DMARDs (including methotrexate). The GDG were also aware of increasing evidence that subcutaneous methotrexate might have greater bioavailability than the oral route, but did not feel there was sufficient evidence to make a recommendation at this stage, particularly as a health economic analysis was not available.

Taking all these considerations into account, the GDG felt that methotrexate should be included as the first DMARD therapy, either as monotherapy or as part of a combination of other therapies. Furthermore, the most successful and cost-effective step-down and combination therapy regimes had all used steroids in one form or another (either orally in a tapered dose, intra-articularly, intra-muscularly or a combination of these approaches) and it was therefore felt that steroids should be specifically mentioned in combination regimes. Although the basecase analysis determined that a strategy of monotherapy plus glucocorticoids is more costly and less effective than DMARD monotherapy (due to the cost-differential not being covered by a significant increase in ACR response rate; please see Appendix C for more information), the GDG felt it was important to note that step up and step down all include glucocorticoids in the regimen, so that no combination regime has been shown to work without steroids in some form (oral, intramuscular or intra-articular). Until studies have demonstrated that combination regimes can be used efficaciously in the absence of steroids, the GDG felt that they should be included in the recommendation.

It was agreed that no lower limit should be placed on the amount of time that needed to pass before the introduction of a DMARD in recent-onset RA; indeed such therapy should be initiated as soon as possible. Although there was no good evidence to support the concept of an upper limit by which time DMARD therapy should have been started in order to achieve long-term benefits on disease outcomes (the 'window of opportunity' referred to in the clinical introduction), the GDG felt that the initiation of DMARD therapy within 3 months of the onset of persistent symptoms was supported by the evidence and should therefore be recommended as an ideal target.

In keeping with this initial aggressive treatment of disease it was noted that there was a need to try to decrease the doses of drugs once satisfactory disease control had been achieved, and that this would in turn involve appropriate monitoring (see recommendations in section 8.1). The GDG agreed that ideally the level of disease control to be aspired to is remission, but this was not always achievable in clinical practice. Therefore a negotiated position needs to be reached by the patients and professional whereby it is determined between these parties what consititues a satisfactory response.

The need for early initiation of therapy would also support the recommendations about the need for urgent referral to specialist care of people with persistent idiopathic synovitis, even in the absence of abnormal tests, and especially if symptoms have already been present for more than 3 months (see recommendations in section 8.2).

Although methotrexate appears to be the drug of choice for use in combination therapies in patients with a recent onset of rheumatoid arthritis, it was acknowledged that would be circumstances under which other drugs would be chosen (such as co-morbidities and contraindications to methotrexate), and perhaps used as monotherapies. Other DMARD monotherapies and combination therapies that exclude methotrexate can work very satisfactorily. It was therefore decided that where combination therapies were not indicated, the type of drug used is less important than the promptness of initiating therapy and the rapid escalation to, and maintenance at a therapeutic dose, of DMARD. The GDG felt that there should be a recommendation that embraced these concepts

RECOMMENDATIONS

R16   In people with newly diagnosed active RA, offer a combination of DMARDs (including methotrexate and at least one other DMARD, plus short-term glucocorticoids) as first-line treatment as soon as possible, ideally within 3 months of the onset of persistent symptoms.

R17   In people with recent-onset RA receiving combination DMARD therapy and in whom sustained and satisfactory levels of disease control have been achieved, cautiously try to reduce drug doses to levels that still maintain disease control.

R18   In people with newly diagnosed RA for whom combination DMARD therapy is not appropriate,* start DMARD monotherapy, placing greater emphasis on fast escalation to a clinically effective dose rather than on the choice of DMARD.

Please see section 10 for the relevant related TA recommendations.

7.1 C   Disease modifying and biological drugs: when to withdraw them

7.1.14   Clinical introduction (withdrawing DMARDs)

There are a variety of reasons for stopping or reducing disease modifying drugs. Some drugs may need to be stopped prior to a patient or their partner conceiving (eg methotrexate and leflunomide) and during pregnancy and breastfeeding. The drugs may be stopped or reduced due to side-effects, or during inter-current illnesses. They may be stopped due to primary or secondary loss of efficacy.

A further category of patients pose questions about the most appropriate approach. These are patients with established RA with minimal or no disease activity. The observation that their disease is controlled may be due to the natural history of the disease, or due to the disease modifying drugs that they are taking. If the former is suspected, it would be good clinical practice to attempt to withdraw the medication. If the latter is the case, then such attempts might result in an increase in disease activity. Furthermore, there is some data to suggest that even in patients in remission, MRI scans can still show disease activity and progression of damage, which might be intensified if the disease modifying drug was withdrawn. However, the significance of this observation is currently unknown.

Once established, it has been argued that RA never completely disappears. Even if the data suggest complete withdrawal of disease modifying drugs is not appropriate for most patients, is there any evidence to support the common clinical approach of keeping patients on the smallest dose of drugs that appears to keep the disease under satisfactory control?

---

* For example, because of comorbidities or pregnancy, during which certain drugs would be contraindicated.

7.1.15 Clinical methodological introduction (withdrawing DMARDs)

We looked for studies that investigated the effect of withdrawing or titrating the dose of DMARDs or biological drugs with respect to symptoms, joint damage, function and quality of life in patients with established RA. Due to the paucity of trials in this area, all study types were included as evidence.

Ten studies[265–274] were found that fulfilled the criteria. The 10 studies consisted of 7 RCTs[265–270,274] and 3 case-series.[271–273] One RCT[274] was excluded due to methodological limitations (unblinded and ITT analysis was not performed). No studies were found that evaluated biological drugs.

▷ RCTs

The 6 included RCTs[265–270] assessed RA patients who had already been treated with DMARDs and were randomised to either continue on the treatment, have treatment withdrawn (be given placebo) or have the dose of DMARD reduced. Patients were then followed up for a period of time and outcomes were then assessed. The RCTs differed with respect to the following:

- Sample size (range: N=10 to N=285)
- Blinding (5 RCTs double blind, 1 RCT single blind)
- Trial length (range: 6 months to 2 years)
- Treatment (1 RCT 2nd line DMARDs vs placebo, 1 RCT MTX, penicillamine or gold DMARDs vs placebo, 1 RCT MTX vs placebo, 1 RCT IM gold vs placebo, 1 RCT azathioprine vs placebo, 1 RCT D-penicillamine at same dose vs D-penicillamine dose titrated)
- Treatment regimen – dose and withdrawal/titration regimen

Although the RCTs were fairly sound methodologically, it is worth noting that most of them were small trials (sample size <40) and were single or double blind and ITT analysis was not performed (5 RCTs). One trial was graded as 1++ as it was both double blind and ITT analysis was performed. Different dosing and titration regimens and the differing populations in the studies may also limit direct comparisons between studies.

▷ Case-series

The 3 case-series[271–273] assessed the effects of dose titration on patients already receiving DMARDs or corticosteroids. The first case-series (Fleischmann et al.)[273] assessed patients already receiving MTX, treated them with infliximab and if clinical improvement was seen at 22 weeks, the dose of MTX was then tapered and patients were followed up and outcomes assessed at 1 year. The second case-series (Tishler et al.)[272] assessed patients already receiving MTX with stable disease, the regime of MTX was then reduced from once/week to once/fortnight. Patients were then followed up and outcomes assessed at 1 year. The third case-series (Bacon et al.)[271] assessed patients already receiving corticosteroids (prednisolone) with stable disease. The dose of corticosteroids was tapered and patients were then followed up and outcomes assessed at 1 year.

7.1.16 Health economic methodological introduction (withdrawing DMARDs)

No health economic papers were identified for this question.

7.1.17 Clinical evidence statements (withdrawing DMARDs)

▷ Established RA

Table 7.27 Symptoms/quality of life (withdrawal vs continue treatment)

Study	Outcomes	Follow-up	Result – best treatment
1 RCT (deSilva et al.)[266] Level 1+	Pain and morning stiffness	16, 24 and 32 weeks	**Continue** (all p <0.05) 16 weeks: MD 0.6 and 31.5 24 weeks: MD 1.0 and 54.3 32 weeks: MD 0.7 and 75.0
1 RCT (Gotzsche et al.)[267] Level 1++	Swollen joints; pain	6 months	**Continue** (MD 2.2, p=0.03; p <0.002)
	Tender joints		**NS**
1 RCT (Kremer et al.)[268] Level 1+	Tender and swollen joints	1 month	**Continue** (MD –0.8 and 6.0, both p <0.05)
	Morning stiffness and evening fatigue		**NS**
1 RCT (Ten Wolde et al.)[269] Level 1+	Pain at rest, morning stiffness and RAI	1 year	**Continue** (MD 0.2 p=0.031, MD 27 p=0.005 and MD 1.9 p=0.000)
1 RCT (Van der Leeden et al.)[270] Level 1+	RAI and number of swollen joints	Over the 3 years	**Early** (values not given, p <0.05)

- 1 case-series[272] found that when the frequency of MTX treatment was reduced in patients with clinical remission, there was no deterioration in morning stiffness and Ritchie Articular Index. **Level 3**
- 1 case-series[273] found that in patients who had infliximab added to their current MTX treatment and who showed ≥40% clinical improvement in arthritis, when MTX was tapered, significant improvements from baseline were seen for tender and swollen joints (median improvement 73%, p <0.001). **Level 3**

Table 7.28 Function (withdrawal vs continue treatment)

Study (All Level 1+)	Outcomes	Follow-up	Result – best treatment
1 RCT (Kremer et al.)[268]	Grip strength	1 month	NS
1 RCT (Ten Wolde et al.)[269]	Grip strength (right and left hands); HAQ score	1 year	Continue (MD –5.2 and –5.0 p <0.05; MD 0.14 p=0.014)

- 1 case-series[272] found that when the frequency of MTX treatment was reduced in patients with clinical remission, there was no deterioration in grip strength. **Level 3**
- 1 case-series[273] found that in patients who and infliximab added to their current MTX treatment and who showed ≥40% clinical improvement in arthritis, when MTX was tapered, significant improvements from baseline were seen for HAQ score (median improvement 40%, p <0.001). **Level 3**

Joint damage (withdrawal vs continue treatment)

- 1 RCT[270] found that there was NS difference between the group withdrawn from gold treatment compared with the group continuing on gold treatment for radiological score. **Level 1+**

Table 7.29 Global assessment (withdrawal vs continue treatment)

Study	Outcomes	Follow-up	Result – best treatment
1 RCT (deSilva et al.)[266] Level 1+	Patient's and clinician's general evaluation of response to therapy	32 weeks	Continue (7% vs 67%)
1 RCT (Gotzsche et al.)[267] Level 1++	Patient's perception of well-being	6 months	Continue (p=0.002)
	Patient's evaluation of the number of painful joints	6 months	NS
1 RCT (Kremer et al.)[268] Level 1+	Physician's and patient's global evaluation of pain and disease activity	1 month	Continue (MD 1.1 and 1.0; 0.9 and 0.4, all p <0.05)

- 1 case-series[272] found that when the frequency of MTX treatment was reduced in patients with clinical remission, there was no deterioration in doctor's and patient's global assessment of pain and disease activity. **Level 3**

Table 7.30 Remission (withdrawal vs continue treatment)

Study	Outcomes	Follow-up	Result – best treatment
1 RCT (Ahern et al.)[265] **Level 1+**	Maintenance of remission	12 months	**Continue** (89% vs 21%)
1 RCT (Gotzsche et al.)[267] **Level 1++**	Number of patients experiencing treatment failure	6 months	**Continue** (60% vs 15.8%, p=0.000001)
1 RCT (Kremer et al.)[268] **Level 1+**	Number of patients experiencing significant flare	1 month	**Continue** (20% vs 100%)

- 1 case-series[271] found that in 26% of patients who were on long-term treatment with corticosteroids and whose arthritis appeared to be in remission, withdrawal of corticosteroid treatment was successful (no reactivation of arthritis), however 61% had to have their corticosteroid treatment reintroduced due to the return of active arthritis. **Level 3**
- 1 case-series[272] found that in patients who were on treatment with MTX and whose arthritis appeared to be in remission, reducing the frequency of treatment was successful (arthritis did not deteriorate) in 87% of patients, however 13% had a flare of arthritis. **Level 3**

Table 7.31 Biochemical markers (withdrawal vs continue treatment)

Study (All level 1+)	Outcomes	Follow-up	Result – best treatment
3 RCTs (deSilva, Kremer and Van der Leeden)[266,268,270]	ESR	32 weeks (deSilva) 1 month (Kremer) Over 3 years (Van der Leeden)	**NS**
1 RCT (Ahern et al.)[265]	Mean CRP level	1 month and 3 months after clinical relapse	**Continue** (values not given, p <0.05)
1 RCT (Ten Wolde et al.)[269]	CRP and ESR	1 year	**Continue** (MD 2 p=0.008 and MD 5 p=0.000)

- 1 case-series[272] found that when the frequency of MTX treatment was reduced in patients with clinical remission, there was no deterioration in ECR or CRP levels. **Level 3**
- 1 case-series[273] found that in patients who had infliximab added to their current treatment MTX treatment and who showed ≥40% clinical improvement in arthritis, when MTX was tapered, significant improvements from baseline were seen for ESR and CRP levels (median improvement 23% and 50%, both p≤0.001). **Level 3**

Table 7.32 Adverse events (withdrawal vs continue treatment)

Study	Outcomes	Follow-up	Result – best treatment
1 RCT (Gotzsche et al.)[267] Level 1++	Severity of reported side-effects	6 months	**NS**
1 RCT (Ten Wolde et al.)[269] Level 1+	AEs	1 year	**Similar** (34% vs 37%)

- 1 case-series[273] found that in patients who had infliximab added to their current MTX treatment and who showed ≥40% clinical improvement in arthritis, when MTX was tapered, there was an 80% incidence of AEs. Specific AEs were not specified but included infection and infusion reactions. **Level 3**

Table 7.33 Withdrawals (withdrawal vs continue treatment)

Study (All Level 1+)	Outcomes	Follow-up	Result – best treatment
1 RCT (deSilva et al.)[266]	Total number of withdrawals; withdrawals due to clinical deterioration	32 weeks	**Continue** (21% vs 39%; 0% vs 33%)
1 RCT (Kremer et al.)[268]	Number of withdrawals (both N=0)	1 month	**NS**
1 RCT (Van der Leeden et al.)[270]	Number of withdrawals	Over the 3 years	**Similar** (N=5 and N=4)

Effect of reintroduction of withdrawn DMARDs

- 1 RCT[265] found that when D-penicillamine was reintroduced at the former dose in patients in the tapered dose group who experienced flare, 87% achieved clinical remission again within 4 months. The remaining 13% achieved remission when given a higher dose. **Level 1+**
- 1 RCT[268] found that when MTX was reintroduced in patients in the withdrawal group who experienced flare, all achieved improvement again in pain, morning stiffness and patient's assessment of global disease activity. **Level 1+**
- 1 case-series[272] found that when MTX treatment was reintroduced at the usual frequency in patients in the reduced dose frequency group who had experienced flare, all achieved control of disease activity. **Level 3**

7.1.18 Summary of evidence statements (withdrawing DMARDs)

- The studies used a variety of withdrawal methods with different DMARDs. In some studies the patients had excellent disease control prior to withdrawal of active DMARD,[265,266,269,271,272] and in others had ongoing active disease.[267,268,270,273,]

- In some of the trials the active DMARD was tapered down,[271–273] but in most was suddenly replaced with placebo.[265–270]

- Whichever method was used, the majority of studies showed the patients on placebo or lower doses of DMARD did not do as well symptomatically, functionally or in quality of life.[265–269,271] There was insufficient data to address any impact on joint damage.

- One study in which methotrexate could be reduced successfully was in patients responding well to infliximab.[273] One study also suggested that restoring the patient back to the original dose controlling drug could result in restoration of disease improvement.[265]

7.1.19 From evidence to recommendations (withdrawing DMARDs)

Based on the available evidence, the GDG felt that when a decision was made to try and reduce dosages of disease modifying drugs, it would be prudent to advise that this should always be done with caution, and that arrangements should be place for an urgent reassessment so that there could be a prompt return to disease-controlling dosages of medication at the first sign of any flare-up. Patient education regarding to know when and how to seek rapid access and help in the event of a flare-up in the context of well controlled established disease is covered by recommendation R36). The GDG nevertheless felt that, for those specific patients in whom a decision had been taken to decrease (or discontinue) their disease modifying drugs, an extra recommendation about the availability of a prompt review (eg by rapid access to the named member of the MDT, see section 6.1) was indicated.

It was also felt appropriate to extrapolate from the available evidence a more general recommendation that the opportunity to try and decrease or discontinue the dosages of current medication should always be explored when additional drugs are being added to a treatment regimen.

RECOMMENDATIONS

R19   In people with established RA whose disease is stable, cautiously reduce dosages of disease-modifying or biological drugs. Return promptly to disease-controlling dosages at the first sign of a flare.

R20   When introducing new drugs to improve disease control into the treatment regimen of a person with established RA, consider decreasing or stopping their pre-existing rheumatological drugs once the disease is controlled.

R21   In any person with established rheumatoid arthritis in whom disease-modifying or biological drug doses are being decreased or stopped, arrangements should be in place for prompt review.

7.2 Glucocorticoids

7.2.1 Clinical introduction

▷ Glucocorticoids in recent-onset and established RA

Glucocorticoids have been used in the management of RA for over 50 years. When first introduced, enthusiasm for the efficacy of these drugs was tempered by the severe side effects of the high dose regimes that were used. Clinicians and patients continue to approach these drugs with caution. However, some aspects of steroid use are standard clinical practice:

- Intra-articular injections have a limited evidence-base, but their users and receivers can testify that they are extremely useful for a flare in one or more joints.
- For polyarticular flares, or at first presentation of the disease, intramuscular/intra-articular, or short oral courses of steroids, can decrease symptoms whilst waiting for other slower-acting drugs to take effect.
- For severe extra-articular manifestations, intravenous steroids can save critical organs (eg eyes in scleritis) or even life-threatening complications on occasions (eg severe serositis or vasculitis), though they should be used with immunosuppressives such as cyclophosphamide.

Questions the GDG asked were:

- Should recent-onset RA patients be treated with some form of steroids (oral or intramuscular)?
- Do the benefits of steroids out-weigh the disadvantages?
- Do steroids have a lasting impact on symptoms, function of joints and quality of life?
- Should steroids be classified as disease modifying drugs?

7.2.2 Clinical methodological introduction

We looked for studies that investigated the efficacy and safety of corticosteroids with respect to symptoms, joint damage, function and quality of life in patients with a recent onset of RA or in patients with established RA. Due to the large volume of evidence, only RCTs were selected which had a sample size of N>50 and compared corticosteroids alone vs placebo or corticosteroids in combination with a DMARD vs DMARD. Only studies that compared steroids with placebo, or steroids plus DMARDs with DMARDs were included in order to attempt to tease out the influence of steroids alone. However, it should be noted that one study[282,283] compared steroids with placebo in the absence of other DMARDs, and that the other studies compared steroids plus a DMARD with a DMARD alone. In some of these studies the DMARDs were fixed by protocol and in others the concomitant DMARDs were left to the treating physician. Disease activity inclusion criteria varied between studies. Some studies included patients with up to 1 year of RA and others up to 2 years. Consequently, because of all of these differences, pooling results needs to be treated with caution.

In order to be included in the established disease trials, patients had to have active disease, but this had different definitions in different trials. It was noted that one trial[275] used penicillamine in both arms, and another[276] used gold injections. Neither of these DMARDs are particularly popular currently because of toxicity concerns. There is no available evidence for much more popular DMARDs such as methotrexate or sulfasalazine. Papers assessing corticosteroids which were published in the 1950s were not included in the evidence because the databases searched only commence with publications from 1966 onwards.

▷ Recent-onset RA

Six RCTs[277–284] were found that fulfilled the criteria. Two of these RCTs (1 RCT;[282,283] 1 RCT[279,280]) were each published as two separate papers reporting different outcomes and so each trial has only been counted once, however results from both papers are reported and referenced here. The methodological limitations of the RCTs were as follows: those graded 1+ were either double blind and ITT analysis was not performed (2 RCTs) or were unblinded and ITT analysis was performed (1 RCT). The trial graded 1++ was blinded and ITT analysis was performed.

All six trials were parallel group studies using the oral corticosteroid prednisolone, but they differed with respect to the following:
- Sample size (range: N=81 to N=259)
- Blinding (5 RCTs double blind, 1 RCT unblinded)
- Trial length (5 RCTs 2 years, 1 RCT 12 weeks; follow-up ranged from immediate to 1-year post-treatment)
- Treatment (1 RCT corticosteroid vs placebo, 5 RCTs corticosteroid + DMARD vs DMARD)
- Treatment regimen – dose.

▷ Established RA

Five RCTs[275,276,285–287] were found that fulfilled the criteria. The methodological limitations of the RCTs were as follows: those graded 1+ were either double blind and ITT analysis was not performed (2 RCTs), unblinded and ITT analysis was performed (1 RCT) or single blind and ITT analysis was performed but had a high drop-out rate (1 RCT). The trial graded 1++ was blinded and the authors performed ITT analysis.

All five trials were parallel group studies using corticosteroids, but they were very variable in design and had variable inclusion criteria. The trials differed with respect to the following:
- Sample size (range: N=59 to N=137)
- Blinding (3 RCTs double blind, 1 RCT single blind, 1 RCT unblinded)\par
- Trial length (range: single injection to 1 year; follow-up ranged from immediate to 7 months post-treatment)
- Treatment (1 RCT corticosteroid vs placebo, 3 RCTs corticosteroid + DMARD vs DMARD)
- Corticosteroid used (2 RCTs methylprednisolone, 1 RCT prednisolone, 1 RCT depomedrone, 1 RCT rimexolone)
- Route of corticosteroid administration (2 RCTs IM, 1 RCT IA, 1 RCT IV, 1 RCT oral)
- Treatment regimen – dose.

7.2.3 Health economic methodological introduction

Two studies were identified and appraised. Bae et al.[288] is a US based cost-utility analysis of low-dose corticosteroids versus Cox-2 inhibitors and non-selective NSAIDs. Verhoeven et al.[241] is a Dutch-based cost-utility analysis of step-down prednisolone, sulphasalazine and methotrexate versus sulphasalazine.

7.2.4 Clinical evidence statements

▷ Recent-onset RA

Symptoms and quality of life

- Three RCTs (1 RCT[279,280] **Level 1+;**[281] 1 RCT[277] **Level 1++**) showed no improvement in pain at 1 year or 2 years for oral prednisolone (and at year 3 for the Hickling and Kirwan trial[279,280] **Level 1+**).
- One RCT[281] showed sustained decreases of disease activity (DAS28) at 6, 12 and 24 months in the prednisolone arm, and a greater proportion of patients in DAS28 remission at the end of 2 years, but not at the end of 1 year. **Level 1+**
- Three RCTs (1 RCT[279,280] **Level 1+**; 1 RCT[282,283] **Level 1++**; 1 RCT [284] **Level 1+**) demonstrated clinical and laboratory measures of joint inflammation, with the exception of joint tenderness in the Van Everidgen study,[282,283] had not improved at 1 or 2 years. However, the Wassenberg study[284] showed no overall patient improvement or significant changes in quality of life measures.
- Three RCTs addressed adverse events and withdrawals over a 2-year period (1 RCT [284] **Level 1+**; 1 RCT[277] **Level 1++**; 1 RCT[281] **Level 1++**) and found similar results for prednisolone versus placebo, although Cappell[277] found more withdrawals due to adverse events in the steroid arm, and Wassenberg[284] more withdrawals due to drug failure in the steroid arm.
- Two RCTs (1 RCT[282,283] **Level 1++**; 1 RCT[281] **Level 1+**) showed that in the prednisolone arms concomitant medication could be reduced. Patients in the Van Everidgen[282,283] and Svensson[281] prednisolone arms were able trial were able to decrease intra-articular steroids, and in the Svensson[281] trial were able to decrease their NSAIDs.

Joint damage

- Four RCTs (1 RCT[279,280] **Level 1+**; 1 RCT[281] **Level 1+**; 1 RCT[282,283] **Level 1++**; 1 RCT[284] **Level 1+**) showed decreased radiological damage (proportion of erosions, progression of radiological damage) in the oral prednisolone arm versus the placebo over 2 years. However, in only the Wassenberg[284] and Svensson[281] trials was this divergence evident at 1 year. Joint space narrowing failed to improve in the prednisolone arms of Wassenberg[284] and Svensson,[281] but other components of composite damage indices did improve. In Kirwan[279,280] the difference in erosions on hand x-rays remained significant at 3 years (1 year after the withdrawal of steroids), but the progression of radiological damage was no different.
- One RCT[277] failed to show an improvement in radiological damage in the prednisolone arm at 1 or 2 years. **Level 1++**

Function

- Three RCTs (1 RCT[282,283] **Level 1++**; 1 RCT[277] **Level 1++**; 1 RCT[284] **Level 1+**) showed that functional scores were no different at 1 and 2 years in the prednisolone arm. Van Everidgen[282,283] showed an improvement in grip strength at 1 year on prednisolone, but this difference was lost at 2 years.
- One RCT[279,280] showed no functional improvements in HAQ for budenoside 3 mg or 9 mg at 3 months compared with placebo. Prednisolone 7.5 mg showed an improvement in HAQ at 3 months, but this was not sustained at 1 or 2 years. **Level 1+**
- One RCT[281] did show significant improvements in the prednisolone arm for HAQ and Signals of Functional Impairment (SOFI index) at 6, 12 and 24 months. **Level 1+**

▷ Established RA

Symptoms and quality of life

- One RCT[285] compared monthly depomedrone to placebo in addition to the usual DMARD and found decreased DAS and swollen joints at 6 months, but both patient and physician's global assessments were no different. More patients withdrew from the placebo arm because of lack of efficacy. Symptomatic benefits were not sustained at 1 or 2 years. No decrease in ESR occurred. Although the steroid arm had more adverse events, there were no greater withdrawals from the trial for these. **Level 1++**
- One RCT[276] looked at IM methylprednisolone at 0, 4 and 8 weeks of initiation of IM gold therapy compared with placebo. Pain and joint counts improved at 12 weeks (4 weeks post last injection), but not at 24 weeks. Joint counts improved at 12 weeks but not 24 weeks. ESR decreased at 4 weeks in the steroid group but was not sustained beyond this. Index of Disease Activity improved up to 12 weeks but not at 24 weeks. The injections were well tolerated with no greater number of withdrawals in the steroid arm. **Level 1+**
- One RCT[275] looked at varied doses of oral prednisolone given in a tapered regime, starting at 30 mg, and tailing this down to a dose between 2.5 mg and 15 mg (determined by the patient) to control disease. Although there were greater numbers of patients with more than 20% and 50% clinical improvement at 3 months, this was not sustained at 6 or 12 months. No improvements in ESR or CRP occurred. **Level 1+**
- One RCT[278] compared 6 IV methylprednisolone injections (15 mg/kg) over 20 weeks with placebo and found no difference for a variety of symptom outcomes after 20 weeks or 1 year (7 months post-treatment). **Level 1+**
- One RCT[286] found that tender and swollen joint counts significantly improved at 4 weeks for oral budesonide 3 mg and 9 mg and oral prednisolone 7.5 mg when added to usual treatment compared with placebo and usual treatment (all p <0.05). At 12 weeks, along with other measures of disease activity and quality of life (physicians and patients global assessments, ACR20, SF-36 physical and mental condition), this was only sustained for budesonide 9 mg and prednisolone 7.5 mg (p <0.05). Pain and morning stiffness did not improve at 12 weeks for oral budesonide 3 mg and 9 mg. For prednisolone 7.5 mg, pain improved at 12 weeks (p <0.001) but morning stiffness did not. CRP and ESR only improved at 12 weeks on prednisolone (both p <0.001). Whilst the numbers of patients with adverse events were similar to placebo, all three steroid arms had greater numbers of adverse events than placebo, but with no greater withdrawals. **Level 1++**

- One RCT[287] looked at different doses of intra-articular rimexolone into RA knees and for higher doses found symptomatic benefit compared to placebo for up to 84 days. The injection was well tolerated. **Level 1+**

Joint damage

- One RCT[285] compared monthly depomedrone to placebo in addition to the usual DMARD, and found decreased radiological damage at 2 years in the steroid arm (analysis used % change from baseline due to baseline differences – however when analysed using change in actual scores there was NS difference between the groups). **Level 1+**
- One RCT[276] looked at IM methylprednisolone at 0, 4 and 8 weeks of initiation of IM gold therapy compared with placebo, and found no difference between the groups at 24 weeks for radiological damage. **Level 1+**
- One RCT[275] looked at varied doses of oral prednisolone given in a tapered regime, starting at 30 mg, and tailing this down to a dose between 2.5 mg and 15 mg (determined by the patient) to control disease. The steroid arm showed less joint damage (delta Larsen score) at 1 year, but a similar number of patients with joint damage and progression of erosions. **Level 1+**

Function

- One RCT[287] looked at different doses of intra-articular rimexolone into RA knees and for higher doses found sustained functional benefits (walking ability, range of movement) compared to placebo for up to 84 days. **Level 1+**
- One RCT[285] compared monthly depomedrone to placebo in addition to the usual DMARD and found improved HAQs at 6 months, but not sustained at 1 or 2 years. **Level 1++**
- One RCT[276] looked at IM methylprednisolone at 0, 4 and 8 weeks of initiation of IM gold therapy compared with placebo. They found improvements in HAQ in the steroid arm at 4 and 12 weeks, but not at 8 and 24 weeks. There was no improvement in grip strength at any stage for the steroid arm. **Level 1+**
- One RCT[275] looked at varied doses of oral prednisolone given in a tapered regime, starting at 30 mg, and tailing this down to a dose between 2.5 mg and 15 mg (determined by the patient) to control disease. There was a significant improvement in HAQ and grip strength in the steroid group at 1 year. **Level 1+**

7.2.5   Health economic evidence statements

Bae et al.[288] concluded that corticosteroids are less costly and more effective than NSAIDs in the long-term treatment of RA patients, but differences between the two treatments in both cost and health outcome are relatively small. The study is US-based hence resources used and their associated costs could be very different in the UK. In the Verhoeven et al. study,[241] the analysis revealed that combined treatment with step-down prednisolone, methotrexate and sulphasalazine to be more effective than sulphasalazine alone at equal or lower cost. The combined treatment group had lower expenses for non-protocol medication and inpatient care and lower costs outside the healthcare system that offset the higher costs for protocol medication and monitoring.

7.2.6 Summary of evidence statements

▷ Recent-onset RA

- In recent-onset RA, low dose oral steroid regimes give symptomatic and quality of life benefit for up to 3 months,[286] but this is usually not sustained at 1 year or beyond.[277,280–284]
- There is no good evidence for functional improvements with steroids.[277,280,282–284]
- Low dose steroids are generally well tolerated,[277,281,284] and small decreases in concomitant medications may be possible.[281–283]
- The majority of the trials suggest that steroids are disease modifying in slowing radiological damage over 2 years.[280–284]

▷ Established RA

- Knee joint injections of steroid give sustained benefit from a symptomatic and functional viewpoint (although the steroid concerned is not used in the UK).[287]
- IM, IV, or oral steroid routes are largely of value in the short term, do not lead to sustained symptomatic benefits.[275,276,278,285]
- Using oral steroids in variable doses to control symptoms may improve function over 1 year.[275]
- The evidence that the use of steroids in established RA may be disease modifying is conflicting, some trials probably underpowered showed no significant effect. This evidence base is not as strong as the evidence base for recent-onset RA.[275,276,285]

▷ Themes from both recent-onset RA and established disease

- Steroids usually only give short-term symptomatic, functional and quality of life benefit.
- Most trials show evidence that steroids are disease modifying

7.2.7 From evidence to recommendations

▷ Recent-onset RA

The GDG noted that there was a considerable mismatch between the available data and what actually happens in clinical practice. For example, both in the initial presentation of disease and during flare-ups, steroids (oral, intra-muscular and intra-articular) are often used to obtain symptomatic benefit and to achieve disease control whilst waiting for the more slowly-acting DMARDS to take effect, despite the lack of evidence to support this. The clinical efficacy of this approach is so well established that it is doubtful that any future randomised controlled clinical trials would ever be conducted, and the GDG felt that there should therefore be a recommendation endorsing this use of steroids, both for those patients with newly diagnosed rheumatoid arthritis who are not already receiving steroids as part of DMARD combination therapy (see recommendation R22), and for the management of flare-ups in those with recent-onset or established disease.

▷ Established RA

The GDG noted that the evidence for the use of steroids in established disease was sparse, of limited quality, and that in two trials the much older drugs penicillamine and gold had been used as comparators. There was a need to establish the merits of combining steroids with drugs such as methotrexate in established disease, where there was much less evidence for disease modification by steroids than in recent-onset disease.

Although a consistent theme for both recent-onset and established disease is that the symptomatic benefit produced by steroids is usually only short lasting, the GDG noted that, in routine clinical practice, there are nevertheless some patients who appear to be reliant on long-term low dose steroids since withdrawing them results in flare-up of disease activity. This use of steroids in this particular group of patients may have to be accepted, even though the situation is not ideal, although attempts should always be made to replace the steroids with other disease modifying drugs and to keep the steroids to the lowest dose that controls symptoms. It was also felt important to emphasise the specific potential serious complications associated with long-term steroid therapy.

RECOMMENDATIONS

R22   Consider offering short-term treatment with glucocorticoids (oral, intramuscular or intra-articular) to rapidly improve symptoms in people with newly diagnosed RA if they are not already receiving glucocorticoids as part of DMARD combination therapy.

R23   Offer short-term treatment with glucocorticoids for managing flares in people with recent-onset or established disease, to rapidly decrease inflammation.

R24   In people with established RA, only continue long-term treatment with glucocorticoids when:
   ● the long-term complications of glucocorticoid therapy have been fully discussed, and
   ● all other treatment options (including biological drugs) have been offered.

7.3   Biologics

7.3A   Biological drugs and conventional DMARDs in patients with established RA where there is ongoing disease activity

7.3.1   Clinical Introduction

Although biological therapies have had a tremendous impact on the management of RA, so too have conventional DMARDs. Furthermore, biological drugs are substantially more expensive than conventional DMARDs. It is appropriate therefore to question the comparative efficacy of these new therapies, and to determine what additional value they add to the management of RA compared with cheaper and more established drugs. Some biological drugs have already completed a NICE technology appraisal such as rituximab[10] and the anti-TNF drugs adalimumab, etanercept and infliximab.[130] Abatacept has recently been appraised and deemed not to be cost-effective for use in the NHS.[11] Other biological drugs such as certolizumab pegol have yet to begin the technology appraisal process.

7.3.2 Clinical methodological introduction

We looked for studies that investigated the efficacy and safety of biological drugs vs DMARDs (singly or in combination) with respect to symptoms, joint damage, function and quality of life in patients with established RA. Due to the large volume of evidence, only RCTs were selected which had a sample size of N≥100 and were of a UK-relevant population.

Two MAs,[289,290] 10 RCTs[291–304] and one extension study[305] of 2 RCTs were found that fulfilled the criteria. One of the RCTs (TEMPO trial) was published as five separate papers[292,293,300,303,304] reporting different outcomes and follow-up times, so the trial has only been counted once, however results from all the papers are reported and referenced here. All trials (including the MAs) were in patients with established RA. The methodological limitations of the RCTs were as follows: those graded 1+ were either double blind and ITT analysis was not performed (2 RCTs) or unblinded but ITT analysis was performed (1 RCT). The trials graded 1++ were both single blind and ITT analysis was performed (7 RCTs).

The first SR/MA[289] focused on 6 double-blind RCTs with N=2,381 patients which compared adalimumab monotherapy or in combination with DMARDs vs placebo or other DMARDs. Both the MA itself and the studies it included were well conducted. Studies included in the analysis differed with respect to:
- Intervention – dose given and regimen
- Study size (range N=54 to N=636)
- Study duration – length of intervention (12 weeks to 52 weeks)

The second SR/MA[290] focused on 3 double-blind RCTs with N=1,040 patients which compared anti-TNF + MTX vs MTX with a treatment time between 50 to 55 weeks. Both the MA itself and the studies it included were well conducted. Studies included in the analysis differed with respect to:
- Intervention (1 RCT infliximab (IFX) + MTX, 1 RCT etanercept (ETN) + MTX, 1 RCT adalimumab (ADA) + MTX)
- Intervention – dose given and regimen
- Study size (range N=174 to N=459)

NOTE: The two MAs[289,290] included RCTs already included in this section. However it was felt important to report the RCTs separately in order to see the effects of the individual drugs for all outcome measures, since the MAs either pooled drug classes together or only pooled data for some outcomes (since not all the trials used the same outcome measures).

All 10 RCTs[291–304] were parallel group but were very variable in terms of type of treatment and had variable inclusion criteria. The trials differed with respect to the following:
- Sample size (range: N=161 to N=2,987)
- Blinding (9 RCTs double blind, 1 RCT unblinded)
- Trial length (range: 16 weeks to 4 years)
- Treatment – type of biologics and DMARDs used
- Treatment regimen – single drugs and combinations compared
- Treatment regimen – dose

The included extension study[305] included patients who were originally randomised to either etanercept (10, 25 or 50 mg) or placebo in 2 RCTs. In the 5-year extension phase, all patients were given etanercept 25 mg twice/week.

NOTE: In most of the trials the population consisted of patients who were not doing well on/not responding to their DMARD therapy. These patients were then randomised to either continue on this DMARD or to take a biological drug. Therefore there may be some bias in the study design in favour of the biologic drug because those in the trial arm that continue on the their usual DMARD which is not working well, are unlikely to do well compared to those who are put onto a biologic drug instead.

7.3.3 Health economic methodological introduction

In the HTA report entitled 'A systematic review of the effectiveness of adalimumab, etanercept and infliximab for the treatment of rheumatoid arthritis in adults and an economic evaluation of their cost-effectiveness' produced by Chen et al. 2006,[237] a review of publications relating to economic evaluations of biologics was performed. In this report publications dated up to February 2005 were reviewed. Details of the search method used can be found in the HTA report. To bring this review up to date we have performed a search for economic evaluations published from 2005–2007.

▷ Results of systematic review of economic evaluations

We performed a search for publications dated Jan 2005 – 1st Oct 2007 using the same search terms used for the clinical review. The 2005–2007 search resulted in 58 references to consider; of these 14 references related to cost-effectiveness studies of DMARDs and biologics. Of the 14 publications related to cost effectiveness studies, 8 references were excluded as they were abstracts or reviews and two references had already been included in the HTA report review, one was excluded because it looked at recent-onset RA. In total 4 new references were found for inclusion in the review – three as a result of the search and one preprint was also found. The study by Jobanputra et al. (2002) is now obsolete and has been replaced by the HTA report of Chen et al. 2006[237] and therefore has been removed from the list of reviewed publications.

Table 7.34 Summary of published economic analyses

Study	Disease duration (years)	Country (sponsor)	TNF inhibitor(s) considered	Form of economic analysis	Model used	Time horizon
Choi et al. (2002)[306]		USA (Not Stated)	Etanercept	Cost-effectiveness	Decision tree	6 months
Brennan et al. (2004)[307]	Not given Failed 3.3. DMARDs	UK (Not Stated, by two authors from Wyeth)	Etanercept	Cost-utility	Patient level	Lifetime
Wong et al. (2002)[308]	Not stated	USA (Schering-Plough, Centocor Corp, National Institutes for Health)	Infliximab	Cost-utility	Markov	Lifetime
Kobelt et al. (2003)[309]	Response: 11yrs Baseline: 8.2 months	Sweden and UK (Schering-Plough)	Infliximab	Cost-utility	Markov	10 years

continued

Table 7.34 Summary of published economic analyses – *continued*

Study	Disease duration (years)	Country (sponsor)	TNF inhibitor(s) considered	Form of economic analysis	Model used	Time horizon
Kobelt et al. (2004)[310]	14.2	Sweden (Österlund and Kock Foundations, the King Gustav V 80-year fund, Reumatikerförbundet.)	Etanercept, infliximab	Cost utility	Not applicable	Not applicable
Chiou et al. (2004)[311]		USA (Not stated)	Etanercept, infliximab, adalimumab	Cost-utility	Decision tree	1 year
Welsing et al. (2004)[312]	3.8 minimum	Netherlands (Not stated, but used data from Wyeth)	Etanercept	Cost-utility	Markov	5 years
Bansback et al. (2005)[313]	Over 8yrs	Sweden (Abbott Laboratories)	Etanercept, infliximab, adalimumab	Cost-utility	Patient level	Lifetime
Kobelt et al. (2005)[314]	6.8	Sweden (Wyeth Research)	Etanercept	Cost-utility	Markov	10 years
Spalding et al. (2006)[239]	3 months	USA (Astellas Pharma)	Adalimumab, etanercept, infliximab + methotrexate, adalimumab + methotrexate	Cost utility	Markov	Lifetime
Tanno et al. (2006)[315]	11	Japan (Ministry of Education, Science, Sports and Culture and the Ministry of Health, Japan)	Etanercept	Cost utility	Markov	Lifetime
Marra et al. (2007)[316]	9	Canada (Canadian Arthritis Network)	Infliximab + methotrexate	Cost utility	Markov	10 years
Chen et al. (2006)[237]	Various	UK (NHS HTA Programme)	Adalimumab, etanercept, infliximab + methotrexate, adalimumab + methotrexate, etanercept+ methotrexate	Cost utility	Patient level	Lifetime
Brennan et al. (2007)[317]	14.1	UK (BSR)	Etanercept, infliximab, adalimumab	Cost utility	Patient level	Lifetime

7.3.4 Clinical evidence statements

▷ Pooled data

Table 7.35 Pooled data – drug class

Study	Intervention	Outcomes	Result – best treatment
1 MA[290] Level 1++	Anti-TNF + MTX vs MTX	ACR 70 (RR 3.43, 95% CI 1.74 to 6.75, p=0.0004); withdrawals due to lack of efficacy (RR 0.38, 95% CI 0.22 to 0.64, p=0.0003)	**Anti-TNF + MTX**
		Withdrawals due to AEs	**NS**
	IFX vs ADA	ACR20, ACR50, ACR70, withdrawals due to AEs or lack of efficacy	**NS**
	ADA vs ETN	ACR20 (RR 0.46, 95% CI 0.34 to 0.61, p <0.0001), ACR50 (RR 0.37, 95% CI 0.22 to 0.60, p <0.0001), ACR70 (RR 0.44, 95% CI 0.21 to 0.93, p=0.003)	**ADA**
		Withdrawals due to AEs (RR 0.38, 95% CI 0.17 to 0.86, p=0.02)	**ETN**
		Withdrawals due to lack of efficacy	**NS**
	IFX vs ETN	ACR20 (RR 0.45, 95% CI 0.27 to 0.73, p=0.001)	**IFX**
		ACR50, ACR70, withdrawals due to AEs or lack of efficacy	**NS**

Table 7.36 Pooled data – adalimumab (ADA)

Study	Intervention	Outcomes	Follow-up	Result – best treatment
1 MA[289] Level 1++	ADA sc 40 mg eow* + MTX (or DMARDs) vs placebo sc* + MTX (or DMARDs)	ACR50 (3 RCTs: RR 3.7, 95% CI 2.2 to 6.3) and ACR70 (3 RCTs: RR 5.1, 95% CI 3.1 to 8.4); HAQ (2 RCTs: RR –0.3, 95% CI –0.4 to –0.2); tender joints (2 RCTs: RR –6.7, 95% CI –9.0 to –4.3); patient pain assessment (2 RCTs: RR –15.8, 95% CI –20.3 to –11.3)	24 weeks	**Arm 1** (all p <0.00001)
		Withdrawals; withdrawals due to AEs; AEs and SAEs (all doses of ADA)		**NS**
		ACR20		**Significant heterogeneity**

continued

Table 7.36 Pooled data – adalimumab (ADA) – *continued*

Study	Intervention	Outcomes	Follow-up	Result – best treatment
	ADA sc 20 mg ew* vs placebo	ACR20 (2 RCTs: RR 6.1, 95% CI 3.2 to 11.5) and ACR50 (2 RCTs: RR 8.8, 95% CI 1.1 to 69.8); withdrawals (ADA all doses)	2 weeks	**ADA** (p <0.0001 and p=0.04; p <0.00001)
	ADA sc 40 mg ew vs placebo	ACR20 (2 RCTs: RR 6.7, 95% CI 2.3 to 19.1) and ACR50 (2 RCTs: RR 15.1, 95% CI 2.0 to 114.0)		**ADA** (p=0.0004 and p=0.009)
	ADA at 40 mg eow vs placebo	ACR20 (2 RCTs: RR 1.9, 95% CI 1.2 to 3.1)	24/46 weeks	**ADA** (p=0.009)
	ADA (all doses) vs placebo	Withdrawals		**ADA** (p <0.00001)
		SAEs, withdrawals due to AEs,		**NS**
		AEs		**Significant heterogeneity**

*eow = every other week, ew = every week, sc=subcutaneous

▷ Data for individual drugs

Etanercept

Table 7.37 Etanercept

Study	Intervention	Outcomes	Follow-up	Result – best treatment
1 RCT[296] **Level 1++**	ETN vs SSZ	ACR20 (MD 45.8%), ACR50 (MD 32.6%), ACR70 (MD 19.4%), DAS score (MD 28.6%), painful joints (MD 42.7%), swollen joints (MD 30.2%), VAS pain (MD 42.3%), morning stiffness (MD 83.9%) and EQ-5D (MD 44.5%), HAQ (MD 26.1%), patient's and physician's global assessments (36.9% and 43.9%), ESR (MD 37.4%), CRP (MD 37.0%)	24 weeks	**ETN** (all p <0.01)
		Withdrawals due to AEs		**NS**
	ETN + SSZ vs SSZ	ACR20 (MD 46.0%), ACR50 (MD 38.0%), ACR70 (MD 23.0%) DAS score (MD 30.3%), painful joints (MD 39.4%), swollen joints (MD 31.6%), VAS pain (MD 40.6%), morning stiffness (MD 89.6%) and EQ-5D (MD 47.5), HAQ (MD 31.0%), patient's and physician's global assessments (MD 46% and 39.9%), ESR (MD 42.8), CRP (MD 33.8)		**ETN + SSZ** (all p <0.01)
		Withdrawals due to AEs		**NS**

continued

Table 7.37 Etanercept – *continued*

Study	Intervention	Outcomes	Follow-up	Result – best treatment
	ETN + SSZ vs ETN	ACR20, ACR50, ACR70, DAS score, painful joints, swollen joints, Pain (VAS), Morning stiffness and EQ-5D, HAQ, patient's and physician's global assessments, ESR, CRP, withdrawals due to AEs		**NS**
1 RCT[292,293, 300,304] **Level 1++**	ETN vs MTX	ACR (AUC) – MD 2.5, 95% CI 0.8 to 4.2, p=0.0034; patients achieving a major improvement of HAQ >0.8 (45% vs 36%, p <0.05)	52 weeks	**ETN**
		Patients achieving remission, HAQ, withdrawals due to AEs		**NS**
		Patients achieving remission – DAS <1.6 (23% vs 16%), Total Sharp Score (MD 2.24), erosion score (MD 1.76), patients with no erosions (75% vs. 66%)	2 years	**ETN** (all p <0.05)
		EQ5D, Patient global assessment of overall RA activity, Patient General Health Assessment, number of swollen joints, Pain (VAS), patient and physicians global assessment, HAQ, CRP, AEs		**NS**
		ACR20, ACR50, ACR70, DAS score	52 weeks and at 2 years	**NS**
		Patients achieving remission (TSS change ≤0.5 units) at 3 years (61% vs 51%), Radiographic progression - TSS (1.6 vs 5.95, p <0.05) and erosion score (0.39 vs 3.25, p <0.05), total number of withdrawals (numbers not given)	3 years	**ETN** (all p <0.05)
		JSN, Patients reporting 1/> AEs or number of SAEs		**NS**
1 RCT[292,293, 300,304] **Level 1++**	ETN + MTX vs. MTX	ACR20, ACR50, ACR70, patients achieving remission (DAS <1.6 and DAS <2.6), modified TSS, JSN, erosion score **3 years**: 85% vs 70%, 67% vs 44%, 47% vs 21%, 41% vs 18% and 40% vs 19%, −0.14 vs 5.95, −0.67 vs 2.7, −0.67 vs 3.25 EQ5D above normal (1 year only reported: 41% vs 24%, p <0.05)	1,2 and 3 years	**ETN + MTX**
		DAS score (2.2 vs. 3.0), HAQ, HAQ clinical improvement of ≥0.22 (**2 years**: 87% vs 74%), HAQ major improvement of >0.8 (**2 years**: 62% vs 35%)	1 and 2 years	**ETN + MTX** (all p <0.05)
		Incidence of AEs, withdrawals due to AEs	1 year	**NS**

continued

Table 7.37 Etanercept – *continued*

Study	Intervention	Outcomes	Follow-up	Result – best treatment
		ACR components (patient global assessment of overall RA activity, swollen joints, painful joints, VAS pain, patients and physicians global assessment, HAQ, CRP); patients with no radiographic progression (78% vs 60%) and no progression of erosions (86% vs 66%)	2 years (all p <0.01)	**ETN + MTX**
		Patients reporting 1/> AEs or number of SAEs		**NS**
		Patients with low disease activity (DAS <2.4: 65% vs 39% and DAS <3.2: 56% vs 29%), HAQ improvement (55% vs 33%), patients with no disability (HAQ score 0 – 48% vs 33%); total number of withdrawals and withdrawals due to lack of efficacy (numbers not given)	3 years	**ETN + MTX** (most: p <0.01)
		Incidence of AEs, patients reporting 1/> AEs or number of SAEs		**NS**
1 RCT[292,293, 300,304] **Level 1++**	ETN + MTX vs etanercept	Patients achieving remission (DAS <1.6 and DAS <2.6) **3 years**: 41% vs 22% and 40% vs 21%	1,2 and 3 years	**ETN + MTX** (p <0.0001, p <0.01, p <0.05)
		ACR20 (86% vs. 75%), ACR50 (71% vs. 54%), ACR70 (49% vs. 27%), and DAS score (2.2 vs. 2.9), HAQ score (p <0.05); patients achieving clinical HAQ improvement of ≥0.22 (87% vs. 76%), HAQ major improvement of >0.8 (62% vs. 42%); modified TSS (MD 1.66) and erosion score (MD 1.12)	1 and 2 years	**ETN + MTX** (Values reported are for 2 years)
		JSN mean change: –0.23, 95% CI –0.45 to –0.02 vs. 0.32, 95% CI 0.00 to 0.63; p=0.0007; EQ5D above normal (41% vs 31%, p <0.05)	1 year	**ETN + MTX**
		Incidence of AEs, withdrawals due to AEs		**NS**
		ACR components (patient global assessment of overall RA activity, swollen joints, painful joints, VAS pain, patients and physicians global assessment, HAQ, CRP); patients with no radiographic progression (78% vs 68%) and no progression of erosions (86% vs 75%)	2 years	**ETN + MTX** (all p <0.05)
		Patients reporting 1/> AEs or number of SAEs	2 years	**NS**

continued

Table 7.37 Etanercept – *continued*

Study	Intervention	Outcomes	Follow-up	Result – best treatment
		ACR20 (85% vs 71%), ACR50 (67% vs 46%), ACR70 (47% vs 26%), patients with low disease activity (DAS <2.4: 65% vs 44% and DAS <3.2: 33% vs 29%); HAQ improvement (55% vs 37%), patients with no disability (HAQ score 0 – 48% vs 35%); Radiographic progression – JSN (–0.67 vs 1.22), erosions (–0.67 vs 0.39), total sharp score (–0.14 vs 1.6), withdrawals and withdrawals due to lack of efficacy (numbers not given)	3 years	**ETN + MTX** (p <0.001; p <0.01; p <0.05)
		Patient satisfaction, patients reporting 1/> AEs or number of SAEs		**NS**
1 RCT[301] **Level 1+**	ETN + MTX vs etanercept	ESR (MD –6.1, 95% CI –9.6 to –2.7)	16 weeks	**ETN + MTX** (p=0.001)
		Patients achieving ACR20, ACR50 or ACR70; proportion of patients with an improvement in DAS28 of >1.2 units, AEs		**NS**
		Number of flares (0.9% and 0%), proportion of patients who experienced a clinical remission (NS), proportion of patients who experienced a 'good' or 'moderate' EULAR response (82.4% vs 80%)		**Similar**

Extension studies: etanercept

- One RCT extension study[305] found that patients treated with etanercept had stable ACR20, ACR50 and ACR70 (all NS); decreased patient's and physician's global assessment (values not given), DAS (value not given) and HAQ scores (39% improvement), ESR and CRP levels (–31.3 mg/l and –19.5 mm/h), improved patient pain scores (49.2%) and reduced number of painful and swollen joints (71% and 72% reduction). Additionally, the two most common reasons for discontinuation were AEs (73%) and unsatisfactory response (58%). There were no predominant AEs leading to discontinuation. **Level 3**
- One RCT extension[303] found that there was NS difference between any of the groups (ETN + MTX vs MTX with ETN vs ETN with MTX added) for the outcomes of DAS remission (<1.6) and DAS low disease activity (<2.4) at 1 year. **Level 1++**

Abatacept (ABA)

Table 7.38 Abatacept (ABA)

Study	Intervention	Outcomes	Follow-up	Result – best treatment
1 RCT[302] **Level 1+**	ABA 2 mg + MTX vs MTX	3 of the 8 components of SF-36 (including physical functioning and bodily pain), SF-36 physical summary scores	1 year	**ABA + MTX** (mean change, range 2.6 to 3.0; all p <0.05)
		Patients improving in all SF-36 scales (significant for 2/11 comparisons)		**ABA + MTX** (better)
	ABA 10 mg + MTX vs MTX	SF-36 bodily pain, vitality and physical functioning components; SF-6D, SF-36 physical and mental		**ABA + MTX** (mean change, range 2.5 to 5.8, p <0.0001; p <0.05)
		All other SF-36 components; patients improving in all SF-36 scales (significant for 10/11 comparisons)		**ABA + MTX** (better)
		Patients improving in all SF-36 scales (significant for 7/11 comparisons).		**ABA + MTX** (better)
1 RCT[298] **Level 1++**	ABA + DMARD vs placebo + DMARD	All SF-36 subscales and composite scores (most p ≤0.0001), VAS fatigue (MD 69.7, p <0.0001), patients 'doing better' (except role functioning and mental component), rate of change for all QoL outcomes (except role emotional, most p <0.001), HAQ-DI (MD 0.4, p <0.0001), rate of change for HAQ and fatigue (values not given, both p ≤0.0001)	1 year	**ABA + DMARD**

Adalimumab (ADA)

Table 7.39 Adalimumab (ADA)

Study	Intervention	Outcomes	Follow-up	Result – best treatment
1 RCT[295] **Level 1++**	ADA + standard antirheumatic therapy vs placebo	ACR20 (52.8% vs 34.9%), ACR50 (28.9% vs 11.3%), ACR70 (14.8% vs 3.5%)	24 weeks	**Arm 1** (all p ≤0.001)
		Incidence of AEs, SAEs, severe or life threatening AEs (all did not vary according to ~ of DMARDs used); withdrawals due to AEs		**NS**
	ADA + 1 or 2 DMARDs vs placebo	ACR20 responses		**Arm 1** (p ≤0.001)
	ADA + 0, 1 or 2 DMARDs vs placebo	ACR50 and ACR70 responses		**Arm 1** (p ≤0.001)

continued

Table 7.39 Adalimumab (ADA) – *continued*

Study	Intervention	Outcomes	Follow-up	Result – best treatment
1 RCT[294] **Level 1++**	ADA 20 mg + MTX vs placebo + MTX	ACR20 (MD 30.7%), ACR50 (MD 28.2%), ACR70 (MD 16.3%), tender (MD 7.2) and swollen joints (MD 6.1), patient's assessment of pain VAS (MD 16.2), patient and physicians' global assessment of disease activity (MD 13.2 and 16.7), SF-36 (all domains, values not given), HAQ (MD 0.36), radiographic progression – TSS (MD 1.9) and joint erosion score (MD 1.2), CRP (MD 0.6)	1 year	**ADA + MTX** (all p ≤0.001)
		Total number of withdrawals (21% vs 30%), withdrawals due to lack of efficacy (8% vs 12%) and due to AEs (3% vs 7%)		**ADA + MTX (better)**
		Joint space narrowing (JSN); patients reporting at least 1 AE and for rate of AEs		**NS; similar**
	ADA 40 mg + MTX vs placebo + MTX	ACR20 (MD 34.9%), ACR50 (MD 32%), ACR70 (MD 19.7%), tender and swollen joints (MD 7 and 6.3), patient's assessment of pain VAS (MD 18.2)), SF-36 (all domains except emotional role, values not given), HAQ (MD 0.34), radiographic progression – TSS (MD 2.6), joint erosion score (MD 1.6) and JSN score (MD 0.9), patient's and physician's global assessment of disease activity (MD 16.6), CRP (MD 0.6)		**ADA + MTX** (all p ≤0.001)
		Total number of withdrawals (23% vs 30%), withdrawals due to AEs (3% and 7%)		**ADA + MTX (better)**
		Patients reporting at least 1 AE and rate of AEs (values not given), withdrawals due to lack of efficacy (13% and 12%)		**Similar**
1 RCT[291] **Level 1++**	ADA 20 mg + MTX vs placebo + MTX	ACR20 (MD 24%), ACR50 ((MD 17%); tender and swollen joints (MD 9.1 and 3.8), patient's assessment of pain VAS (MD 16.2), patient's and physician's global assessment of disease activity (MD 19.5 and 24.5), CRP (MD –1.5); HAQ (MD 0.27); better for SF-36 scores (values not given)	24 weeks	**ADA + MTX** (p=0.003; p=0.002; p ≤0.001; p=0.004)
		ACR70 and Fatigue; withdrawals due to AEs (6% and 3%)		**NS; placebo + MTX (better)**
	ADA 40 mg + MTX vs placebo + MTX	ACR20 (MD 36%), ACR50 (MD 32%), ACR70 (MD 4%), tender and swollen joints (MD 9.1 and 7.5), patient's assessment of pain VAS (MD 16.5), fatigue FACIT (MD 5.5), SF-36 (better, values not given), HAQ (MD 0.35), patient's and physician's global assessment of disease activity (MD 17.7 and 41.4), CRP (MD –1.7)		**ADA + MTX** (all p ≤0.001)
		Withdrawals due to AEs (0% and 3%)		**ADA + MTX (better)**

continued

Table 7.39 Adalimumab (ADA) – *continued*

Study	Intervention	Outcomes	Follow-up	Result – best treatment
	ADA 80 mg + MTX vs placebo + MTX	ACR20 (MD 11%), ACR50 (MD, ACR70 (MD 11%); tender and swollen joints (MD 11.5 and 7.9)), patient's assessment of pain VAS (MD 19), Fatigue FACIT (MD 6.5), HAQ (MD 0.32), patient's and physician's global assessment of disease activity (MD 14.6 and 31.2), CRP (MD –1.4), SF-36 score (better, values not given)		**ADA + MTX** (p=0.02; all p ≤0.001)
		Withdrawals due to AEs (1.4% and 3%)		**Similar**

Rituximab (RTX)

Table 7.40 Rituximab (RTX)

Study	Intervention	Outcomes	Follow-up	Result – best treatment
1 RCT[299] **Level 1++**	RTX vs placebo + MTX	ACR20 (MD 27%)	24 weeks	**RTX** (p <0.01 or not given)
		Percentage of patients with HAQ-DI reductions ≥0.25 (68% vs 45%)		**RTX (better)**
		ACR50, ACR70, SAEs or withdrawals due to AEs		**NS**
	RTX + CTX vs placebo + MTX	ACR20 (MD 38%) and ACR50 (MD 28%)	24 and 48 weeks	**RTX + CTX c** (p <0.01 and p <0.05)
		Percentage of patients with HAQ-DI reductions ≥0.25 (59% vs 45%)		**RTX + CTX (better)**
		SAEs or withdrawals due to AEs		**NS**
	RTX + MTX vs placebo + MTX	ACR20 (35%), ACR50 (MD 30%) and ACR70 (MD 18%)		**RTX + MTX** (p <0.01 and p <0.05)
		Percentage of patients with HAQ-DI reductions ≥0.25 (63% vs 45%)		**RTX + MTX** (better)
		SAEs or withdrawals due to AEs		**NS**

Infliximab (IFX)

Table 7.41 Infliximab (IFX)

Study	Intervention	Outcomes	Follow-up	Result – best treatment
1 RCT[297] **Level 1++**	IFX 3 mg/kg + MTX vs MTX + placebo	ACR20 (MD 31.5%), ACR50 (MD 22.4%), ACR70 (MD 32%), DAS28 score (MD 0.9%), proportion of patients in remission DAS28 <2.6 (MD 17%)	22 weeks	**IFX + MTX** (all p <0.0001)
		AEs		**NS**
		When IFX dose increased: numbers and types of SAEs (both 7.5%), AEs (69.7% vs 66.2%) and rates of AEs		**Similar**
	IFX 10 mg/kg + MTX vs MTX + placebo	ACR20 (MD 35.5%), ACR50 (MD 25.7%), ACR70 (MD 11.4%), DAS28 score (MD 1.1%), proportion of patients in remission DAS28 <2.6 (MD 17%)		**IFX + MTX** (all p <0.0001)
		AEs		**NS**
		When IFX dose increased: numbers and types of SAEs (7.8% vs 7.5), AEs (72.3% vs 66.2%) and rates of AEs		**Similar**

7.3.5   Health economic evidence statements

Table 7.42 Health economic studies assessing biologics

Drug	Comparator	Study	Date	Time horizon	ICER
Adalimumab	DMARD sequence	Bansback	2005	Lifetime	ACR50/DAS28 good: €34,167 per QALY (MTX) €34,922 per QALY (MTX) (from pooled analysis) €41,561 per QALY (monotherapy) ACR20/DAS28 moderate: €40,875 per QALY (+ MTX) €44,018 per QALY (+ MTX) (from pooled analysis) €65,499 per QALY (monotherapy)
	Anakinra	Chiou	2004	1 year	Adalimumab alone dominated Adalimumab + MTX dominated
	DMARDs	Chen[237]	2006	Lifetime	Adalimumab (no MTX) £140,000 per QALY Adalimumab (with MTX) £64,000 per QALY (Third line (late RA data))

continued

Table 7.42 Health economic studies assessing biologics – *continued*

Drug	Comparator	Study	Date	Time horizon	ICER
Etanercept	Anakinra	Chiou	2004	1 year	US$13,387 per QALY (monotherapy) US$7,925 per QALY (+ MTX)
	DMARD sequence	Brennan (industry Sponsored)	2004	Lifetime	£16,330 per QALY
	DMARD sequence	Bansback (industry Sponsored)	2005	Lifetime	ACR50/DAS28 good: €35,760 per QALY(+ MTX) €36,927 per QALY (monotherapy) ACR20/DAS28 moderate: €51,976 per QALY (+ MTX) €42,480 per QALY (monotherapy)
	Baseline level (failed at least 2 DMARDs, including methotrexate)	Kobelt	2004	Not applicable	After 3 months treatment:€43,500 per QALY After 6 weeks treatment: €36,900 per QALY
	Methotrexate	Kobelt (industry Sponsored)	2005	10 years	Etanercept alone dominated. Treatment for 2 years, extrapolation to 10 years: Etan-MTX €37,331 per QALY. Treatment for 2 years, extrapolation to 5 years: Etan-MTX €54,548 per QALY. Treatment for 10 years: Etan-MTX €46494 per QALY. Treatment for 5 years, extrapolation to 10 years. Etan-MTX €47,316 per QALY
	Usual treatment, leflunomide,	Welsing	2004	5 years	Etanercept monotherapy dominated by leflunomide/ etanercept combinations Etanercept vs usual treatment: €163,556 per QALY for Lef-Etan €297,151 per QALY for Etan-Lef Etanercept vs leflunomide €317,627 per QALY for Lef-Etan €517,061 per QALY for Etan-Lef
	Monotherapy leflunomide, methotrexate, sulfasalazine, no second line agent	Choi	2002	6 months	Etanercept – sulfasalazine: $41,900 per ACR20 Etanercept - methotrexate: $40,800 per ACR70WR

continued

Table 7.42 Health economic studies assessing biologics – *continued*

Drug	Comparator	Study	Date	Time horizon	ICER
	Standard therapy for Japanese RA patients (methotrexate or sulfasalazine or methotrexate + sulfasalazine)	Tanno	2006	Lifetime	Etanercept Y2.50 million per QALY
	DMARDs	Chen[237]	2006	Lifetime	Etanercept (no MTX) £47,000 per QALY Etanercept (with MTX) £50,000 per QALY (Third line (late RA data))
Infliximab	Placebo and methotrexate	Wong (industry Sponsored)	2002	Lifetime	$30,500 per QALY
	Methotrexate	Kobelt (industry Sponsored)	2003	10 years	For 1 year of treatment: €3,440 per QALY in Sweden €34,800 per QALY in UK
	Baseline level (failed at least 2 DMARDs, including methotrexate)	Kobelt	2004	Not applicable	After 3 months treatment €43,500 per QALY After 6 weeks treatment: €36,900 per QALY
	DMARD sequence	Bansback (industry Sponsored)	2005	Lifetime	ACR50/DAS28 good: €48,333 per QALY (+ MTX) ACR20/DAS28 moderate: €64,935 per QALY (+ MTX)
	Anakinra	Chiou	2004	1 year	Infliximab + MTX dominated
	Methotrexate	Marra	2007	10 years	Incremental cost per QALY depending on utilities used: HUI2-QALY $53,429 HUI3-QALY $32,018 SF-6D-QALY $69,826 EQ-5D-QALY $46,322
	DMARDs	Chen[237]	2006	Lifetime	Infliximab (with MTX) £140,000 per QALY (Third line (late RA data))
Adalimumab/ etanercept/ infliximab	DMARDs	Brennan	2007	Lifetime	£23,882 per QALY (prob cost effective = 0.84) (£32,013 at current discount rates, prob cost effective = 0.36)

Of the reviewed studies, only four[237,307,309,317] are UK based. In England and Wales, the usual incremental cost-effectiveness threshold is considered to be in the region of £20,000 to £30,000 per QALY gained. Of the four economic analyses performed in a UK setting the following results hold whichever threshold is considered:

- adalimumab – Chen 2006 reported an ICER greater than the NICE threshold[237]
- etanercept – Brennan et al. 2004[307] reported an ICER below the threshold, but Chen et al.[237] reported an ICER above the threshold
- infliximab – the Kobelt et al. ICER was under the threshold but the Chen et al. ICER was above.

As a group of anti-TNF drugs, Brennan et al. 2007[317] reported an ICER between £20–£30k. This study directly models from the British Society for Rheumatology Biologics Registry, but using the updated NICE discount rates the ICER would exceed £30k.

We see that the results of published economic evaluations vary: some analyses suggest that use of TNF inhibitors may fall within the usual acceptable cost-effectiveness ranges, others report very high ICERs. A direct comparison of ICERs between studies is not possible because of different approaches to modelling, in particular time horizon, cycle length, country of origin, perspective chosen, source of preference weights and comparator drugs.

Drug manufacturers have sponsored four published analyses, with a further one having links with a drug company. Two studies do not state the sponsors of the study and the six remaining studies were not linked with any drug manufacturers. All but one economic analysis used a decision analytic model. Published models vary in some important aspects; for example, type of model used, whether switching of therapy is considered, drug combinations, comparator therapies and time horizon and cycle length. Different studies apply different discount rates. Some studies use a 3% or 4% rate for both costs and QALYs and some use a rate of 6% for costs and 1.5% for QALYs. In model-based analyses, costs and benefits were modelled over a number of different time horizons including: 6 months, 1 year, 5 years, 10 years and lifetime. Four studies carried out a cost-effectiveness analysis using a patient-level simulation model.

7.3.6 Summary of evidence statements

- In patients with established active disease despite conventional disease modifying drugs, the addition of a biological drug generally adds significant benefits for symptom control, function and quality of life.[291–296,298–300,302,305]
- In those studies addressing radiological damage, the combination of biological drug and methotrexate compared to methotrexate alone favour the combination.[292,294,300]
- The combination of anti-TNF with methotrexate was superior to anti-TNF drug alone for symptomatic benefit, and in studies that measured them, functional outcomes, quality of life and joint damage.[291–294,298,300]
- The only studies to compare biological therapy directly with conventional disease modifying drug in established RA suggest that etanercept is superior to sulphasalazine,[296] and rituximab is superior to methotrexate,[299] for symptom control and functional benefit.
- Comparisons of etanercept with methotrexate in established RA showed few differences in symptom control or functional benefit, though etanercept was superior to methotrexate for decreased radiological progression.[292,300]

7.3.7 From evidence to recommendations

The available data does not answer the clinical question of whether a patient who is not responding to DMARD therapy should go onto other conventional DMARDs or onto a biological drug. There are no head to head trials of these comparators.

The only studies to compare biological directly with conventional disease modifying drugs suggest that etanercept is superior to sulphasalazine, and rituximab is superior to methotrexate, for symptom control and functional benefit. However, a comparison of etanercept with methotrexate showed few differences in symptom control or functional benefit, though etanercept was superior to methotrexate for decreased radiological progression. This suggests a disconnection between the ability of drugs on the one hand to influence disease activity, and on the other to slow radiological progression.

All the other studies show that in patients with active disease despite conventional disease modifying drugs, the addition of a biological drug such as anti-TNF or rituximab, generally adds significant benefits for symptom control, function and quality of life. This is in comparison with continuing on methotrexate, the response to which had not been ideal, because the patient had sufficiently active disease on the methotrexate to be included in the trial. In those studies addressing radiological damage, the combination of biological drug and methotrexate with methotrexate alone favour the combination. The combination of etanercept and methotrexate was superior to either drug alone for symptomatic and functional benefit, quality of life and joint damage. This is reflected in the licences for etanercept and adalimumab that in the absence of contraindications, methotrexate should be co-prescribed. The sequential use of adalimumab, etanercept and infliximab for the treatment of rheumatoid arthritis was not covered within this guideline as it was the subject of a NICE technology appraisal. For more information on the status of this appraisal, please see the NICE website at www.nice.org.uk

RECOMMENDATIONS

Please see Chapter 10 for the relevant related TA recommendations.

7.3 B Anakinra

7.3.9 Clinical introduction

Interleukin-1 (IL-1) is a pro-inflammatory cytokine. There is much evidence to implicate this molecule in the pathogenesis of RA where it promotes cartilage destruction and bone resorption. Anakinra is a recombinant form of human IL-1 receptor antagonist that inhibits the activity of IL-1, thus theoretically protecting both cartilage and bone. It is licensed for use in combination with methotrexate in patients who have had an inadequate response to methotrexate alone. NICE published a technology appraisal of anakinra in November 2003 (TA 72).[9] The appraisal committee could not recommend anakinra on the balance of its clinical benefits and cost effectiveness, with the cost per QALY estimated to be in excess of £69,000. The technology appraisal recommended further studies to evaluate the long-term effectiveness and safety of anakinra, and comparative trials with DMARDs and TNF-inhibitors to guide clinical practice. The GDG have been asked to update this anakinra technology appraisal within this guideline.

7.3.10 Clinical methodological introduction

We looked for studies that investigated the efficacy and safety of anakinra alone or in combination with another DMARD versus placebo or other drug treatment with respect to symptoms, function, quality of life and ability to beneficially modify structural changes of RA. Studies were selected in accordance with the criteria used for the NICE HTA on anakinra[318] as it was within the remit of this guideline to update the HTA. All studies published after the cut-off date used in the HTA were considered as evidence. Two RCTs[319,320] were found that fulfilled the criteria. The Cohen paper[319] was the same trial as one already included in the HTA, but has reported additional outcomes. The GDG wished to address the issue of longer-term effects of anakinra on patients with RA and identified 3 additional papers which were extension studies of RCTs. One of these[321] was excluded since it solely reported AEs, the second and third[322,323] were results of one trial but reported different outcomes. These were thus included as additional evidence.

The 2 RCTs[319,320] were both double blind, (but ITT analysis was not performed), parallel group studies and assessed patients who concurrently continued with their usual MTX treatment.

The first RCT (Cohen et al.)[319] was a 6-arm study comparing anakinra vs placebo in N=419 patients. Patients were treated once a day with either anakinra (5 groups with doses ranging from 0.04 mg/kg to 2.0 mg/kg) or placebo (1 group) in a 12-week or 24-week treatment phase. The second RCT (Genovese et al.)[320] was a 3-arm study comparing anakinra + biologic vs biologic in N=244 patients. Patients were treated with anakinra (100 mg four times/week) + biologic (2 groups: etanercept 25 mg either once or twice/week) vs biologic (1 group: etanercept, 25 mg twice/week) in a 24 week treatment phase with follow-up at 4 weeks post-treatment or at time of early discontinuation.

The extension study[322,323] included patients who were originally randomised to either anakinra or placebo for 24 weeks of treatment. In the extension phase (which lasted 52 weeks – ie total study was 76 weeks) all patients were given anakinra (30 mg, 75 mg, 150 mg). Patients in the placebo group were randomised to anakinra and those already in the anakinra groups remained on the dose they were originally randomised to (30 mg, 75 mg, 150 mg). Results are reported for week 48 (ie 24 weeks into the extension phase).

7.3.11 Health economic methodological introduction

Health economic evidence was not formally reviewed as there is an existing technology appraisal model. Drug costs and clinical evidence have not changed enough for anakinra to become a cost-effective therapy.[9]

7.3.12 Clinical evidence statements

▷ Anakinra – extension studies (all studies were graded as level 3 evidence)

Symptoms

- The extension study[322,323] found the following at 48 weeks (24 weeks into the extension phase of anakinra treatment):
  - In the original placebo group there was a significantly higher proportion of patients who achieved an ACR20 response (p=0.007) and sustained ACR20 response (p <0.001)

compared with the response at week 24. For the individual doses of anakinra there were no significant differences in number of patients achieving ACR20 response compared with week 24. However there were significant differences in number of patients achieving sustained ACR20 response for anakinra 75 mg (p=0.016) and anakinra 150 mg (p=0.022).

– In the original placebo group ACR50 increased compared to week 24, however ACR70 remained unchanged.

– In the original placebo group there was a significant improvement compared to week 24 for the number of swollen joints (p <0.001), number of tender joints (p <0.001), pain assessment (p <0.005), CRP (p <0.005), and ESR (p <0.001). For the individual doses of anakinra there were significant improvements compared to week 24 for anakinra 30 mg: CRP (p <0.05), and ESR (p <0.005); anakinra 75 mg: number of swollen joints (p <0.05), number of tender joints (p <0.005), and ESR (p <0.001); anakinra 150 mg: number of swollen joints (<0.005), number of tender joints (p <0.05).

– In the original anakinra groups combined, compared to week 24 there was NS difference in the proportion of patients who achieved an ACR20 response or sustained ACR20 response. There was also NS difference at week 24 for each of the individual doses of anakinra. ACR50 increased compared to week 24, however ACR70 remained unchanged.

– In the original anakinra groups combined, compared to week 24 there was no difference for number of swollen joints, number of tender joints, pain assessment, CRP (p <0.005), and ESR. In the anakinra 150 mg group there was a significant deterioration in assessment of pain (p <0.05).

• The extension study[322,323] found the following at 48 weeks (24 weeks into the extension phase of anakinra treatment):

– There was significantly less joint damage in all groups (those originally randomised to placebo or anakinra) compared to that at 24 weeks (p <0.001).

– In the original placebo group there was a significant reduction in TMSS, modified Sharp erosion score and modified Sharp joint narrowing score for all anakinra doses (p <0.001).

– In the original anakinra groups TMSS and modified Sharp erosion score were significantly lower for the higher anakinra doses (75 and 150 mg/day), with no significant difference for the 30 mg/day dose and for the modified Sharp joint narrowing score at any dose.

Function

• The extension study[322,323] found the following at 48 weeks (24 weeks into the extension phase of anakinra treatment):

– In the original placebo group there was a significant improvement compared to week 24 for HAQ score (p <0.001). For the individual doses of anakinra there were significant improvements compared to week 24 for anakinra 30 mg: HAQ (p <0.005); anakinra 150 mg: HAQ (p <0.005).

– In the original anakinra groups combined, compared to week 24 there was a significant deterioration in the HAQ score (p <0.05). In the anakinra 150 mg group there was a significant deterioration in HAQ (p <0.05).

Global assessment

- The extension study[322,323] found the following at 48 weeks (24 weeks into the extension phase of anakinra treatment):
  - In the original placebo group there was a significant improvement compared to week 24 for patient global assessment (p <0.05) and investigator assessment (p <0.05). For the individual doses of anakinra there were significant improvements compared to week 24 for anakinra 30 mg: patient global assessment (p <0.05).
  - In the original anakinra groups combined, compared to week 24 there was a significant deterioration in patient global assessment and investigator assessment. In the anakinra 150 mg group there was a significant deterioration in patient global assessment.

Study withdrawals

- The extension study[322,323] found the following at 48 weeks (24 weeks into the extension phase of anakinra treatment):
  - Rates of withdrawal were similar compared to 24 weeks
  - Withdrawals due to AEs were similar compared to 24 weeks
  - Arthritis flare was the most common reason for withdrawal due to AEs.

▷ Anakinra vs placebo

Function

- One RCT[319] (N=419) found that for the outcome of HAQ-DI (change from baseline), anakinra 1.0 mg/kg and 2.0 mg/kg were significantly better than placebo at 12 weeks (1.0 mg: −0.35, p <0.05; 2.0 mg: −0.39, p <0.01) and 24 weeks, end of study (1.0 mg: −0.37, p <0.05; 2.0 mg: −0.51, p <0.01). However, there were NS differences between anakinra 0.04 mg/kg, 0.1 mg/kg, 0.4 mg/kg and placebo. **Level 1++**
- The same RCT[319] (N=419) found that for the outcome of percentage of patients reporting no impairment of function (HAQ-DI = 0), anakinra 1.0 mg/kg was significantly better than placebo at week 24, end of study (18.6% and 5.4% respectively, p <0.05; OR 4.76, 95% CI 1.1 to 20.0). However, there were NS differences between anakinra 0.04 mg/kg, 0.1 mg/kg, 0.4 mg/kg, 2.0 mg/kg and placebo. **Level 1++**

▷ Anakinra + biologic vs biologic

Symptoms (all Level 1+)

- One RCT[320] (N=244) found that for the outcome of ACR 20, etanercept was significantly better than anakinra + etanercept once/week (68% and 51% respectively; OR 1.98, 95% CI 1.05 to 3.78; p=0.037) at 24 weeks (end of treatment). However there was NS difference between etanercept and anakinra + etanercept (twice/week).
- The same RCT[320] (N=244) found that for the outcome of ACR 50, there was NS difference between etanercept and anakinra + etanercept (once/week or twice/week) at 24 weeks (end of treatment). The same RCT[320] (N=244) found that for the outcome of ACR 70, there was NS difference between etanercept and anakinra + etanercept (once/week or twice/week) at 24 weeks (end of treatment).

- The same RCT[320] (N=244) found that for the outcome of EULAR response, etanercept was better than anakinra + etanercept once/week (79% and 66% patients respectively) and twice/week (79% and 73% patients respectively) at 24 weeks (end of treatment).
- The same RCT[320] (N=244) found that for the outcome of DAS score (% reduction), etanercept was similar to anakinra + etanercept once/week (39% and 40% patients respectively) and twice/week (39% and 41% patients respectively) at 24 weeks (end of treatment).

Adverse events

- One RCT[320] (N=244) found that for the outcomes of Number of SAEs, number of infections and number of serious infections, etanercept was better than anakinra + etanercept once/week and twice/week over 24 weeks (end of treatment). **Level 1+**

Study withdrawals

- One RCT[320] (N=244) found that for the outcome of number of withdrawals due to AEs, etanercept was significantly better than anakinra + etanercept once/week (0% and 8.6% respectively, p-value not given) and twice/week (0% and 7.4% respectively, p value not given) at 24 weeks (end of treatment).
- The same RCT[320] (N=244) found that for the outcome of number of withdrawals, etanercept was better than anakinra + etanercept once/week (7% and 12% respectively) and twice/week (7% and 20% respectively) at 24 weeks (end of treatment).

7.3.13 Summary of evidence statements

- Anakinra in different doses works well in an extension study in patients previously randomised to placebo for a variety of disease activity measures, radiological [322,323] and functional outcomes.[319,322,323]
- The drug appears to be well tolerated.[322,323]
- Etanercept was better alone than in combination with anakinra for some measures of efficacy, tolerability and a reduced rate of infections.[320]

7.3.14 From evidence to recommendations

Since publication of the NICE Technology Appraisal on anakinra in 2003, new high quality data has been sparse. Extension studies have not shown any evidence to suggest a significant improvement in efficacy of anakinra after the first 24 weeks of treatment, or of any effect on decline in HAQ (the driver of economic modelling in the NICE TA) after 24 weeks of follow-up. The GDG noted that the cost of anakinra had reduced, but did not feel that this was likely to bring it within the NICE cost effectiveness range if new health economic modelling was undertaken.

It was also noted that the addition of anakinra to etanercept resulted in no improvement of efficacy, with many outcome measures suggesting that the combination was inferior to using etanercept alone. The combination also resulted in a significant increase in serious infections. The GDG felt that it was reasonable to extrapolate this finding to all anti-TNF therapies, given that they all have a similar propensity for increasing the risk of infection.

The GDG concluded that, on the basis of the evidence reviewed, the current TA recommendations should stand, but with an additional recommendation cautioning against the co-prescribing of anakinra and anti-TNF therapy.

RECOMMENDATIONS

R25   On the balance of its clinical benefits and cost effectiveness, anakinra is not recommended for the treatment of RA, except in the context of a controlled, long-term clinical study.*

R26   Patients currently receiving anakinra for RA may suffer loss of wellbeing if their treatment were discontinued at a time they did not anticipate. Therefore, patients should continue therapy with anakinra until they and their consultant consider it is appropriate to stop.*

R27   Do not offer the combination of tumour necrosis factor-α (TNF-α) inhibitor therapy and anakinra for RA.

7.4   Symptom control

7.4 A   Analgesics

7.4.1   Clinical introduction

When people with RA are asked to list their priorities for the management of RA, pain relief is almost always in first place. Pain is a cardinal sign of inflammation, and therefore adequate disease control will result in satisfactory pain relief in many people with RA. However, others will not gain sufficient disease-control to relieve symptoms, or will develop mechanical pain due to damage to joints or surrounding structures. Analgesics will be used by all patients with RA at some time during the course of their disease. Key questions include:

● Are analgesics helpful for the pain of RA?

● Are there any particular side effects of analgesics that are a problem in the RA population?

● Does the addition of analgesics to other pain-relieving medication (particularly NSAIDs) add anything to pain-control?

● Are analgesics better than NSAIDs for some aspects of pain control?

● Is there any evidence to support the use of low dose anti-depressants in RA, in keeping with their use in other diseases associated with chronic pain?

7.4.2   Clinical methodological introduction

We looked for studies that investigated the efficacy and safety of analgesic drugs with respect to symptoms, function and quality of life in patients with a recent onset of rheumatoid arthritis, and in established disease. Due to the large volume of evidence on analgesics, studies were selected which fulfilled the following criteria: were of a UK-relevant population; if the population was mixed arthritis there had to be >75% RA or RA subgroup analysis; for opioids

---

* These recommendations are from 'Anakinra for rheumatoid arthritis'. NICE technology appraisal 72. The GDG reviewed the evidence on anakinra but made no changes to the recommendations.

or opioid-paracetamol comparisons – sample size >50; for anti-depressant comparisons – all papers were considered apart from those in patients who were already depressed and those which used doses of anti-depressants which were greater than those used in clinical practice for their analgesic effect.

Eight studies[324–331] were found that fulfilled the criteria. Studies were found which looked at opioids, opioids + paracetamol, NSAIDs + paracetamol, anti-depressants, and other analgesics (nefopam). No suitable studies were found which looked at paracetamol alone. All studies were methodologically sound.

NOTE: all studies found looked at either patients with established RA or duration not mentioned, no studies were found which specifically mentioned patients with a recent onset of RA.

▷ Opioids and opioid-paracetamol

One RCT[324] and two case-series (prospective)[325,326] were found which fulfilled the criteria for opioids and opioid-paracetamol analgesics.

The RCT[324] was a double-blind, parallel group study looking at opioids or opioid-paracetamol analgesics in patients with established RA or disease duration not mentioned. It compared 2 different treatment arms (codeine 90 mg/day + paracetamol 1500 mg/day + Diclofenac 50 mg once/day vs Diclofenac 100 mg/day) in N=60 patients with RA in a 7 day treatment phase.

The two case-series [325] both looked at transdermal fentanyl (TF) and compared treatment outcome with baseline values. The first case-series[325] assessed N=104 patients (disease duration not mentioned) in a 28 day treatment phase and the second[326] assessed N=226 patients with established RA in both a 30-day and 12-month treatment phase.

▷ NSAIDs + paracetamol

Two RCTs[327,328] (both double blind, no ITT analysis, and N=20 patients) were found which looked at NSAIDs + paracetamol. The first RCT[328] was a parallel group study comparing 2 different treatment arms (Indomethacin 50 mg/day + paracetamol 4 g/day vs Indomethacin 150 mg/day) in a 4-week treatment phase. The second RCT[327] was a cross-over study comparing 6 different treatment arms (Naproxen 500 mg/day, 1000 mg/day or 1500 mg/day + paracetamol 4 g/day vs Naproxen 500 mg/day, 1000 mg/day or 1500 mg/day) in a 2-week treatment phase.

▷ Anti-depressants

Two RCTs[329,331] (both double-blind, no ITT analysis, and disease duration not mentioned) were found which looked at anti-depressants as analgesics. The first RCT[329] was a cross-over trial of N=256 patients comparing 3 arms: amitriptyline (1 mg/kg/day for 3 days then 1.5 mg/kg/day thereafter) vs trazodone 1.5 mg/kg/day for 3 days then 3 mg/kg/day thereafter) vs placebo in a 7-week treatment phase. The second RCT[331] was a parallel study in N=36 patients comparing 2 arms: amitriptyline (25 mg/day for 1 week then increased to 50 mg/day for week 2 then 75 mg/day thereafter) vs placebo in a 12-week treatment phase.

▷ Other analgesics

One RCT[330] was found which looked at other analgesics. The RCT was a double blind, cross-over study (ITT analysis was not performed) comparing nefopam 180 mg/day vs placebo in N=27 patients with established RA in a 4-week treatment phase.

7.4.3 Health economic methodological introduction

No health economic papers were identified.

7.4.4 Clinical evidence statements

▷ Opioids and opioid-paracetamol

Symptoms, function, quality of life and global assessment

- One RCT[332] found that the opioid Sativex was significantly better than placebo for: DAS, Pain on movement and at rest, Quality of sleep and SF-MPQ. However, there was NS different for morning stiffness and SF-MPQ dimensions of total intensity of pain at present and intensity of pain at present. **Level 1+**
- One RCT[324] found that there was NS difference between codeine + paracetamol + diclofenac vs diclofenac for: Pain (VAS), morning stiffness, Ritchie Index, Patient's global judgement of efficacy and physician's global assessment of tolerability and Number of nocturnal awakenings on the disability score. **Level 1+**
- One case-series[326] found that TF treatment was significantly better than baseline values for: ADLs, social activities, pain intensity and sleep disturbance due to pain, Quality of sleep and satisfaction with pain treatment at 30 days; better for general well being at 30 days and satisfaction, pain intensity, ADLs and social activities remained stable at 12 months and 85% of symptoms disappeared by the end of the study. **Level 3**
- One case-series[325] found that TF treatment was significantly better than baseline values for: Pain control, WBPI pain, pain recorded in patients' diaries, patient's assessment of treatment, HAQ score and HAQ components of eating, activities and arising. **Level 3**

Use of rescue medication, withdrawals and adverse events

- One RCT[332] found that the opioid Sativex was better than placebo for: withdrawals due to AEs and SAEs, and was similar for AEs of nausea and arthritic pains. **Level 1+**
- One RCT[324] found that there was NS difference between codeine + paracetamol + diclofenac vs diclofenac for: AEs and withdrawals due to AEs. **Level 1+**
- One case-series[325] found that of patients who received TF treatment, 27% withdrew due to AEs, 65% had AEs but there were no SAEs. **Level 3**
- One case-series[326] found that of patients who received TF treatment, 17% had AEs, 10% withdrew due to AEs and 40% used rescue medication. **Level 3**

▷ NSAIDs + paracetamol

- One RCT[328] found that there was NS difference between Indomethacin + paracetamol and Indomethacin for: morning Pain (VAS), Night Pain, morning stiffness, Joint movement, patient's assessment of therapeutic efficacy and Ritchie articular index. The 2 groups were also similar for ESR, CRP and AEs. **Level 1+**
- One RCT[327] found that Naproxen 500 mg/day + paracetamol was significantly better than Naproxen (500, 1000 and 1500 mg/day) for: Joint index, Joint pain, Morning stiffness and Global assessment of disease activity. However there was NS difference for ADLs. **Level 1+**
- The same RCT[327] found that Naproxen 1000 mg/day + paracetamol was significantly better than Naproxen (500, 1000 and 1500 mg/day) for: Number of painful joints (Ritchie); morning stiffness; pain at rest and movement (VAS) and for Global assessment of disease activity. **Level 1+**
- The same RCT[327] found that Naproxen 500 mg/day + paracetamol was significantly better than Naproxen 1000 mg/day) for: Number of AEs. Additionally, AEs were significantly related to dose of naproxen. **Level 1+**

▷ Anti-depressants

- One RCT[329] found that amitriptyline was significantly better than placebo for: present pain intensity, worst pain, number of painful and tender joints, severity rating summary of painful and tender joints but there was NS difference for least pain (VAS). However, there was NS difference for physical incapacitation. **Level 1+**
- The same RCT[329] found that trazodone was significantly better than placebo for depression. However, there was NS difference for: least pain (VAS) or physical incapacitation. **Level 1+**
- One RCT[331] found that there was NS difference between amitryptiline and placebo at 12 weeks for Pain and joint tenderness, and the groups were similar for: Total number of withdrawals (both N=4), withdrawals due to AEs (N=2 and N=3 respectively) and withdrawals due to lack of efficacy (N=2 and N=1 respectively). **Level 1+**

▷ Other analgesics

- One RCT[330] found that nefopam was significantly better than placebo for: Pain, Morning stiffness, grip strength and joint tenderness. However it was worse for AEs and there was NS difference for ESR. **Level 1+**

7.4.5 Summary of evidence statements

- There are very few good quality trials of analgesics in RA. Most of the available studies were over very short time periods, and some in small populations
- A variety of analgesics provide symptomatic benefit in RA (eg decreased pain, better sleep, improved activities of daily living, improved social activities, satisfaction with medication)[325,326,330,332]
- Analgesics appear to be well tolerated[325,326,332]
- Some studies suggest decreases in more 'inflammatory' symptoms such as morning stiffness and grip strength[324,330]

- Amitriptyline (in quite high doses) has been shown to be successful in reducing joint swelling, and help to lift a low mood and chronic fatigue[329]
- There was no evidence to show that low dose amitryptiline was helpful in a study over a 3-month period[331]
- 100 mg of diclofenac did not show any increased benefit over 50 mg diclofenac plus paracetamol and codeine[324]
- 150 mg of indomethacin did not show any increased benefit over 50 mg indomethacin plus paracetamol[328]
- The addition of paracetamol to naproxen improved pain control.[327]

7.4.6   From evidence to recommendations

Although the evidence for analgesics being helpful in RA was sparse, the GDG considered that there was nevertheless sufficient data to suggest that they are effective in controlling pain, and that there should accordingly be a recommendation that these drugs should be offered where other approaches have not resulted in satisfactory pain control. In addition, bearing in mind the need to use NSAIDs and COX2 inhibitors in the lowest effective doses for the shortest periods of time (see recommendation 29), it was also felt important to emphasise that analgesics should be considered as a way to decrease reliance on these drugs

The GDG also noted that, although low dose antidepressants are commonly used in clinical practice to treat pain and sleep disturbance in RA patients, there was surprisingly no evidence to support this despite the observation that patients and their healthcare professionals can testify to their benefits. It was agreed that there should be a research recommendation to address this issue.

RECOMMENDATION

R28   Offer analgesics (for example, paracetamol, codeine or compound analgesics) to people with RA whose pain control is not adequate, to potentially reduce their need for long-term treatment with non-steroidal anti-inflammatory drugs (NSAIDs) or cyclo-oxygenase-2 (COX-2) inhibitors.

7.4 B   NSAIDs

7.4.8   Clinical introduction

NSAIDs (for example, ibuprofen, diclofenac, naproxen) and COX2 inhibitor drugs (for example, rofecoxib, celecoxib and etoricoxib) have anti-inflammatory and analgesic properties, and many people with RA can testify to their effectiveness in controlling their symptoms. Indeed the quality of life of many would be diminished for many people by not allowing continuing treatment with NSAIDs that they may need to take in significant doses over many years. There is no evidence to suggest that NSAIDs modify the course of RA, and they are purely for symptomatic benefit.

For some decades it has been clear that NSAIDs also have major disadvantages, with evidence of increased toxicity, particularly in the gastro-intestinal tract, but in other organ systems also (such as the propensity for impairing renal function, and aggravating asthma), and interactions with other commonly prescribed medications (such as warfarin, diuretics, ACE inhibitors). The COX2 selective drugs were designed to decrease gastrointestinal morbidity and mortality, and there is some evidence that they may have been successful in this regard. However, a concern over selectively blocking COX2 is that this might lead to an imbalance in the ratio of prostacyclin to thromboxane, and lead to an increased risk of cardiovascular morbidity and mortality. The VIGOR trial showed clear and early divergence between rofecoxib and naproxen for adverse cardiovascular outcomes, and eventually was instrumental in the withdrawal of rofecoxib due to increasing concerns over the balance of efficacy to toxicity. The data for celecoxib is rather mixed, with some trials suggesting increased cardiovascular risk, but other trials, and observational databases, showing no increased risk. For etoricoxib the MEDAL study showed no increased risk for cardiovascular mortality when compared with traditional NSAIDs, but the COX2 inhibitor was associated with more peripheral oedema and hypertension. More recently evidence has emerged to show increased cardiovascular risk for all NSAIDs, irrespective of their COX2 specificity, and regulatory bodies around the world have added to the cautions before using any of these drugs. Therefore all NSAIDs and COX2 inhibitor drugs should be considered to be similar for cardiovascular risk.

Against the background of these concerns, one would be forgiven for trying to avoid NSAIDs and COX2 drugs altogether, but this runs the risk of denying patients access to useful symptom controlling drugs. Clearly caution needs to be exercised in ensuring that people with RA are screened to ensure that these drugs are not contra-indicated for any reason. If their use is appropriate, existing guidelines from regulatory authorities such as the MHRA advise the lowest dose be used over the shortest period of time. This should also discourage an over-reliance on drugs where there is no evidence to suggest that they treat the underlying disease process. In the early stages of RA a person may need high doses of NSAIDs for symptomatic benefit, but if this need continues, this may be a sign that disease control is not adequate. Evidence of efficacy of DMARDs is the ability to decrease NSAID use, and this needs to be reviewed throughout the course of the disease.

The GDG has been asked to update the current technology appraisal guideline on COX2 drugs, and to consider the conclusions drawn by our colleagues on the NICE osteoarthritis guidelines to determine whether factors related to differences in efficacy or toxicity would be likely to result in conclusions that are different from the OA guidelines. The key questions are:

- How clinically and cost-effective are NSAIDs and COX2s in decreasing the symptoms of RA?
- What risks are associated with the use of NSAIDs and COX2s in RA?
- Are there any differences between NSAIDs and COX2s for clinical- and cost-efficacy and toxicity in RA?
- Are there differences between individual drugs within the classes for toxicity and clinical- and cost-efficacy in RA?
- Is the combination of NSAID and proton-pump inhibitor more cost-effective than COX2 selective drugs?
- Are there any circumstances under which a combination of proton-pump inhibitor and COX2 selective drug might be cost-effective in RA?

7.4.9 Clinical methodological introduction

We looked for studies that investigated the efficacy and safety of NSAIDs and Cox-2 selective drugs with respect to symptoms, function and quality of life in patients with a recent onset of rheumatoid arthritis, and in established disease. Trials on Cox-2 selective drugs were selected in accordance with the criteria used for the NICE HTA on Cox-2s[333] as it was within the remit of this guideline to update the HTA. All trials published after the cut-off date used in the HTA were considered as evidence. The criteria used in the TA were as follows:

1. Cox-2s: celecoxib, rofecoxib, meloxicam and etodolac
2. Comparators: placebo, NSAIDs, other Cox-2s
3. Doses: licensed doses per day – celecoxib (200–400 mg), rofecoxib (not specified for RA), meloxicam (15 mg) and etodolac (600 mg)
4. Treatment length: ≥4 weeks
5. Trial type: RCTs/SR/MA (level 1 studies)
6. Trial size: N >50 in each arm
7. Population: RA (any duration), any country.

Papers looking at rofecoxib were excluded as evidence because rofecoxib is no longer licensed in the UK.

Due to the large volume of evidence on NSAIDs and other Cox-2s not listed in the TA, only RCTs/MA were selected which had been published in 1997 onwards, were of a UK-relevant population, if the population was mixed arthritis there had to be >75% RA or RA subgroup analysis and looked at the following comparisons: NSAIDs or Cox-2s vs placebo, analgesics or NSAIDs (different or same NSAIDs including diff routes of administration and diff doses). Some papers on COX-2s also report NSAID vs placebo arms and thus these have been included in the NSAIDs evidence.

Twelve studies (11 RCTs and 1 extension of an RCT)[334–346] were found that fulfilled the criteria. One of the RCTs was published as two separate papers[343,345] reporting different outcomes and so the trial has only been counted once. However results from both papers are reported and referenced here. One of the studies[346] was an extension study of an included trial[338] and was included as additional evidence. Two of the studies[335,336] were excluded due to methodological limitations.

NOTE: all trials found looked at patients with established RA patients, no studies were found for patients with a recent onset of RA.

▷ Cox-2 selective drugs (TA update)

One MA[335] and one RCT[336] were found which fulfilled the criteria to update the NICE TA on Cox-2s in RA patients. Both of these studies[335,336] were excluded due to methodological limitations (the MA reported significant heterogeneity; the RCT was unblinded and ITT analysis was not performed) and thus there were no papers included to update the TA.

▷ Other Cox-2s

Two RCTs[337,338] and one extension study of an RCT[346] were found which looked at other Cox-2s in RA patients. Both RCTs were methodologically sound randomised, parallel group studies with a 12-week treatment phase. The first RCT[337] looked at Cox-2s in N=891 patients with established RA. The trial compared 3 different treatment arms (etoricoxib 90 mg, naproxen 1000 mg and placebo). The naproxen vs placebo arm will be reported in the NSAIDs section. The second RCT[338] looked at Cox-2s in N=816 patients with established RA. The trial compared 3 different treatment arms (etoricoxib 90 mg, naproxen 1000 mg and placebo). The naproxen vs placebo arm will be reported in the NSAIDs section. The extension study reported results of patients who remained on etoricoxib 90 mg vs naproxen 1000 mg for the full trial and extension period (121 weeks).

▷ NSAIDs

Nine RCTs[334,337–345] were found which looked at NSAIDs in RA patients. Three of these RCTs[334,337,338] have been included in the Cox-2 sections, but they additionally looked at NSAIDs vs placebo, and therefore these comparisons are included as evidence in this section. One of the RCTs was published as two separate papers[343,345] reporting different outcomes and so the trial has only been counted once. However results from both papers are reported and referenced here.

All 9 included RCTs were randomised, double blind, fairly large (range: N=346 to N=1,149) parallel group studies comparing naproxen 100 mg (500 mg twice/day) vs placebo in patients with established RA in a 12-week treatment phase (except for 1 RCT – Geussens et al.[334] which had a 26-week treatment phase and 1 RCT – Krug et al.[342] which compared naproxen vs nabumetone). Some of the studies also had Cox-2 arms which were either reported as evidence in the previous Cox-2 sections or consisted of Cox-2s that are not licensed in the UK. The methodological limitations of the RCTs were as follows: all except one was graded as 1+ since they were double blind but ITT analysis was not performed. The remaining study was given a 1++ because it was blinded and the authors performed ITT analysis.

7.4.10 Health economic methodological introduction

In the Brown et al. HTA report[347] a systematic review of economic evaluations of Cox-2 drugs was performed. The nine papers found in this report were appraised.[348–356] A search was performed looking for economic evaluations published subsequent to the HTA report but no papers were found.

7.4.11 Clinical evidence statements

▷ Cox-2 selective drugs (TA update)

No papers were included to update the NICE TA.

▷ Other Cox-2s

Table 7.43 Symptoms

Study	Treatment	Follow-up	Outcomes	Result – best treatment
2 RCTs[337,338] **Level 1+**	Etoricoxib 90 mg vs placebo	12 weeks	Tender and swollen joint count, pain (VAS) and ACR20 completers	**Etoricoxib** (1 RCT all p <0.001, 1 RCT all p <0.01).
1 RCT and its extension study[338,346] **Level 1+**	Etoricoxib 90 mg vs naproxen	12 weeks	Tender and swollen joint count, pain (VAS) and ACR20 completers at 12 weeks	**Etoricoxib** (all p <0.01 except swollen joints p=0.05)
		121 weeks	Tender and swollen joint count	**NS**

Table 7.44 Function

Study	Treatment	Follow-up	Outcomes	Result – best treatment
2 RCTs[337,338] **Level 1+**	Etoricoxib 90 mg vs placebo	12 weeks	HAQ score/modified HAQ score	**Etoricoxib** (1 RCT p <0.001, 1 RCT p <0.01)
1 RCT[337] **Level 1+**	Etoricoxib 90 mg vs naproxen	12 weeks	HAQ score	**NS**
1 RCT [338] **Level 1+**		12 weeks	Modified HAQ score	**Etoricoxib** (p <0.01)

Table 7.45 Global assessment

Study	Treatment	Follow-up	Outcomes	Result – best treatment
2 RCTs[337,338] **Level 1+**	Etoricoxib 90 mg vs placebo	12 weeks	Patient's and investigator's global assessment of disease activity	**Etoricoxib** (p <0.001)
1 RCT[337] **Level 1+**	Etoricoxib 90 mg vs naproxen	12 weeks	Patient's and investigator's global assessment of disease activity	**NS**
1 RCT and its extension study[338,346]		12 weeks	Patient's and investigator's global assessment of disease activity	**Etoricoxib** (p <0.01)
Level 1+		121 weeks	Patient's and investigator's global assessment of disease activity	**NS**

Table 7.46 Biochemical markers

Study	Treatment	Follow-up	Outcomes	Result – best treatment
2 RCTs[337,338] **Level 1+**	Etoricoxib 90 mg vs placebo	12 weeks	CRP	**Etoricoxib** (1 RCT p <0.05, 1 RCT p <0.01)
2 RCTs[337,338] **Level 1+**	Etoricoxib 90 mg vs naproxen	12 weeks	CRP	**NS**

Table 7.47 Withdrawals

Study	Treatment	Follow-up	Outcomes	Result – best treatment
1 RCT[337] **Level 1+**	Etoricoxib 90 mg vs placebo	12 weeks	Withdrawals due to lack of efficacy; total number of withdrawals	**Etoricoxib** (1 RCT p <0.001, 1 RCT p <0.01); similar
1 RCT[338] **Level 1+**			Total number of withdrawals	**Etoricoxib** (better)
2 RCTs[337,338] **Level 1+**			Withdrawals due to AEs	**NS**
1 RCT[337] **Level 1+**	Etoricoxib 90 mg vs naproxen	12 weeks	Withdrawals due to lack of efficacy; total number of withdrawals; withdrawals due to AEs	**NS; similar; similar**
1 RCT [338] **Level 1+**		12 weeks	Withdrawals due to lack of efficacy; total number of withdrawals	**Etoricoxib** (p <0.01; better)

Table 7.48 Adverse events

Study	Treatment	Follow-up	Outcomes	Result – best treatment
1 RCT[337] Level 1+	Etoricoxib 90 mg vs placebo	12 weeks		NS
			Number of patients with SAEs	Similar
			GI nuisance symptoms	Placebo
			Number of patients with drug-related AEs and hypertension AEs	Better
1 RCT[338] Level 1+				NS
			Number of patients with drug-related AEs and for SAEs	Similar
			Dyspepsia AEs	Placebo
			Hypertension AEs	Better
1 RCT[337] Level 1+	Etoricoxib 90 mg vs naproxen	12 weeks	Number of patients with: drug-related AEs, SAEs, GI nuisance symptoms and hypertension AEs	Similar
1 RCT and its extension study[338,346] Level 1+		12 weeks	Dyspepsia AEs and hypertension AEs	Similar
		121 weeks	Total number of AEs	Similar

▷ NSAIDs

Table 7.49 Symptoms

Study	Treatment	Follow-up	Outcomes	Result – best treatment
2 RCTs[337,338] Level 1+	Naproxen vs placebo	12 weeks	Tender and swollen joint count, pain (VAS) and ACR20 completers	Naproxen (1 RCT all $p < 0.001$ except swollen joints $p < 0.05$; 1 RCT $p < 0.01$)
1 RCT[334] Level 1++			Tender joint count, ACR20 responder index, Pain (VAS), Morning stiffness	Naproxen (all $p < 0.05$)
			Swollen joint count	NS
1 RCT[340] Level 1+		26 weeks	Swollen joint count	Naproxen ($p < 0.05$)
		13 and 26 weeks	Tender joint count; pain (VAS)	Naproxen ($p < 0.05$; $p < 0.01$)

continued

Table 7.49 Symptoms – *continued*

Study	Treatment	Follow-up	Outcomes	Result – best treatment
1 RCT[343,345] **Level 1+**	Naproxen vs placebo	12 weeks	Swollen joint count, ACR20 responders, pain (VAS) and morning stiffness	**Naproxen** (all: $p < 0.05$)
1 RCT[339] **Level 1+**		12 weeks	ACR20, reduction in the number of tender/painful joints, tender/painful Joints; pain (VAS), morning stiffness	**Naproxen** ($p \geq 0.01$; $p < 0.001$)
1 RCT[341] **Level 1+**		12 weeks	Tender and painful joint count, tender and painful joint score, swollen joint count and swollen joint score, ACR20 responders, ACR-N; Pain (VAS); Morning stiffness	**Naproxen** (all $p \geq 0.001$)
1 RCT[344] **Level 1+**		12 weeks	ACR20 responders, Tender /painful joint score; reduction in the number of tender/painful joints	**Naproxen** ($p \geq 0.001$; $p=0.03$)
1 RCT[342] **Level 1+**	Naproxen vs nabumetone	12 weeks	Change in number of tender, swollen and painful joints; pain (VAS) and AIMS2 dimensions, clinical change in number of joints involved (?50% reduction) and clinical change in number of tender, swollen and painful joints ($\geq$50% reduction) and RADAR dimensions	**NS**

Table 7.50 Function

Study	Treatment	Follow-up	Outcomes	Result – best treatment
4 RTCs[337,338] **Level 1+**	Naproxen vs placebo	12 weeks	HAQ or modified HAQ	**Naproxen** (2 RCTs $p \leq 0.001$; 1 RCT $p < 0.01$; 1 RCT $p < 0.05$)
1 RCT[340] **Level 1+**		13 and 26 weeks		**Naproxen** ($p < 0.05$)

Table 7.51 Global assessment

Study	Treatment	Follow-up	Outcomes	Result – best treatment
7 RCTs[337,338, 340,339,341,344] **Level 1+** and [334] **Level 1++**	Naproxen vs placebo	All 12 weeks (except Geusens[340] – 13 and 26 weeks)	Patient's and investigator's global assessment of disease activity	**Naproxen** (3 RCTs p≤0.001; 1 RCT p <0.01; 1 RCT p <0.05; 1 RCT p <0.01 13 weeks and p <0.05 26 weeks)
1 RCT[343,345] **Level 1+**		12 weeks	Patient's and investigator's global assessment of disease activity	**NS**
1 RCT[342] **Level 1+**	Naproxen vs nabumetone	12 weeks	Patient's and investigator's global assessment of disease activity	**NS**

Table 7.52 Quality of life

Study	Treatment	Follow-up	Outcomes	Result – best treatment
1 RCT[341] **Level 1+**	Naproxen vs placebo	12 weeks	PTSS, SF-36 physical (all domains except general health); SF-36 mental (all domains except role-emotional)	**Naproxen** (p≤0.001; p≤0.001; p <0.01)
1 RCT[343,345] **Level 1+**		12 weeks	SF-36 physical (all domains); SF-36 mental (all domains)	**Naproxen** (p <0.01; p <0.05)

Table 7.53 Biochemical markers

Study	Treatment	Follow-up	Outcomes	Result – best treatment
1 RCT[338] **Level 1+**		12 weeks	CRP	**Naproxen** (p <0.01)
7 RCTs[337,339, 340,341,343–345] **Level 1+** and [334] **Level 1++**	Naproxen vs placebo	All 12 weeks (except Geusens[340] – 13 and 26 weeks)	CRP	**NS**

Table 7.54 Withdrawals

Study	Treatment	Follow-up	Outcomes	Result – best treatment
5 RCTs[337,343, 345,339,341] **Level 1+** and [334] **Level 1++**	Naproxen vs placebo	12 weeks	Withdrawals due to lack of efficacy	**Naproxen** (all SS except Gibofsky = better)
1 RCT[340] **Level 1+**		26 weeks		**Naproxen (better)**
2 RCTs[338, 343,345] **Level 1+**		12 weeks	Total number of withdrawals	**Naproxen (better)**
1 RCT[337] **Level 1+**				**Similar**
1 RCT[340] **Level 1+**		26 weeks		**Naproxen (better)**
4 RCTs[337,338, 343,345] **Level 1+** and [334] **Level 1++**		12 weeks	Withdrawals due to AEs	**NS**
1 RCT[341] **Level 1+**				**Placebo (better)**
1 RCT[340] **Level 1+**		26 weeks		**Naproxen (better)**
1 RCT[343,345] **Level 1+**		12 weeks	Withdrawals due to GI AEs	**Placebo (better)**
1 RCT[342] **Level 1+**	Naproxen vs nabumetone	12 weeks	Withdrawals due to lack of efficacy	**Similar**
			Withdrawals due to treatment-related AEs and Total withdrawals	**NS**

Table 7.55 Adverse events

Study	Treatment	Follow-up	Outcomes	Result – best treatment
3 RCTs[337,338] Level 1+ and [334] Level 1++	Naproxen vs placebo	12 weeks	Drug-related AEs and SAEs	NS
3 RCTs[339,343–345] Level 1+			Total AEs	Placebo (better)
2 RCTs[338,341] Level 1+			Dyspepsia AEs	Placebo (better)
1 RCT[334] Level 1++			1 or more AEs	NS
1 RCT[341] Level 1+		12 weeks	Percentage of patients with AEs	Similar
1 RCT[340] Level 1+		26 weeks		Placebo (better)
3 RCTs[337–339] Level 1+		12 weeks	Hypertension AEs	Placebo (better)
3 RCTs[341,343,345] Level 1+ and [334] Level 1++				NS or similar
1 RCT[340] Level 1+		26 weeks		Placebo (better)
1 RCT[337] Level 1+		12 weeks	GI AEs or nuisance symptoms	Similar
2 RCTs[343–345] Level 1+				Placebo (better)
1 RCT[340] Level 1+		26 weeks		Placebo (better)
1 RCT[342] Level 1+	Naproxen vs nabumetone	12 weeks	Number of patients with ≥1 AE; Serious GI AEs	Similar; NS

Table 7.56 Use of rescue medication

Study	Treatment	Follow-up	Outcomes	Result – best treatment
1 RCT[334] Level 1++	Naproxen vs placebo	12 weeks	Use of rescue medication	NS
1 RCT[340] Level 1+		26 weeks	Use of rescue medication	NS
1 RCT[342] Level 1+	Naproxen vs nabumetone	12 weeks	Use of rescue paracetamol	NS

7.1.12 Health economic evidence statements

Table 7.57 COX-2 inhibitors – taken from the Brown HTA Report and the NICE TA COX-2 Assessment Report

Study	Country	Comparators	Patients	Time Horizon	Model used	ICER	Conclusions
Svarvar 2000[349]	Norway	Celecoxib vs NSAID	OA and RA	1 year	ACCES Decision Analytic model	Per GI event averted, per LYG	Celecoxib dominates
Chancellor 2001[355]	Switzerland	Celecoxib vs NSAID	Arthritis	6 months	Decision Analytic with Monte Carlo	Per adverse event	Celecoxib dominates
You 2002[352]	Hong Kong	Celecoxib vs NSAID	OA and RA	6 months	Decision Analytic	Expected Cost	Celecoxib has lowest expected cost
El-Serag 2002[356]	USA	Celecoxib vs NSAID	Cox-I users	1 year	Decision Analytic	Per UGI event	Cox-2 are dominant in high-risk patients
Spiegel 2003[348]	USA	Celecoxib or rofecoxib vs naproxen	OA and RA	Lifetime	Decision Analytic	Per QALY	Rofecoxib and celecoxib are cost-effective in high-risk patients (US$55k). Average risk US$275k
Zabinski 2001[353]	Canada	Celecoxib vs NSAID	OA and RA	6 months	Decision Analytic	Expected cost	Celecoxib has lower expected cost than NSAID+H2RA, NSAID+misoprostol, NSAID+PPI but more costly than NSAID

continued

Table 7.57 COX-2 inhibitors – taken from the Brown HTA Report and the NICE TA COX-2 Assessment Report – *continued*

Study	Country	Comparators	Patients	Time Horizon	Model used	ICER	Conclusions
Maetzel 2003[351]	Canada	Naproxen vs rofecoxib, diclofenac vs celecoxib, Ibuprofen vs celecoxib. High risk are same as above + PPI	OA and RA	5 years	Markov	Per QALY	Average risk. Celecoxib and rofecoxib unlikely to be cost-effective (Can$271k and Can$125k respectively). High risk Rofecoxib dominates naproxen +PPI. Celecoxib dominates ibuprofen +PPI
Fendrick 2002[354]	US	Cox-2 vs generic NSAID switched to safer NSAID after AE Cox-2 vs safer NSAIDs as first line	Long-term NSAID users	1 year	Markov	Per symptomatic ulcer avoided	US$32k per symptomatic ulcer avoided US$57k per complicated ulcer avoided
Brown 2006[347]	UK	Cox-2 vs Cox-I, along with principal GPA strategies (PPI, H2RA and misoprostol)	OA and RA	6 months	Probabilistic Decision Analytic model	Per ulcer avoided, per serious GI event avoided and per LYG	Mean ICER: £301 per endoscopic ulcer avoided, £22,843 per serious GI event averted, £12742 per LYG
Non selective NSAIDs							
McCabe 1998[350]	UK	Nabumetone, ibuprofen	OA and RA	3 months	Decision tree	Per LYG	Co prescription after minor AE: £2517per LYG. Switching after minor AE: £1880 per LYG

Of the ten papers appraised the only UK Cox-2 economic evaluation was Brown et al.,[347] and the only non-selective NSAID economic evaluation was McCabe et al.[350] Direct comparison of the ICERs is impossible due to differences in comparator arms, model assumptions, cost data and health system setting. Three studies[348,351,356] concluded that Cox-2s are cost effective for patients at a high risk of a gastrointestinal event. Two papers[349,355] concluded that Cox-2s are dominant therapies over non selective NSAIDs. Two papers[348,351] determine that Cox-2s are not cost effective for patients with a normal risk of a gastrointestinal event. None of the papers provide cost effectiveness analysis for an RA only population.

7.4.13 Summary of evidence statements and tables

- NSAIDs and COX2 inhibitor drugs are useful in reducing symptoms of RA (tender and swollen joint counts, pain (VAS), morning stiffness, withdrawals due to lack of efficacy, achievement of ACR20, improvement in function, patients and investigators global assessment of disease activity)[334,337–339,341,343–345]

- Trials on large numbers of RA patients on NSAIDs and COX2 inhibitor drugs are available, but often over relatively short periods of time, and in patients satisfying a number of exclusion criteria that makes them only partially representative of RA patients in clinic[334,337–339,341,343–345]

- In selected populations eligible to enter NSAID and COX2 trials, the drugs are generally well tolerated,[334] though increased hypertension and dyspepsia were reported in the active arms of some trials[337–339,341,343–345]

- There is no consistent evidence of differences in efficacy when NSAIDs are compared with other individual NSAIDs or COX2 inhibitor drugs[337,342]

- The health economic evidence for Cox-2 inhibitors is contradictory, but they may be cost effective in patients at high risk of a gastrointestinal event.[248,251,256] None of the evidence reviewed is specific to RA populations.

7.4.14 From evidence to recommendations

There is clear evidence to show that both NSAIDs and COX2 inhibitors are effective in treating the symptoms of RA. The benefits obtained from these drugs need to be balanced against their adverse effects, mainly on the gastro-intestinal and cardiovascular systems. It was felt that whilst the data did not suggest any consistent differences between NSAID and COX2 inhibitor for efficacy, there were differences in toxicity profiles. There will be some patients in whom these drugs are contraindicated, and others in whom they should only be used with caution if they are clearly efficacious. In all cases, the GDG felt that these drugs should be used in the lowest effective dose over the shortest period of time, and on a 'when necessary' basis rather than regularly. In clinical practice, although there was no specific clinical trial evidence to support this, strategies to minimise the use of these drugs were considered to be important.

In symptomatic patients, the emphasis needs to be on monitoring disease activity (see section 8.1), and if patients are requiring high doses of NSAIDS or COX2 inhibitors on a regular basis, this should be regarded as an indication that disease modifying therapy may not be working satisfactorily, and that changes in treatment might be needed.

The GDG was cognisant of the changes that had been made to the NICE Technology Appraisal Guidance on COX2 inhibitors for patients with osteoarthritis,[8] and bore these in mind when updating this guidance for RA patients. It was felt that, in comparing the RA and OA populations, it was likely that gastrointestinal risks would be similar (unless the risk had been increased by patients being co-prescribed steroids) but that cardiovascular risks would be greater in the RA population (see section 8.2). The extensive health modelling which had taken place for the OA Guideline was regarded as unlikely to be very different for a RA population, and there should therefore be a similar recommendation about the potential benefit of co-prescribing protein pump inhibitors, which had been an important element of the cost-effectiveness analysis. NSAID gels in RA have a much more limited role and evidence base than in OA, largely due to the polyarticular nature of the disease. The OA Guideline recommendations relevant to these were not felt to be appropriate for RA.

The GDG also felt that there should be a recommendation for RA patients similar to that for OA patients already receiving concomitant low-dose aspirin, in that other analgesics should be considered before giving NSAIDs or COX2 inhibitors.

RECOMMENDATIONS

R29   Oral NSAIDs/Cox-2 inhibitors should be used at the lowest effective dose for the shortest possible period of time.

R30   When offering treatment with an oral NSAID/Cox-2 inhibitor, the first choice should be either a standard NSAID or a COX-2 inhibitor (other than etoricoxib 60 mg). In either case, these should be coprescribed with a PPI, choosing the one with the lowest acquisition cost.

R31   All oral NSAIDs/COX-2 inhibitors have analgesic effects of a similar magnitude but vary in their potential gastrointestinal, liver and cardio-renal toxicity; therefore, when choosing the agent and dose, healthcare professionals should take into account individual patient risk factors, including age. When prescribing these drugs, consideration should be given to appropriate assessment and/or ongoing monitoring of these risk factors.

R32   If a person with RA needs to take low-dose aspirin, healthcare professionals should consider other analgesics before substituting or adding an NSAID or COX-2 inhibitor (with a PPI) if pain relief is ineffective or insufficient.

R33   If NSAIDs or COX-2 inhibitors are not providing satisfactory symptom control, review the disease-modifying or biological drug regimen.

8 | Monitoring rheumatoid arthritis

8.1 Monitoring disease

8.1.1 Clinical introduction

Monitoring of disease activity in RA has traditionally been performed subjectively, and based on information about the inflammation shared between the patient and health care professional, such as the symptoms (pain, swelling, duration of morning stiffness, fever, weight loss), and the signs (joint swelling, heat and tenderness). This can be made more objective by laboratory tests of the inflammatory activity such as the C-reactive protein (CRP), erythrocyte sedimentation rate (ESR). It has been acknowledged that any individual measure of disease activity has limitations. For example, pain is exclusively perceived by the patient, and this perception is influenced by a host of factors beyond disease activity. Acute phase markers may be elevated due to other intercurrent disease such as infection. No single measure of disease activity satisfactorily encapsulates the complexity of the concept, or is free from confounding so as to just measure RA disease activity. Consequently amalgamations of single measures have been validated for use in RA. Many of these originated from trials, but have increasingly been used in clinical practice to more objectively inform decision making.

Because of the fluctuating and chronic nature of RA, there is limited information from measuring disease activity at a single moment in time, and evidence to show that the 'area under the curve'* of ongoing inflammation is closely related to accumulating damage and disability. Furthermore, there is no point in measuring disease activity if the results are ignored. High disease activity suggests disease control is inadequate and demands an appropriate response. Sustained low disease activity or remission may enable a cautious reduction in medication (see recommendation 20). In this section the best methods of assessing ongoing disease activity are considered, and the appropriate response to the information produced by these methods.

8.1.2 Clinical methodological introduction

We looked for studies that assessed what are the most effective methods of measuring the ongoing disease activity of patients with RA (established and recent onset of disease). Due to the large volume of evidence, studies were selected that were of a UK relevant population, sample size N>70. For papers assessing treatment adjusted by disease activity scores, only those looking at composite scores were included and for papers assessing disease activity measures, measurements had to have been taken over time (ie >2 time point assessments). Three RCTs,[242,357,358] one pooled analysis,[359] and 4 case-series[360–363] were found that fulfilled the inclusion criteria. The methodological limitations of the remaining included RCTs were as follows: the pooled analysis of RCTs and the cluster RCT were both graded as 1+ since the RCTs were all unblinded but ITT analysis was not performed. The remaining 2 RCTs were given a 1++ was blinded and the authors performed an ITT analysis.

---

* ie cumulative summation of measurements over time.

▷ Recent-onset RA

Two RCTs[242,358] and one case-series[364] were found. The RCTs were both single blind, parallel group studies looking at adjusting treatment based on monitoring disease activity. The first RCT[242] was performed in N=111 patients who were randomised to 2 different arms: intensive monitoring (every month) by disease activity versus routine monitoring (every 3 months) over 18 months. The second RCT[358] was performed in N=299 patients who were randomised to 2 different arms: intensive monitoring (every month) by 20% response versus conventional monitoring (every 3 months) over 2 years. The case-series[358] looked at monitoring disease activity measures over at least 3 years in N=110 patients.

▷ Established RA

One cluster RCT,[357] 1 pooled analysis of 3 RCTs,[359] and 4 case-series'[360–363] were found. The cluster RCT[357] was a single blind, parallel group trial looking at adjusting treatment based on monitoring disease activity in N=205 patients who were randomised to 2 different arms: systematic monitoring by DAS28 versus usual care (no monitoring/adjustment) over 24 weeks. The pooled analysis[359] looked at the data from 3 RCTs of leflunomide and monitored disease activity measures over 1 year in N=1839 patients.

The 4 case-series[360–363] all looked at monitoring disease activity measures over time and differed with respect to: sample size (range N=71 to N=233) and length of follow-up (range: 24 weeks to 30 months).

8.1.3 Health economic methodological introduction

No health economic papers were identified.

8.1.4 Clinical evidence statements

▷ Recent-onset RA

Table 8.1 Monitoring: disease activity measures

Study	Outcomes	Follow-up	Result – best measure
1 case-series[364] **Level 3**	Correlation between time integrated CRP and radiological progression	All times up to 3 years	**Correlation** (values not given)

Table 8.2 Treatment monitoring: adjustment by disease activity

Study	Outcomes	Follow-up	Result – best treatment
1 RCT[242] Level 1++	**EULAR good response** (OR 5.8, 95% CI 2.4 to 13.9) **and remission** (OR 9.7, 95% CI 3.9 to 23.9), **ACR20** (OR 5.7, 95% CI 1.9 to 16.7), **ACR50** (OR 6.1, 95% CI 2.5 to 14.9) **and ACR70** (OR 11, 95% CI 4.5 to 27); **disease activity score** (MD 1.6, 95% CI 1.1 to 2.1); **joint swelling** (MD 3, 95% CI 1 to 5, p=0.0028), **joint tenderness** (MD 8, 95% CI 4 to 12, p=0.0003), **patient's global assessment** (MD 30, 95% CI 17 to 42), **and assessor's global assessment of disease activity** (MD 24, 95% CI 14 to 34; **VAS pain** (MD 25, 95% CI 14 to 36); **HAQ** (MD 0.5, 95% CI 0.2 to 0.8, p=0.0025); **ESR** (MD 18, 95% CI 8 to 28, p=0.0007); **SF-12 physical domain** (MD 5.3, 95% CI 0.8 to 9.8, p=0.021); **erosion score** (MD 2.5, p=0.002) and **total Sharp score** (MD 4.0, p=0.02).	18 months	**Intensive** (p <0.0001 unless stated)
	Number of AEs, Higher prescription of IM and IA corticosteroids and of combination DMARDs (67% vs 11%) and **higher doses of MTX** (17.6 mg vs 13.6 mg/week)		**Intensive (better)**
	CRP; SF-12 mental domain; JSN and doses of SSZ		NS
1 RCT[358] Level 1+	**Number of patients reaching remission for 3 months**	1 and 2 years	**Intensive** Year 1: 35% vs 14%, p <0.001; Year 2: 50% vs 37%, p=0.029.
	Mean time until first period of remission (10.4 vs 14.3 months); **duration of all periods of remission** (11.6 vs 9.1 months, p=0.025); **median AUC for morning stiffness** (MD 6.7, p=0.009), **ESR** (MD 3.9, p=0.007), **tender joints** (MD 1.09), **swollen joints** (MD 2.0), **VAS general well-being** (MD 12.2), **VAS pain** (MD 7.0), **modified ACR50** (58% vs 43%, p=0.018)	1 year	**Intensive** (p≤0.001 unless stated)
	Use of NSAIDs	6 months and 2 years	**Intensive** 6 months: 79% vs 93% (p=0.002) 2 years: 46% vs 71%, p <0.001)
	Number of patients with AEs (87% vs 94%)	2 years	**Intensive (better)**
	Median AUC for functional disability; modified ACR50; radiographic progression and number of IA CS	2 years	NS

MD=mean difference, SD=standardised difference)
Note: all studies compared intensive strategy (adjusted by disease activity measure response) vs routine strategy (adjusted by rheumatologist's criteria)

▷ Established RA

Table 8.3 Monitoring: disease activity measures

Study	Outcomes	Follow-up	Result – best measure
1 pooled analysis[359] **Level 1+**	**Correlation between SDAI change and HAQ change**	All times up to 1 year	**Correlation** (range: r=0.53 to 0.66, all p <0.0001)
	Correlation between SDAI and DAS28	All time-points up to 6 months	**Correlation** (range: r=0.91 to 0.93, all p <0.0001)
1 case-series[360] **Level 3**	**Measures that changed the most and the fastest: RAI** (4 weeks), **summated change score** (4 weeks)	24 weeks	**Best clinical measures** (p <0.05)
	Measures that changed the most and the fastest: ESR and plasma viscosity (4 and 8 weeks respectively)	24 weeks	**Best laboratory measures** (p <0.05)
	Grip strength and joint size	24 weeks	**Not good**
1 case-series[361] **Level 3**	**CRP and articular index** (range 64% to 95% correlations) **compared to ESR and articular index** (range 53% to 85% correlation)	24 weeks	**Best significant correlation with all drug groups**
1 case-series[362] **Level 3**	**Correlation between change in KFI with therapy and: change in RAI** (r=0.4, p=0.001), **morning stiffness** (r=0.27, p=0.004), **swollen joint count** (r=0.3, p=0.0005), **CRP** (r=0.21, p=0.03) and **LSI** (r=0.35, p=0.002),	18 months	**Correlation**
	Correlation between change in KFI with therapy and: ESR or change in time to onset of fatigue.		**Not correlate (NS)**
	Correlation between change in HFI and: change in RAI (r=0.02, p=0.02), **morning stiffness** (r=0.11, NS), **swollen joint count** (r=0.29, p=0.002), **CRP** (r=0.17, NS) and **LSI** (r=0.18, NS)		**Correlation (but not as good as KFI)**
1 case-series[363] **Level 3**	**Correlation between clinical status (physical disability measured by rheumatologists) and: disease activity score** (r=0.44) **followed by the Mallya index** (r=0.43) **and the RAI** (r=0.42).	2 years	**Best correlations**
	Discriminate between high and low disease activity (based on use of DMARDs): disease activity score (SD 1.66), **followed by Riel index** (SD 1.46) **and the Mallya Index** (SD 1.37)		**Best discriminators**
	Correlation between increase in joint damage (erosions, JSN and total score) and: CRP (r=0.40, 0.52 and 0.50), **swollen joints** (r=0.54, 0.39 and 0.48), **ESR** (r=0.19, 0.36 and 0.29), **disease activity score** (0.31, 0.26 and 0.30), **Mallya index** (0.25, 0.30 and 0.31), **Riel Index** (0.22, 0.21 and 0.24) **and grip strength** (−0.32, −0.39 and −0.38).		**Best correlation**

Table 8.4 Treatment monitoring: adjustment by disease activity

Study	Outcomes	Follow-up	Result – best measure
1 RCT[357] Level 1+	**Mean difference in proportion of patients with low disease activity (DAS28 <3.2,** MD 15, 95% CI 3 to 27); **DMARD changes** (MD 9%, 95% CI 2% to 16%); **patient global assessment of disease activity** (data not given)	24 weeks	**Systematic monitoring** (all p <0.05)
	Mean dose of non-oral steroids, prednisone and MTX dose; AEs; pain (VAS) and disability		**NS**

Note: this study compared systematic monitoring + treatment adjustment vs usual care (no systematic monitoring or treatment adjustment)

8.1.5 Summary of evidence statements

- In recent-onset RA time-integrated CRP predicts radiological progression[364] and mean CRP correlates with articular index[361]

- In two studies of recent-onset RA, intensive treatment strategies with the aim of keeping the Disease Activity Score to low levels of activity resulted in substantially better outcomes when compared with usual care for most measures of disease activity, remission, function and radiological progression[2,42,358] A similar approach in established disease also resulted in improved disease control.[357]

- In established disease, studies show high correlations between indices of disease activity.[359]

- In established disease changes in disease activity correlate with changes in function[362] and indices that amalgamate several measures of disease activity show greater validity than out-perform single measures of disease activity.[360,362]

- In established disease that disease activity index performs better than the Riel Index and Mallya index for correlations with clinical status and joint damage, and the ability to differentiate between low and high disease activity.[363]

8.1.6 From evidence to recommendations

The GDG noted that whilst there was no single measure nor composite measure which was better than any other it seemed logical to recommend both a laboratory measure of disease activity such as CRP and a well validated composite score of disease activity such as DAS 28. It was also noted that measurements of DAS28 were mandatory for initiating and monitoring anti-TNF therapy according to current NICE guidance (see section 10). The GDG felt very strongly that such numerical assessments were preferable to descriptive words such as 'better', 'worse'. Furthermore such measurements would need to be made serially in order to inform clinical decision-making; this could include increasing therapy to suppress disease activity when present or conversely cautiously decreasing medication when disease activity was judged to be acceptably low.

The GDG were very impressed by the evidence for frequent (monthly) measurements in patients with recent-onset active disease, where aggressive treatment strategies aimed at keeping DAS28 to low levels produced substantially better outcomes. Frequent monitoring of such patients in the early stages of their disease were judged important in terms of better outcome but patients with stable chronic well controlled disease would only need such measurements infrequently.

RECOMMENDATIONS

R34   Measure CRP and key components of disease activity (using a composite score such as DAS28) regularly in people with RA to inform decision-making about:
- increasing treatment to control disease
- cautiously decreasing treatment when disease is controlled.

R35   In people with recent-onset active RA, measure CRP and key components of disease activity (using a composite score such as DAS28) monthly until treatment has controlled the disease to a level previously agreed with the person with RA.

8.2   Content and frequency of review

8.2.1   Clinical introduction

RA is a chronic and unpredictable disease with fluctuations in activity. When active, it has the propensity to damage the musculoskeletal and other systems. The traditional approach to long-term management has been to see the patient at a frequency determined:
- by the problems at any one visit (active problems leading to more frequent visits),
- the practicalities of when clinic space allows appointments to be made.

Such reviews have tended to focus on the immediate problems, lacked structure, and have not paid enough attention to other less obvious disease processes that might influence morbidity and mortality. The ARMA standards of care have suggested an annual review should take place (ARMA Standards of Care for people with Inflammatory Arthritis.[365] An annual review could be used to ensure that
- the disease status is addressed, with formal measures of disease activity, remission, damage and function
- current medications, educational needs, physical and psychosocial issues, depression and fatigue are all addressed
- assessment and screening for complications of RA and other co-morbidities takes place, especially osteoporosis and atherosclerosis.

In RA, problems outside the musculoskeletal system may be directly related to the disease. For some patients the term RA is a misnomer, in that the disease affects systems other than the musculoskeletal system. These manifestations are related to:
- the joint inflammatory process itself, such as irreversible damage to the cervical spine causing bone instability and deformity and potential myelopathy
- the inflammatory process occurring in other organs and systems, such as the eye (scleritis), the lung (pulmonary fibrosis and pleural effusion), and vasculitis.

This section addresses the evidence for the content and frequency of a regular review in order to ensure that disease control is optimised, and problems directly and indirectly related to the disease are formally assessed and objectively addressed, to ensure that no overt or covert problems lead to a preventable impact on the quality of life for the patient.

8.2.2 Clinical methodological introduction

We looked for studies that assessed what should be the content of a regular review of patients with established RA. Due to the sparsity of evidence, all study types were looked at. Three RCTs[366–369] were found that fulfilled the inclusion criteria and no studies were found which addressed regular review in terms of comorbidities. One of the RCTs[3,67,369] was published as two separate papers, reporting different follow-up times and so these have only been counted once, however results from both the papers are reported and referenced here.

▷ Established RA

The 3 included RCTs[366,367,368] were single blind (but ITT analysis was not performed), parallel group trials. The first RCT[366] looked at annual and 4-monthly review of N=466 patients who were randomised to 2 different arms: symptom control/shared care setting versus aggressive treatment/hospital setting. Patients in the symptom control group were assessed for HAQ score every 4 months and annually for OMERACT, OSRA, DAS28 and extra-articular features. Patients in the aggressive treatment group were assessed for HAQ score, ESR, CRP and tender/swollen joints every 4 months and annually for OMERACT, OSRA, DAS28 and extra-articular features. The trial length was 3 years. The second RCT[367,369] looked at review of N=209 patients who were randomised to 2 different arms: shared care with GP (no routine hospital review but rapid access on request) setting versus traditional hospital care (regular planned review every 3–4 months). The trial length was 2 years and had a follow-up at 4 years. The third RCT[368] looked at review of N=132 patients who were randomised to 3 different arms: GP follow-up (review on request) vs routine hospital follow-up (3-monthly review) vs OT follow-up (3-monthly review). The trial length was 2 years.

8.2.3 Health economic methodological introduction

No health economic papers were identified.

8.2.4 Clinical evidence statements

▷ Established RA

Rapid access (shared care with GP) vs 3–4-month regular review (traditional hospital care)

- One RCT[367,369] found that rapid access was significantly better than traditional hospital regular review (every 3–4 months) for: pain (VAS), change in pain (VAS) and self-efficacy score at 2 years (all p <0.05) and for ROM (right elbow, p <0.05) and patient satisfaction and confidence (p <0.01) at 4 years. However, there was NS difference for HAQ, radiographic progression (Larsen scores) and anxiety and depression at 2 years and for HAQ, pain (VAS), morning stiffness, ROM (left elbow and both knees) and patient's opinion of disease activity at 4 years. **Level 1+**

Symptom control vs aggressive treatment (both assessed at least every 4 months)

- One RCT[366] found that at 3 years, aggressive treatment was significantly better than symptom control for OSRA disease activity score (OR –0.40, 95% CI –0.71 to –0.10, p=0.01). However, there was NS difference for: HAQ, patient's and physician's global assessment, tender and swollen joint count, pain (VAS), DAS-28, radiographic progression (Larsen score), OSRA damage score, eroded joint count and ESR. **Level 1+**

GP follow-up (on request) vs routine hospital follow-up (3-monthly) vs OT follow-up (3-monthly)

- One RCT[368] found that OT follow-up (3-monthly) was significantly better than GP follow-up (on request) and routine hospital follow-up (3-monthly) for: articular Index at 2 years (p <0.05). However, there were NS differences between the groups for: articular Index at 1 year and functional capacity and ESR at 1 year and 2 years. **Level 1+**

8.2.5 Evidence to recommendations

The GDG noted the lack of consistency in the evidence relating to frequency of review, place of review and assessment of aggressive treatment. It was noted that no one approach would be suitable for everybody; regular review may be suitable for some, whilst patient initiated review may be more suitable for others. It was specifically felt that, for those people where it was thought appropriate to offer patient initiated follow-up when needed rather than routine regular follow-up, it was essential that they were well educated about their disease and knew when and how to obtain further help, for example by contacting the named designated member of the MDT (see recommendations in section 6.1). The GDG also noted that it was equally essential that where patient-initiated follow-up was deemed appropriate, routine drug monitoring must still take place as these people might otherwise only receive a routine annual review.

The GDG were disappointed that there was no published evidence found for the elements of what should be covered in a follow up. The GDG discussed the GP Quality Outcomes Framework (QOF) points and a table from the unpublished RA BSR guideline* that considers the interface between primary and secondary care. GDG members who had been involved in drawing up the BSR RA guidelines pointed out the lack of evidence to support the content of reviews. In the absence of any evidence, it was felt by the GDG that an annual review of the disease (with objective measures of activity, damage and function), complications and co-morbidities, was reasonable and that the content of the review should include assessment of disease status, primary prevention of ischaemic heart disease, osteoporosis assessment, making sure patient are not depressed, ensuring their cervical spine is stable, and checking for other possible organ involvement (eg eye, lung, vasculitis).

The GDG discussed that patients and healthcare professionals looking after them are often unaware that they are at increased cardiovascular risk with RA. Secondary care practitioners RA clinics need to be much more aware of this and the GDG felt that the input of the RA Nurse Specialist is important here. GDG felt that there was a need for awareness-raising in relation to RA and co-morbid risks. All practitioners need to be aware that management of RA is not just about managing the RA disease but also being much more aware of the co-morbidities of ischaemic heart disease, depression and osteoporosis.

---

* Unpublished at present but will be published by February 2009.

RECOMMENDATIONS

R36   Offer people with satisfactorily controlled established RA review appointments at a frequency and location suitable to their needs. In addition, make sure they:

- have access to additional visits for disease flares
- know when and how to get rapid access to specialist care, and
- have ongoing drug monitoring.

R37   Offer people with RA an annual review to:

- assess disease activity and damage, and measure functional ability (using, for example Health Assessment Questionnaire [HAQ])
- check for the development of comorbidities, such as hypertension, ischaemic heart disease, osteoporosis and depression
- assess symptoms that suggest complications, such as vasculitis and disease of the cervical spine, lung or eyes
- organise appropriate cross referral within the multidisciplinary team
- assess the need for referral for surgery (see section 8.3)
- assess the effect the disease is having on a person's life.

8.3 Timing and referral for surgery

8.3.1 Clinical introduction

Despite recent advances in medical management of RA leading to a reduction in the requirement for surgery, significant numbers of people with the disease still go on to develop irreversible damage to joints and tendons. For patients with irreversible, or localised non-responding damage to the musculoskeletal system, surgical interventions can be an effective solution for pain relief, restoration of function, prevention of progressive deformity, and improvement in the quality of life. The timing of a surgical referral will clearly depend on the clinical urgency of the underlying problem. Myelopathy due to pressure on the spinal cord from cervical spine instability can at worst result in death. Short of this, the result can be irreversible neurological damage with a resultant disability. Clearly therefore cervical spine instability causing myelopathy requires urgent intervention. By contrast pressure on peripheral nerves, (for example, carpal tunnel syndrome) can result in pain and weakness but the urgency for intervention is less than that of pressure on the spinal cord.

Some operations become technically more difficult or have worse outcomes if the damage or deformity has progressed too far. This is one of many reasons why a surgical opinion may need to be obtained early in disease progression, in consultation with other appropriate members of the MDT.

As with all treatment, medical or surgical, the decision to undertake surgery must be discussed with the patient. The potential risks and benefits of the operation should be balanced against the risks and benefits of continuing conservative management and the wishes of the informed patient.

Surgical and anaesthetic techniques have improved considerably. The risks of intervention have decreased substantially, and the outcomes of most operations are excellent with prolonged benefits (particularly hip and knee replacements). Because RA affects many joints, it is important that the surgeon has the knowledge to assess the overall problems of the RA patient, be aware of the multisystem nature of the disease, the drugs that patients are on and has the time and resources to assess patients in detail. While the surgeon should have an overall ability to assess the patients needs, physical and psychological, it is unlikely that any one surgeon will have the skillset necessary to perform all the operations that may be necessary.

In this section, the focus is not on the type of intervention, which goes well beyond the scope of this guideline, but on the timing of referral for a surgical opinion.

8.3.2 Clinical methodological introduction

We looked for studies that assessed factors that determine the timing of referral for surgery. Due to the small amount of evidence, all study types were selected that were of a UK relevant population. Four cross-sectional studies[370–374] and one retrospective case-series[375] were found that fulfilled the inclusion criteria. One study[370,371] was published as 2 separate papers looking at different outcomes and different populations (physicians or patients) and so has only been counted once but results from both papers have been included and referenced here.

The first cross-sectional study[370] performed a survey of N=1000 physicians (N=500 rheumatologists and N=500 surgeons) and N=126 patients. The survey focused on the physicians' indications and timing of different types of surgery for rheumatoid hand disease and patients' priorities and willingness to have hand surgery. The second cross-sectional study[373] performed a survey of N=1379 RA patients and focused on the variables associated with having orthopaedic surgery or TJR. The third and fourth cross-sectional studies[372,374] performed surveys on N=62 and N=56 patients respectively and focused on predictors of RA patients having surgery.

The retrospective case-series[375] assessed the symptomology of N=111 patients with rheumatoid cervical myelopathy who had undergone MRI or cervical spine surgery or both.

8.3.3 Health economic methodological introduction

No health economic papers were identified.

8.3.4 Clinical evidence statements

All studies were given an evidence grading of Level 3.

Table 8.5 Indications for RA joint surgery – physicians

Study	Type of surgery	Experts opinion	Indications
1 cross-sectional study[370,371]	MCP joint arthroplasty	Hand surgeons and rheumatologists	**Most important: impaired hand function followed by MCP joint pain**
	Small joint synovectomy	Hand surgeons Rheumatologists	**Progressive joint synovitis Never indicated**
	Resection of the distal ulna	Hand surgeons and rheumatologists	**Impending tendon rupture followed by wrist pain**

Table 8.6 Indications for RA joint surgery – patients

Study	Patients' opinion	Patients	Indications
1 cross-sectional study[370,371]	Willingness to have surgery	Men and women (NS difference)	**Main concern: hand pain followed by hand function Some concern: hand appearance**
	Concerns of inconveniences, pain, risk of anaesthesia and surgical complications	Women and men	**Women more concerned than men**
1 cross-sectional study[372]	Choosing MCP arthroplasty	All patients	**Associations: age (patients older than 50 years) and gender (female patients more likely). Predictors: function followed by pain Not predictor: aesthetic consideration**
1 cross-sectional study[373]	Probability of undergoing surgery	All patients	Highest (univariate): female patients, younger patients, those with long-term disease, a poor functional ability, persistent active disease despite treatment, RF+ and presence of extraarticular complications and significant comorbidity **Highest (multivariate): female gender, long-term disease (≥10 years), ACR functional grade III/IV and the presence of extraarticular complications**
	Probability of undergoing TJR	All patients	Highest (univariate): female patients, those with long-term disease, functional class III/IV, persistent active disease despite treatment, presence of extraarticular complications and/or significant comorbidity **Highest (multivariate): long-term disease (≥10 years), ACR functional grade III/IV and the presence of extraarticular complications**

continued

Table 8.6 Indications for RA joint surgery – patients – *continued*

Study	Patients' opinion	Patients	Indications
1 cross-sectional study[374]	Hopes of what surgery will do	All patients	**Improving appearance and function (44%), reducing pain (27%) and improving strength (15%)**
	Important aspects	All patients	**Ability to perform everyday activities (75%), improvement of hand weakness (73%), ability to do one's normal work (71%), reduction in hand (50%) and improvement of hand appearance (35%)**
	What bothered patients most (hand RA)	All patients	**Function, pain, appearance and weakness**
		Patients who chose to have surgery	**Inability to work or do things with their hands**
		Patients who chose not to have surgery	**Hand weakness and appearance**
	Patients' post-operative expectations	Patients who chose to have surgery vs not have surgery	**Surgery patients less likely to expect difficulty with post-operative rehabilitation; NS for belief in chance of post-op complications**
	Patients' expectations for status 1 year into the future	Patients who chose to have surgery vs not have surgery	**Surgery patients more likely to expect the ability to do more with their hands in 1 year, to do more of their work, have les pain and improved hand appearance**
	Most important person to influence surgical decision	Patients who chose to have surgery vs not have surgery	**NS difference. However non-surgical patients valued their own opinion as moist important and surgical valued expert opinion more**
1 case-series[375]	Patients with rheumatoid cervical myelopathy who underwent surgery vs conservative treatment		**Symptoms present (more): paraesthesia, weakness, unsteadiness, and to exhibit extensor plantar reflexes, gait disturbances and reduced power; Ranawat grades II (NS) or III (SS) and not have normal examination findings (SS)**
			MRI findings (more likely present): cord compression and impingement on cord. Less likely present: cervical spondylosis; abnormal neurological findings (but no compression or impingement)

Table 8.7 Timing for joint surgery

Study	Type of surgery	Experts opinion	Timing
1 cross-sectional study[370,371]	MCP joint arthroplasty	Hand surgeons and rheumatologists	**Most appropriate time: Stage 3 MCP joint disease**
	Extensor tenosynovectomy	Hand surgeons and Rheumatologists	**Most appropriate time: 3–6 months if the synovitis is resistant to medical therapy**
		Rheumatologists vs Hand surgeons	**Appropriate after 12 months or more (26% vs 2%) and never appropriate (8% vs 2%)**

8.3.5 Summary of evidence statements

- The amount of evidence to address the timing of surgical referral is scanty and of limited quality. A survey of hand surgeons and rheumatologists agreed on stage 3 MCP joint disease being the most appropriate time for surgery, and 3–6 months of resistant synovitis for extensor tenosynovectomy[370,371]

- A survey of rheumatologists and hand surgeons found agreement on MCP joint arthroplasty being indicated for function and pain, and resection of the distal ulna indicated for tendon rupture and wrist pain. However there was disagreement on the value of small joint synovectomy with hand surgeons feeling that progressive joint synovitis was an indication, and most rheumatologists feeling it was never indicated[370,371]

- Most patients rank hand function and pain as the main concerns[370,371,372] and it is their hope that surgery will relieve these[374]

- Hand appearance was of little importance in considering surgery in one study,[370,371] but improving function and appearance were main hopes in another.[374]

8.3.6 From evidence to recommendations

The GDG noted the lack of evidence which really addressed this question and felt that it was extremely unlikely that any appropriate clinical trials would specifically address this issue. Indeed the GDG felt that in some cases it would be unethical in doing such trials. It was felt that there was currently an enormous variation in thresholds for seeking surgeon's involvement in the formulation of management plans for patients who might eventually need surgery.

The GDG felt that it would be appropriate to involve surgeons early, even if possible surgery was not urgently indicated. It was noted that assessment for referral for surgery was already recommended as part of an annual review (see chapter 6 and section 8.2.6). It was agreed that there were 4 primary reasons for considering referral for surgery:

- Persistent pain due to joint damage or other identifiable soft tissue cause
- Worsening function
- Progressive deformity
- Persisting localised synovitis.

Additional reasons included tendon rupture, nerve compression, joint instability (eg cervical), infection and incidental radiological findings such as stress fracture. Although the need and urgency for possible surgical intervention would vary with the underlying condition, the GDG felt that an early surgical opinion should always be obtained, particularly in cases where the outcome of a surgical procedure could be jeopardised by a delay in surgical referral.

For tendon rupture, localised non-responding synovitis, nerve compression, septic arthritis and stress fractures it was felt appropriate to refer for a surgical opinion before damage had progressed too far. Multiple tendon rupture, persisting neurological deficit and uncorrectable deformity causing disability could be seen as a failure for the team. For more long-term problems such as pain, function and deformity the need for referral was not so urgent but again should not be delayed until further irreversible changes had occurred.

There were some instances for example cervical myelopathy where urgent action was clearly needed and even though the evidence for this condition was from a retrospective study, the GDG felt that an urgent MRI scan and surgical opinion would be needed in presence of appropriate symptoms or signs.

The GDG noted that while in general the indications for joint replacement for people with RA should be regarded in the same way as for people with OA.[8] RA patients might be considerably younger and the wear and tear in the arthroplasty could well be less in view of the polyarthritic nature of their disease and reduced demands on the joint as a result. The GDG therefore felt that there should be a specific recommendation pointing out that, in comparison with patients with OA the comparative youthfulness of an RA patient should not preclude consideration for joint replacement.

RECOMMENDATIONS

R38   Offer to refer people with RA for an early specialist surgical opinion if any of the following do not respond to optimal non-surgical management:
- persistent pain due to joint damage or other identifiable soft tissue cause
- worsening joint function
- progressive deformity
- persistent localised synovitis.

R39   Offer to refer people with the following complications for a specialist surgical opinion before damage or deformity becomes irreversible:
- imminent or actual tendon rupture
- nerve compression (for example, carpal tunnel syndrome)
- stress fracture.

R40   When surgery is offered to people with RA, explain that the main* expected benefits are:
- pain relief,
- improvement, or prevention of further deterioration, of joint function, and
- prevention of deformity.

R41   Offer urgent combined medical and surgical management to people with RA who have suspected or proven septic arthritis (especially in a prosthetic joint).

R42   If a person with RA develops any symptoms or signs that suggest cervical myelopathy:**
- request an urgent MRI scan, and
- refer for a specialist surgical opinion.

R43   Do not let concerns about the long-term durability of prosthetic joints influence decisions to offer joint replacements to younger people with RA.

---

* Cosmetic improvements should not be the dominant concern.
** For example, paraesthesiae, weakness, unsteadiness, reduced power, extensor plantars.

9 | Other aspects and treatment

9.1 Diet

9.1.1 Clinical introduction

Every healthcare professional will know of people with rheumatoid arthritis who have experimented with their diet, and can testify to improvements in their disease activity. Some patients seem to have specific intolerances, where certain foods or drinks seem to cause flare-ups in their joints, and therefore they avoid them. Other books and internet sites advocate special inclusion or exclusion diets that make great claims about their efficacy. Experimenting with diet gives the person with RA the opportunity to exercise control over an important aspect of their life, and determine whether certain foods included or excluded benefit them and their disease. This section does not focus on weight reduction but looks at whether there is any evidence to support the beneficial effects of specific dietary manipulations in helping to control rheumatoid arthritis? Weight reduction was not specifically addressed within this evidence review. Weight reduction is covered within the Osteoarthritis guideline.[211]

9.1.2 Clinical methodological introduction

We looked for studies that investigated the efficacy of different types of diet or dietary supplements with respect to symptoms, joint damage, function and quality of life in patients with RA (recent-onset and established disease). Due to the large volume of evidence, only MA and RCTs were selected which were of a UK-relevant population and if the population was mixed arthritis there had to be >75% RA or RA subgroup analysis.

Three MAs[376–378] and 14 RCTs[379–394] were found that fulfilled the inclusion criteria. One of these RCTs was published as three separate papers[389–391] reporting different outcomes and so the trial has only been counted once, however results from all three papers are reported and referenced here. One RCT[394] was excluded due to methodological limitations (unblinded and ITT analysis was not performed). The methodological limitations of the remaining included RCTs and MAs were as follows: the RCTs graded 1+ were either blinded and ITT analysis was not performed or unblinded but ITT analysis was performed. The RCTs graded 1++ were both blinded and ITT analysis was performed. The MAs graded 1++ performed both quality assessment of the trials and tests for heterogeneity. No studies were found looking at patients with a recent onset of RA, all trials were conducted using patients with established RA, and the two MAs used a trials which were of a mixed population (recent-onset and established RA).

▷ Mixed population (recent-onset and established RA)

Three MAs[376–378] were found that fulfilled the criteria and focused on RCTs which compared either omega-3 supplements and fish-oils,[377] herbal therapies,[376] or lacto-vegetarian, vegan or Mediterranean diets[378] in patients with RA.

The first SR/MA[376] included 11 RCTs which were all double blind, placebo-controlled trials. However, they differed with respect to:

- intervention – N=7 RCTs used Gamma-linolenic acid, GLA (sources: evening primrose oil, blackcurrant seed oil, borage seed oil); N=1 RCT used feverfew, N=1 RCT used Trypterygium wilfordii hook F, N=1 RCT used topical capsaicin and N=1 RCT used Reumalex (contains willow bark)]
- study size (range N=20 to N=70)
- study quality – max score of 5 (N=10 studies reasonable to good quality; N=1 study poor quality)
- study duration – length of intervention (4 weeks to 15 months).

The second SR/MA[377] included 17 RCTs which were all double blind, placebo (inert-substance) controlled trials. However, they differed with respect to:
- intervention – total omega-PUFA (not reported and range 1.7 g to 9.6 g)
- study size (range N=12 to N=90)
- study quality – max score of 5 (N=12 studies reasonable to good quality; N=5 studies poor quality)
- study duration – length of intervention (1 month to 15 months).

The third MA[378] was not a systematic review but a pooled analysis of 3 unblinded, placebo-controlled RCTs which differed with respect to:
- design – (2 RCTs parallel; 1 RCT cross-over)
- intervention – (1 RCT Mediterranean diet vs western diet, 1 RCT lacto-vegetarian diet vs normal diet, 1 RCT vegan diet vs control period)
- study size (range N=22 to N=56)
- study duration – length of intervention (9 weeks to 4 months).

▷ Established RA

Fourteen RCTs[378–393] were found that fulfilled the inclusion criteria. One of these RCTs was published as three separate papers[389–391] reporting different outcomes and so the trial has only been counted once, however results from all three papers are reported and referenced here.

All 14 RCTs were parallel group studies, but they differed with respect to the following:
- sample size (range: N=30 to N=116)
- blinding (6 RCTs double blind, 6 RCTs single blind, 2 RCTs unblended/blinding not mentioned)
- trial length (range: 4 weeks to 9 months; follow-up ranged from 2 months to 1 year post-treatment)
- treatment – diets (4 RCTs food intolerance and allergy; 4 RCTs vegetarian or vegan; 2 RCTs vitamin and mineral supplements; 1 RCT fish oils;1 RCT Mediterranean; 1 RCT experimental; 1 RCT calorie-restricted)
- treatment regimen – dose and comparison.

9.1.3 Health economic methodological introduction

No health economic papers were identified.

9.1.4 Clinical evidence statements

▷ Mixed population (recent-onset and established RA)

GLA vs placebo

- One MA[376] found that GLA was significantly better than placebo for: pain (VAS) and pain scale (0–4); patient's global evaluation, morning stiffness and joint tenderness. However there was NS difference for: pain (absolute score), morning stiffness (absolute score), joint swelling and reduction in NSAID consumption. There was significant heterogeneity for physician's global evaluation. **Level 1++**

Omega-3 PUFAs vs placebo

- One MA[377] found that omega-3 PUFAs were significantly better than placebo for: patient's assessment of pain, morning stiffness, number of painful/tender joints, NSAID consumption. However there was NS difference for RAI and physician's assessment of pain. **Level 1++**

Vegetarian and Mediterranean diets

- One pooled analysis[378] found that lacto-vegetarian, strictly vegetarian and modified Cretan-Mediterranean diets were significantly better than control diets for: univariate analysis – weight loss and pain. **Level 1+**

▷ Established RA

Gluten-free vegan diet followed by lacto-vegetarian diet

- One RCT[389–391] found that responders were significantly better than non-responders and controls for: pain, morning stiffness, HAQ, number of tender and swollen joints, global assessment and RAI. However there was NS difference for radiographic score, grip strength and ESR. **Level 1++**

Table 9.1 Other comparisons for established RA

Study	Treatment	Follow-up	Outcomes	Result – best treatment
1 RCT[393] Level 1++	Fish oil supplements vs placebo	36 weeks	Pain (VAS); reduction in daily NSAID requirement >30%	**Fish**
			HAQ, morning stiffness, DAS28-CRP, CRP, grip strength, number or type of AEs, number of withdrawals and type of AEs leading to withdrawal	**NS**

continued

Table 9.1 Other comparisons for established RA – *continued*

Study	Treatment	Follow-up	Outcomes	Result – best treatment
1 RCT[379] Level 1+	Mediterranean diet vs usual diet	12 weeks	DAS28, HAQ score, SF-36, swollen joint count, pain (VAS), CRP level, withdrawals and weight loss	**Mediterranean**
			Tender joint count, ESR, patients' global assessment of disease activity, morning stiffness, SOFI score and GAT score	**NS**
1 RCT[380] Level 1+	Experimental diet (to maintain or reduce weight) vs placebo diet	10 weeks	Morning stiffness, grip strength, walk time, tender and swollen joints, patient's and physician's global assessment, ESR and RF	
1 RCT[381] Level 1+	Experimental calorie-restricted diet vs usual diet	6 weeks	Swollen joint count, morning stiffness and pain	**Experimental**
			BMI, weight, tender joint count, physician's global assessment, HAQ score and Larsen Score	**NS**
			Withdrawals	**Usual**
1 RCT[386] Level 1++	Vitamin E supplementation vs placebo	12 weeks	Pain (morning, evening and after chosen activity), response rates (pain in morning and after chosen activity), patient's and investigator's global assessment of efficacy	**Vitamin E**
			Response rates (pain in the evening), RAI, morning stiffness, swollen joints and AEs	**NS**
		20 weeks	RAI, pain measures, morning stiffness, swollen joints and global assessment of efficacy	**NS**
1 RCT[387] Level 1+	Selenium vs placebo	90 days	CRP, QoL (arm movements and health perception)	**Selenium**
			Pain (VAS), RAI, tender and swollen joints, morning stiffness QoL (daily and social activities, mood, physical activity, symptoms and work) and AEs	**NS**
1 RCT[382] Level 1+	Elemental diet (hypoallergenic) vs usual diet	4 weeks	Swollen joint count, ESR, general assessment of health and BMI	**Elemental**
		4 and 12 weeks	CRP, RAI, morning stiffness, pain	**NS**
		12 weeks	Swollen joint count, BMI, ESR, general assessment of health	**NS**
1 RCT[383] Level 1+	Elemental diet vs usual diet	4 weeks	Average grip strength, RAI, and weight loss	**Elemental**
			CRP	**NS**

continued

Table 9.1 Other comparisons for established RA – *continued*

Study	Treatment	Follow-up	Outcomes	Result – best treatment
1 RCT[384] Level 1+	Hypoallergenic, non-allergenic diet vs control diet	24 weeks	Tender joint count, RAI, ESR	**Hypoallergenic**
			BMI, weight, swollen joint count, morning stiffness, pain severity (VAS), HAQ, CRP, responders (Paulus index – 20% and 50%), patient's global assessment of disease	**NS**
1 RCT[385] Level 1+	Allergen-free diet vs allergen-restricted diet	4 weeks	Weight reduction	**Allergen-free** (all p <0.05)
			Swollen and tender joints, global assessment, morning stiffness, RAI, fatigue, grip strength, walking time, ESR, CRP, RF	**NS**
1 RCT[388] Level 1++	Vegan vs non-vegan diet	1 year	ACR20 responders	**Vegan** (p <0.05)
			Radiographic progression	**NS**
1 RCT[392] Level 1+	Vegan vs non-vegan diet	3 months	Weight reduction, rheumatic pains, joint swelling and morning stiffness	**Vegan** (all p <0.01)
			CRP, ESR, changes in disease activity, mean amount of deterioration and ability to move	**NS**
1 RCT[389–391] Level 1++	Vegan vs non-vegan diet Gluten-free vegan diet followed by lacto-vegetarian diet vs omnivorous diet	13 months	Swollen and tender joints, pain (VAS), grip strength, weight reduction; global assessment, morning stiffness, HAQ, CRP, ESR, RF (IgM), RAI	**Gluten-free** (all p <0.02; p <0.001)
			RF	**NS**

9.1.5 Summary of evidence statements

- Most trials show some benefit with a variety of dietary modifications or supplementary additions, but no modifications seemed to exert global improvements in disease activity and function.[376–379,381–391]
- The most effective diet appeared to be gluten free diet followed by vegetarian diet, although these patients also had physiotherapy.[389–391] Other diets with benefits in disease activity include the 'allergen–free' diet,[385] elemental diet,[382] and allergen restricted diet in some patients,[384] Mediterranean diet,[378,379] omega-3 and PUFA's.[377]

9.1.6 From evidence to recommendations

The GDG noted that many of the dietary interventions did seem to have benefit when taken with conventional therapies. However, no diet produced positive results for a broad diversity of outcome measures and there was insufficient evidence to support the recommendation of a single diet. There was no consistent evidence of benefit of any one particular diet. Some of the diets might be unpopular with some patients, such as vegetarian diets, and some might be unpalatable with understandably poor compliance, such as elemental diets. It was felt that it would be helpful in a recommendation to give some direction to RA patients. There was discussion about the evidence to show that the principles of a Mediterranean diet* might be beneficial in people with RA especially because of the impact of such a diet on cardiovascular risk factors. Because:

- people with RA are at an even greater risk of cardiovascular disease than the rest of the population,
- such a diet might be beneficial to the musculoskeletal symptoms of RA,
- this type of diet is more likely to be followed than some of the other more unpalatable alternatives.

RECOMMENDATION

R44   Inform people with RA who wish to experiment with their diet that there is no strong evidence that their arthritis will benefit. However, they could be encouraged to follow the principles of a Mediterranean diet (more bread, fruit, vegetables and fish; less meat; and replace butter and cheese with products based on vegetable and plant oils).

9.2   Complementary therapies

9.2.1   Clinical introduction

Conventional approaches to the management of RA are not always as successful as either healthcare professionals or patients would wish. Patients are frequently concerned about side-effects with prescribed drugs, as witnessed by calls to the National Rheumatoid Arthritis Society helpline on this issue. With the combination of less than total efficacy, and concern over toxicity with conventional drugs, it is understandable therefore that people with RA will explore other approaches to try to help themselves with their disease. They are not short of suggested solutions, with a plethora of articles and advertisements in newspapers, magazines, the internet, television and radio, giving information on complementary, alternative and other non-pharmacological interventions which are claimed to relieve or (misleadingly) cure their arthritis. Surveys have shown that a substantial proportion of people with RA will try complementary and alternative interventions,[395] perhaps reflecting the lack of complete satisfaction with conventional approaches, and also a desire to help themselves. Patients with a recent onset of inflammatory arthritis may try alternative remedies first before presenting to their GP. Out of all of the various therapies available, 100 NRAS (National Rheumatoid Arthritis Society) members and 100 NRAS volunteers were randomly selected from across the UK from the NRAS database and were asked to list their preferences, and the top six were selected from these for literature searches. The top six therapies were: acupuncture, copper bracelets, aromatherapy, massage, reflexology and homeopathy.

---

* It was felt reasonable to recommend the principles of a Mediterranean diet.

9.2.2 Clinical methodological introduction

We looked for studies that assessed which aspects of complementary, alternative and other non-pharmacological interventions are effective in patients with RA (recent-onset and established disease). Due to the small volume of evidence, trials of all types were selected that were of a UK relevant population.

One MA,[396] 2 RCTs,[397–399] and 1 case-series[400] were found that fulfilled the inclusion criteria. One RCT[398,399] was published as two separate papers reporting different follow-up times but was excluded due to methodological limitations (unblinded and ITT analysis was not performed). The methodological limitations of the remaining studies were as follows: the RCT graded 1+ was unblinded and had no dropouts. The MA graded 1++ performed quality assessment of the included trials and tested for heterogeneity.

▷ Mixed arthritis (recent-onset and established RA)

The Cochrane SR/MA[396] was well conducted. The 2 RCTs included in the analysis compared acupuncture vs placebo. However, they differed with respect to:
- intervention [N=1 RCT used acupuncture (needles manipulated); N=1 RCT used electroacupuncture]
- study size (range N=20 and N=64)
- study quality – max score of 5 (N=1 study good quality; n=1 study reasonable quality)
- study duration – length of intervention (N=1 RCT 5 weeks; N=1 RCT 3 months).

The additional RCT[397] assessed massage therapy vs standard care in N=22 patients (disease duration of patients not mentioned) in a 4-week treatment phase.

▷ Established RA

The case-series[400] looked at plant-based homeopathic preparations + antioxidants (vitamin C 1,000 mg and vitamin E 800 mg intramuscularly) in N=30 patients in a 5-week treatment phase.

9.2.3 Health economic methodological introduction

No health economic papers were identified.

9.2.4 Clinical evidence statements

▷ Mixed arthritis (recent-onset and established RA)

- One MA[396] found that electroacupuncture was significantly better than placebo for: pain (0–4 scale) at end of treatment – 24 hours and at 4-month follow-up. **Level 1++**
- The same MA[396] found that there was NS difference between Acupuncture and placebo at end of treatment – 5 weeks for: pain (VAS) at end of treatment – 5 weeks; swollen and tender joints at end of treatment – 5 weeks; disease activity (DAS); global health questionnaire; ESR; CRP; analgesic uptake; patient's global assessment. **Level 1++**
- One RCT[397] found that Hand massage was significantly better than control (standard treatment) at 4 weeks (end of treatment, change from baseline) for: pain (VAS), anxiety (STAI), depression (POMS) and grip strength. **Level 1+**

▷ Established RA

- One case-series[400] found that at 5 weeks (end of study, change from baseline), patients treated with Plant-based homeopathic preparations + antioxidants had decreased pain (VAS) change from baseline –1.5, increased level of well-being (VAS) and decreased restriction of movement. Additionally, there was successful reduction of drugs that patients' had been previously taking (all drugs causing AEs were immediately eliminated – NSAIDs, MTX and/or paracetamol). **Level 3**

9.2.5 From evidence to recommendations

The GDG felt that the evidence for any complementary therapy or medicines being effective was lacking; the GDG was disappointed by this given the overall popularity of these treatments. The only positive evidence surrounded a small short-term study of electroacupuncture and a 4-week study of hand massage. A mixture of plant based homeopathic preparations in a short-term study allowed a reduction in analgesia. However the feeling of the GDG was that none of this constituted strong evidence for sound recommendations. The GDG found that the benefit of complementary therapies was akin to that of analgesics in providing short-term benefit and that this should be reflected in the recommendations. It was felt that the information on the lack of evidence should be shared with patients, but if they chose to try complementary or alternative treatments then it should be ensured that they do not take these to the exclusion of conventional therapies. Some members mentioned that in their experience a bias could develop against patients trying complementary therapies and that this might influence the care given by the MDT. The GDG felt that this attitude should be discouraged

RECOMMENDATIONS

R45   Inform people with RA who wish to try complementary therapies that although some may provide short-term symptomatic benefit, there is little or no evidence for their long-term efficacy.

R46   If a person with RA decides to try complementary therapies, advise them:
- these approaches should not replace conventional treatment
- this should not prejudice the attitudes of members of the multidisciplinary team, or affect the care offered.

10 NICE technology appraisal related recommendations

The recommendations in this section are existing NICE technology appraisal guidance. They were formulated as part of the technology appraisals and not by the guideline developers. They have been incorporated into this guideline in line with NICE procedures for developing clinical guidelines, and the evidence to support the recommendations can be found with the individual appraisals.

▷ Rheumatoid arthritis (refractory) – rituximab (NICE technology appraisal guidance 126)

Available at www.nice.org.uk/TA126

Rituximab in combination with methotrexate is recommended as an option for the treatment of adults with severe active rheumatoid arthritis who have had an inadequate response to or intolerance of other disease modifying antirheumatic drugs (DMARDs), including treatment with at least one tumour necrosis factor α (TNF-α) inhibitor therapy.

Treatment with rituximab plus methotrexate should be continued only if there is an adequate response following initiation of therapy. An adequate response is defined as an improvement in disease activity score (DAS28) of 1.2 points or more. Repeat courses of treatment with rituximab plus methotrexate should be given no more frequently than every 6 months.

Treatment with rituximab plus methotrexate should be initiated, supervised and treatment response assessed by specialist physicians experienced in the diagnosis and treatment of rheumatoid arthritis.

▷ Rheumatoid arthritis (refractory) – abatacept (NICE technology appraisal guidance 141)

Available at www.nice.org.uk/TA141

Abatacept is not recommended (within its marketing authorisation) for the treatment of people with rheumatoid arthritis.

Patients currently receiving abatacept for the treatment of rheumatoid arthritis should have the option to continue therapy until they and their clinicians consider it appropriate to stop.

▷ Adalimumab, etanercept and infliximab for the treatment of rheumatoid arthritis' (NICE technology appraisal guidance 130)

Available at www.nice.org.uk/TA130

The tumour necrosis factor alpha (TNF-α) inhibitors adalimumab, etanercept and infliximab are recommended as options for the treatment of adults who have both of the following characteristics:

- Active rheumatoid arthritis as measured by disease activity score (DAS28) greater than 5.1 confirmed on at least two occasions, 1 month apart
- Have undergone trials of two disease modifying antirheumatic drugs (DMARDs), including methotrexate (unless contraindicated). A trial of a DMARD is defined as being normally of 6 months, with 2 months at standard dose, unless significant toxicity has limited the dose or duration of treatment.*

TNF-α inhibitors[12] should normally be used in combination with methotrexate. Where a patient is intolerant of methotrexate or where methotrexate treatment is considered to be inappropriate, adalimumab and etanercept may be given as monotherapy.[11]

Treatment with TNF-α inhibitors[12] should be continued only if there is an adequate response at 6 months following initiation of therapy. An adequate response is defined as an improvement in DAS28 of 1.2 points or more.[11,12]

After initial response, treatment** should be monitored no less frequently than 6-monthly intervals with assessment of DAS28. Treatment should be withdrawn if an adequate response (as defined in 1.4.4.6) is not maintained.[11]

An alternative TNF-α inhibitor[12] may be considered for patients in whom treatment is withdrawn due to an adverse event before the initial 6-month assessment of efficacy, provided the risks and benefits have been fully discussed with the patient and documented.[11]

Escalation of dose of the TNF-α inhibitors[12] above their licensed starting dose is not recommended.[11]

Treatment[12] should normally be initiated with the least expensive drug (taking into account administration costs, required dose and product price per dose). This may need to be varied in individual cases due to differences in the mode of administration and treatment schedules.[11]

Use of the TNF-α-inhibitors[12] for the treatment of severe, active and progressive rheumatoid arthritis in adults not previously treated with methotrexate or other DMARDs is not recommended.[11]

Initiation of TNF-α inhibitors[12] and follow-up of treatment response and adverse events should be undertaken only by a specialist rheumatological team with experience in the use of these agents.[11]

---

* These recommendations are from 'Adalimumab, etanercept and infliximab for the treatment of rheumatoid arthritis' (NICE technology appraisal guidance 130).
** 'Treatment' and 'TNF-α inhibitors' refer to adalimumab, etanercept and infliximab.

11 | Areas for future research

How cost effective are MRI and ultrasound in establishing the diagnosis and prognosis of small joint synovitis?

How cost effective is the use of anti-CCP in establishing the diagnosis and prognosis of early inflammatory arthritis?

Further evaluations, including cost-effectiveness studies, should take place of the following in people with rheumatoid arthritis:

- Disease-related written information in recent-onset disease
- Written self-management materials in recent-onset and established disease
- Structured 1:1 information giving in recent-onset and established disease
- Refresher courses and updates
- Long-term benefits of group behavioural programmes
- The Arthritis Self Management Programme and the Chronic Disease Self Management Programme in recent-onset and established disease with study populations recruited from out-patient clinics.

The following further evaluations, including cost-effectiveness studies, should take place of in people with rheumatoid arthritis:

- For exercise, the best methods of delivery, the optimal mode and level of activity, and methods of maximising long-term concordance
- The individual components of comprehensive physiotherapy, with particular reference to the effectiveness of electrophysical agents, and their optimal timing throughout the course of the disease.

The following further evaluations, including cost-effectiveness studies, should take place in people with rheumatoid arthritis:

- Comprehensive occupational therapy interventions
- The usefulness of work rehabilitation programmes, both for those currently in work but at risk of job loss and for those already unemployed but needing help in returning to work.

The role of DMARDs in the treatment of mild rheumatoid arthritis should be assessed.

The cost effectiveness of early management with biological drugs (prior to the failure of two conventional DMARDs) should be assessed.

What is the effect of symptom duration on patient outcomes?

What is the most appropriate treatment strategy when the first anti-TNF-α inhibitor fails?

The components of the nurse specialist's role that exert the greatest benefits on outcomes in recent-onset and established RA should be investigated.

References

1. National Institute for Health and Clinical Excellence. *The Guidelines Manual 2007*. London: NICE, 2007.

2. Arnett FC, Edworthy SM, Bloch DA et al. The American Rheumatism Association 1987 revised criteria for the classification of rheumatoid arthritis. *Arthritis & Rheumatism*. 1988;31(3):315–324.

3. Combe B, Landewe R, Lukas C et al. EULAR recommendations for the management of early arthritis: report of a task force of the European Standing Committee for International Clinical Studies Including Therapeutics (ESCISIT). *Annals of the Rheumatic Diseases*. 2007;66(1):34–45.

4. Lawrence JS. Prevalence of rheumatoid arthritis. *Annals of the Rheumatic Diseases*. 1961;20:11–17.

5. Symmons D, Turner G, Webb R et al. The prevalence of rheumatoid arthritis in the United Kingdom: new estimates for a new century. *Rheumatology*. 2002;41(7):793–800.

6. Symmons DP, Barrett EM, Bankhead CR et al. The incidence of rheumatoid arthritis in the United Kingdom: Results from the Norfolk Arthritis Register. *British Journal of Rheumatology*. 1994;33(8): 735–739.

7. British Society for Rheumatology. *Clinical Guidelines: Rheumatoid Arthritis*. Available from: British Society for Rheumatology. Last accessed on: 2008 July 30.

8. National Institute for Health and Clinical Excellence. *Osteoarthritis: the care and management of Osteoarthritis in adults*. (59). London: NICE, 2008.

9. National Institute for Clinical Excellence. *Anakinra for Rheumatoid Arthritis*. (TA72). London: NICE, 2003.

10. National Institute for Health and Clinical Excellence. *Rituximab for the treatment of Rheumatoid Arthritis*. (TA126). London: NICE, 2007.

11. National Institute for Health and Clinical Excellence. *Abatacept for the Treatment of Rheumatoid Arthritis*. (TA141). London: NICE, 2008.

12. Pugner KM, Scott DI, Holmes JW et al. The costs of rheumatoid arthritis: an international long-term view. *Seminars in Arthritis & Rheumatism*. 2000;29(5):305–320.

13. National Rheumatoid Arthritis Society. *I want to work:a self-help guide for people with Rheumatoid Arthritis*. 2007. London, NRAS.

14. Emery P, Breedveld FC, Dougados M et al. Early referral recommendation for newly diagnosed rheumatoid arthritis: evidence based development of a clinical guide. *Annals of the Rheumatic Diseases*. 2002;61(4):290–297.

15. Kumar K, Daley E, Carruthers DM et al. Delay in presentation to primary care physicians is the main reason why patients with rheumatoid arthritis are seen late by rheumatologists. *Rheumatology*. 2007; 46(9):1438–1440.

16. Van der Horst-Bruinsma IE, Speyer I, Visser H et al. Diagnosis and course of early-onset arthritis: Results of a special early arthritis clinic compared to routine patient care. *British Journal of Rheumatology*. 1998;37(10):1084–1088.

17. Kaarela K. Prognostic factors and diagnostic criteria in early rheumatoid arthritis. *Scandinavian Journal of Rheumatology – Supplement*. 1985;57:1–54.

18. Machold KP, Stamm TA, Eberl GJM et al. Very recent onset arthritis – Clinical, laboratory, and radiological findings during the first year of disease. *Journal of Rheumatology*. 2002;29(11):2278–2287.

19. Arndt U, Behrens F, Ziswiler HR et al. Observational study of a patient and doctor directed pre-referral questionnaire for an early arthritis clinic. *Rheumatology International*. 2007;28(1):21–26.

20. Devlin J, Gough A, Huissoon A et al. The outcome of knee synovitis in early arthritis provides guidelines for management. *Clinical Rheumatology*. 2000;19(2):82–85.

21. Harrison BJ, Symmons DPM, Barrett EM et al. The performance of the 1987 ARA classification criteria for rheumatoid arthritis in a population based cohort of patients with early inflammatory polyarthritis. *Journal of Rheumatology*. 1998;25(12):2324–2330.

22. Kaarela K, Hameenkorpi R, Isomaki H. The value of the diagnostic criteria in rheumatoid arthritis. *Scandinavian Journal of Rheumatology*. 1983;12(1):43–45.

23. El Miedany Y, Palmer D, El Gaafary M. Diagnosis of early arthritis: outcomes of a nurse-led clinic. *British Journal of Nursing*. 2006;15(7):394–399.

24. Alarcon GS, Willkens RF, Ward JR et al. Early undifferentiated connective tissue disease. IV. Musculo-skeletal manifestations in a large cohort of patients with undifferentiated connective tissue diseases compared with cohorts of patients with well-established connective tissue diseases: followup analyses in patients with unexplained polyarthritis and patients with rheumatoid arthritis at baseline. *Arthritis & Rheumatism*. 1996;39(3):403–414.

25. Gormley GJ, Steele WK, Gilliland A et al. Can diagnostic triage by general practitioners or rheumatology nurses improve the positive predictive value of referrals to early arthritis clinics? *Rheumatology*. 2003; 42(6):763–768.

26. Houssien DA, Scott DL. Early referral and outcome in rheumatoid arthritis. *Scandinavian Journal of Rheumatology*. 1998;27(4):300–302.

27. Irvine S, Munro R, Porter D. Early referral, diagnosis, and treatment of rheumatoid arthritis: evidence for changing medical practice. *Annals of the Rheumatic Diseases*. 1999;58(8):510–513.

28. Duer A, Ostergaard M, Horslev PK et al. Magnetic resonance imaging and bone scintigraphy in the differential diagnosis of unclassified arthritis. *Annals of the Rheumatic Diseases*. 2008;67(1):48–51.

29. Van der Helm-van Mil AH, Le Cessie S, Van Dongen H et al. A prediction rule for disease outcome in patients with recent-onset undifferentiated arthritis: how to guide individual treatment decisions. *Arthritis & Rheumatism*. 2007;56(2):433–440.

30. Turesson C, O'Fallon WM, Crowson CS et al. Occurrence of extraarticular disease manifestations is associated with excess mortality in a community based cohort of patients with rheumatoid arthritis. *Journal of Rheumatology*. 2002;29(1):62–67.

31. Uhlig T, Smedstad LM, Vaglum P. The course of rheumatoid arthritis and predictors of psychological, physical and radiographic outcome after 5 years of follow-up. *Rheumatology*. 2000;39(7):732–741.

32. Wallberg-Jonsson S, Johansson H, Ohman ML et al. Extent of inflammation predicts cardiovascular disease and overall mortality in seropositive rheumatoid arthritis. A retrospective cohort study from disease onset. *Journal of Rheumatology*. 1999;26(12):2562–2571.

33. Wolfe F, Sharp JT. Radiographic outcome of recent-onset rheumatoid arthritis. A 19-year study of radiographic progression. *Arthritis & Rheumatism*. 1998;41(9):1571–1582.

34. Wolfe F, Michaud K, Gefeller O et al. Predicting mortality in patients with rheumatoid arthritis. *Arthritis & Rheumatism*. 2003;48(6):1530–1542.

35. Wolfe F, Ross K, Hawley DJ et al. The prognosis of rheumatoid arthritis and undifferentiated polyarthritis syndrome in the clinic: a study of 1141 patients. *Journal of Rheumatology*. 1993;20(12):2005–2009.

36. Young A, Bielawska C, Corbett M et al. A prospective study of early onset rheumatoid arthritis over fifteen years: prognostic features and outcome. *Clinical Rheumatology*. 1987;6(suppl 2):12–19.

37. Innala L, Kokkonen H, Eriksson C et al. Antibodies against mutated citrullinated vimentin are a better predictor of disease activity at 24 months in early rheumatoid arthritis than antibodies against cyclic citrullinated peptides. *Journal of Rheumatology*. 2008;35(6):1002–1008.

38. Mathsson L, Mullazehi M, Wick MC et al. Antibodies against citrullinated vimentin in rheumatoid arthritis: Higher sensitivity and extended prognostic value concerning future radiographic progression as compared with antibodies against cyclic citrullinated peptides. *Arthritis & Rheumatism*. 2008;58(1): 36–45.

39. Syversen SW, Gaarder PI, Goll GL et al. High anti-cyclic citrullinated peptide levels and an algorithm of four variables predict radiographic progression in patients with rheumatoid arthritis: Results from a 10-year longitudinal study. *Annals of the Rheumatic Diseases*. 2008;67(2):212–217.

40. De Vries-Bouwstra JK, Goekoop-Ruiterman YP, Verpoort KN et al. Progression of joint damage in early rheumatoid arthritis: association with HLA-DRB1, rheumatoid factor, and anti-citrullinated protein antibodies in relation to different treatment strategies. *Arthritis & Rheumatism*. 2008;58(5):1293–1298.

41. Bukhari M, Lunt M, Harrison BJ et al. Rheumatoid factor is the major predictor of increasing severity of radiographic erosions in rheumatoid arthritis: results from the Norfolk Arthritis Register Study, a large inception cohort. *Arthritis & Rheumatism.* 2002;46(4):906–912.

42. Dixey J, Solymossy C, Young A. Is it possible to predict radiological damage in early rheumatoid arthritis (RA)? A report on the occurrence, progression, and prognostic factors of radiological erosions over the first 3 years in 866 patients from the early RA study (ERAS). *Journal of Rheumatology.* 2004;31(suppl 69): 48–54.

43. Forslind K, Hafstrom I, Ahlmen M et al. Sex: a major predictor of remission in early rheumatoid arthritis? *Annals of the Rheumatic Diseases.* 2007;66(1):46–52.

44. Forslind K, Ahlmen M, Eberhardt K et al. Prediction of radiological outcome in early rheumatoid arthritis in clinical practice: Role of antibodies to citrullinated peptides (anti-CCP). *Annals of the Rheumatic Diseases.* 2004;63(9):1090–1095.

45. Guillemin F, Gerard N, van LM et al. Prognostic factors for joint destruction in rheumatoid arthritis: a prospective longitudinal study of 318 patients. *Journal of Rheumatology.* 2003;30(12):2585–2589.

46. Van Jaarsveld CH, ter Borg EJ, Jacobs JW et al. The prognostic value of the antiperinuclear factor, anti-citrullinated peptide antibodies and rheumatoid factor in early rheumatoid arthritis. *Clinical & Experimental Rheumatology.* 1999;17(6):689–697.

47. Kroot EJ, De Jong B, Van Leeuwen MA et al. The prognostic value of anti-cyclic citrullinated peptide antibody in patients with recent-onset rheumatoid arthritis. *Arthritis & Rheumatism.* 2000;43(8): 1831–1835.

48. Linn-Rasker SP, Van der Helm-van Mil AH, Breedveld FC et al. Arthritis of the large joints – in particular, the knee – at first presentation is predictive for a high level of radiological destruction of the small joints in rheumatoid arthritis. *Annals of the Rheumatic Diseases.* 2007;66(5):646–650.

49. Odegard S, Landewe R, van d et al. Association of early radiographic damage with impaired physical function in rheumatoid arthritis: A ten-year, longitudinal observational study in 238 patients. *Arthritis & Rheumatism.* 2006;54(1):68–75.

50. Plant MJ, Williams AL, O'Sullivan MM et al. Relationship between time-integrated C-reactive protein levels and radiologic progression in patients with rheumatoid arthritis. *Arthritis & Rheumatism.* 2000; 43(7):1473–1477.

51. Priolo F, Bacarini L, Cammisa M et al. Radiographic changes in the feet of patients with early rheumatoid arthritis. GRISAR (Gruppo Reumatologi Italiani Studio Artrite Reumatoide). *Journal of Rheumatology.* 1997;24(11):2113–2118.

52. Ronnelid J, Wick MC, Lampa J et al. Longitudinal analysis of citrullinated protein/peptide antibodies (anti-CP) during 5 year follow up in early rheumatoid arthritis: anti-CP status predicts worse disease activity and greater radiological progression. *Annals of the Rheumatic Diseases.* 2005;64(12):1744–1749.

53. Bas S, Perneger TV, Mikhnevitch E et al. Association of rheumatoid factors and anti-filaggrin antibodies with severity of erosions in rheumatoid arthritis. *Rheumatology.* 2000;39(10):1082–1088.

54. Leigh JP, Fries JF. Mortality predictors among 263 patients with rheumatoid arthritis. *Journal of Rheumatology.* 1991;18(9):1307–1312.

55. Leigh JP, Fries JF. Predictors of disability in a longitudinal sample of patients with rheumatoid arthritis. *Annals of the Rheumatic Diseases.* 1992;51(5):581–587.

56. Plant MJ, O'Sullivan MM, Lewis PA et al. What factors influence functional ability in patients with rheumatoid arthritis. Do they alter over time? *Rheumatology.* 2005;44(9):1181–1185.

57. Sherrer YS, Bloch DA, Mitchell DM et al. Disability in rheumatoid arthritis: comparison of prognostic factors across three populations. *Journal of Rheumatology.* 1987;14(4):705–709.

58. Sihvonen S, Korpela M, Mustila A et al. The predictive value of rheumatoid factor isotypes, anti-cyclic citrullinated peptide antibodies, and antineutrophil cytoplasmic antibodies for mortality in patients with rheumatoid arthritis. *Journal of Rheumatology.* 2005;32(11):2089–2094.

59. Strating MM, Van Schuur WH, Suurmeijer TP. Predictors of functional disability in rheumatoid arthritis: results from a 13-year prospective study. *Disability & Rehabilitation.* 2007;29(10):805–815.

60. Turesson C, McClelland RL, Christianson TJH et al. Severe extra-articular disease manifestations are associated with an increased risk of first ever cardiovascular events in patients with rheumatoid arthritis. *Annals of the Rheumatic Diseases.* 2007;66(1):70–75.

61. Wolfe F, Zwillich SH. The long-term outcomes of rheumatoid arthritis: a 23-year prospective, longitudinal study of total joint replacement and its predictors in 1,600 patients with rheumatoid arthritis. *Arthritis & Rheumatism.* 1998;41(6):1072–1082.

62. Mancarella L, Bobbio PF, Ceccarelli F et al. Good clinical response, remission, and predictors of remission in rheumatoid arthritis patients treated with tumor necrosis factor-alpha blockers: the GISEA study. [erratum appears in *J Rheumatol.* 2007 Sep;34(9):1947]. *Journal of Rheumatology.* 2007;34(8):1670–1673.

63. Proudman SM, Conaghan PG, Richardson C et al. Treatment of poor-prognosis early rheumatoid arthritis. A randomized study of treatment with methotrexate, cyclosporin A, and intraarticular corticosteroids compared with sulfasalazine alone. *Arthritis & Rheumatism.* 2000;43(8):1809–1819.

64. Quinn MA, Conaghan PG, O'Connor PJ et al. Very early treatment with infliximab in addition to methotrexate in early, poor-prognosis rheumatoid arthritis reduces magnetic resonance imaging evidence of synovitis and damage, with sustained benefit after infliximab withdrawal: results from a twelve-month randomized, double-blind, placebo-controlled trial. *Arthritis & Rheumatism.* 2005;52(1):27–35.

65. Van Dongen H, Van Aken J, Lard LR et al. *Efficacy of methotrexate treatment in patients with probable rheumatoid arthritis: A double-blind, randomized, placebo-controlled trial. Arthritis & Rheumatism.* 56;1424–1432. 2008.

66. Van Aken J, Lard LR, Le Cessie S et al. Radiological outcome after four years of early versus delayed treatment strategy in patients with recent onset rheumatoid arthritis. *Annals of the Rheumatic Diseases.* 2004;63(3):274–279.

67. Lard LR, Visser H, Speyer I et al. Early versus delayed treatment in patients with recent-onset rheumatoid arthritis: comparison of two cohorts who received different treatment strategies. *American Journal of Medicine.* 2001;111(6):446–451.

68. Konnopka A, Conrad K, Baerwald C et al. Cost effectiveness of the determination of autoantibodies against cyclic citrullinated peptide in the early diagnosis of rheumatoid arthritis. *Annals of the Rheumatic Diseases.* 2008;67(10):1399–1405.

69. Conaghan PG, O'Connor P, McGonagle D et al. Elucidation of the relationship between synovitis and bone damage: a randomized magnetic resonance imaging study of individual joints in patients with early rheumatoid arthritis. *Arthritis & Rheumatism.* 2003;48(1):64–71.

70. Wakefield RJ, Gibbon WW, Conaghan PG et al. The value of sonography in the detection of bone erosions in patients with rheumatoid arthritis: a comparison with conventional radiography. *Arthritis & Rheumatism.* 2000;43(12):2762–2770.

71. Avouac J, Gossec L, Dougados M. Diagnostic and predictive value of anti-cyclic citrullinated protein antibodies in rheumatoid arthritis: a systematic literature review. *Annals of the Rheumatic Diseases.* 2006;65(7):845–851.

72. Nishimura K, Sugiyama D, Kogata Y et al. Meta-analysis: diagnostic accuracy of anti-cyclic citrullinated peptide antibody and rheumatoid factor for rheumatoid arthritis. *ANN INTERN MED.* 2007;146(11):797–808.

73. Aho K, Palosuo T, Heliovaara M et al. Antifilaggrin antibodies within 'normal' range predict rheumatoid arthritis in a linear fashion. *Journal of Rheumatology.* 2000;27(12):2743–2746.

74. Aho K, Palosuo T, Knekt P et al. Serum C-reactive protein does not predict rheumatoid arthritis. *Journal of Rheumatology.* 2000;27(5):1136–1138.

75. Koivula MK, Heliovaara M, Ramberg J et al. Autoantibodies binding to citrullinated telopeptide of type II collagen and to cyclic citrullinated peptides predict synergistically the development of seropositive rheumatoid arthritis. *Annals of the Rheumatic Diseases.* 2007;66(11):1450–1455.

76. Van Aken J, Van Dongen H, Le Cessie S et al. Comparison of long term outcome of patients with rheumatoid arthritis presenting with undifferentiated arthritis or with rheumatoid arthritis: an observational cohort study. *Annals of the Rheumatic Diseases.* 2006;65(1):20–25.

77. Aho K, Palosuo T, Lukka M et al. Antifilaggrin antibodies in recent-onset arthritis. *Scandinavian Journal of Rheumatology.* 1999;28(2):113–116.

78. Bayliss CE, Dawkins RL, Cullity G et al. Laboratory diagnosis of rheumatoid arthritis. Prospective study of 85 patients. *Annals of the Rheumatic Diseases.* 1975;34(5):395–402.

79. Devauchelle-Pensec V, Berthelot JM, Jousse S et al. Performance of hand radiographs in predicting the diagnosis in patients with early arthritis. *Journal of Rheumatology.* 2006;33(8):1511–1515.

80. Hoffman IE, Peene I, Pottel H et al. Diagnostic performance and predictive value of rheumatoid factor, anti-citrullinated peptide antibodies, and the HLA shared epitope for diagnosis of rheumatoid arthritis. *Clinical Chemistry.* 2005;51(1):261–263.

81. Quinn MA, Green MJ, Marzo OH et al. Prognostic factors in a large cohort of patients with early undifferentiated inflammatory arthritis after application of a structured management protocol. *Arthritis & Rheumatism.* 2003;48(11):3039–3045.

82. Saraux A, Valls I, Voisin V et al. How useful are tests for rheumatoid factors, antiperinuclear factors, antikeratin antibody, and the HLA DR4 antigen for the diagnosis of rheumatoid arthritis? *Revue du Rhumatisme (English Edition).* 1995;62(1):16–20.

83. Solau-Gervais E, Legrand JL, Cortet B et al. Magnetic resonance imaging of the hand for the diagnosis of rheumatoid arthritis in the absence of anti-cyclic citrullinated peptide antibodies: A prospective study. *Journal of Rheumatology.* 2006;33(9):1760–1765.

84. Verpoort KN, Jol-Van D, Papendrecht-Van D et al. Isotype distribution of anti-cyclic citrullinated peptide antibodies in undifferentiated arthritis and rheumatoid arthritis reflects an ongoing immune response. *Arthritis & Rheumatism.* 2006;54(12):3799–3808.

85. Young A, Sumar N, Bodman K et al. Agalactosyl IgG: an aid to differential diagnosis in early synovitis. *Arthritis & Rheumatism.* 1991;34(11):1425–1429.

86. Van der Cruyssen B, Hoffman IEA, Peene I et al. Prediction models for rheumatoid arthritis during diagnostic investigation: Evaluation of combinations of rheumatoid factor, anti-citrullinated protein/peptide antibodies and the human leucocyte antigen-shared epitope. *Annals of the Rheumatic Diseases.* 2007;66(3):364–369.

87. Blalock SJ, Orlando M, Mutran EJ et al. Effect of satisfaction with one's abilities on positive and negative affect among individuals with recently diagnosed rheumatoid arthritis. *Arthritis Care & Research.* 1998; 11(3):158–165.

88. Nagyova I, Stewart RE, Macejova Z et al. The impact of pain on psychological well-being in rheumatoid arthritis: the mediating effects of self-esteem and adjustment to disease. *Patient Education & Counseling.* 2005;58(1):55–62.

89. Smedstad LM, Kvien TK, Moum T et al. Correlates of patients' global assessment of arthritis impact. A 2-year study of 216 patients with RA. *Scandinavian Journal of Rheumatology.* 1997;26(4):259–265.

90. Suurmeijer TP, Waltz M, Moum T et al. Quality of life profiles in the first years of rheumatoid arthritis: results from the EURIDISS longitudinal study. *Arthritis & Rheumatism.* 2001;45(2):111–121.

91. Thyberg I, Skogh T, Hass UAM et al. Recent-onset rheumatoid arthritis: A 1-year observational study of correlations between health-related quality of life and clinical/laboratory data. *Journal of Rehabilitation Medicine.* 2005;37(3):159–165.

92. Wong M, Mulherin D, Sousa KH. The influence of medication beliefs and other psychosocial factors on early discontinuation of disease-modifying anti-rheumatic drugs. *Musculoskeletal Care.* 2007;5(3): 148–159.

93. Goekoop-Ruiterman YP dV-BJACKPGBdJMHKS. Patient preferences for treatment: report from a randomised comparison of treatment strategies in early rheumatoid arthritis (BeSt trial). *Annals of the Rheumatic Diseases.* 2007;66(9):1227–1232.

94. Bath J, Hooper J, Giles M et al. Patient perceptions of rheumatoid arthritis. *Nursing Standard.* 1999;14(3): 35–38.

95. Carr A, Hewlett S, Hughes R et al. Rheumatology outcomes: the patient's perspective. *Journal of Rheumatology.* 2003;30(4):880–883.

96. Covic T, Adamson B, Hough M. The impact of passive coping on rheumatoid arthritis pain. *Rheumatology*. 2000;39(9):1027.

97. Heiberg T, Kvien TK. Preferences for improved health examined in 1,024 patients with rheumatoid arthritis: pain has highest priority. *Arthritis & Rheumatism*. 2002;47(4):391–397.

98. Iaquinta ML, Larrabee JH. Phenomenological lived experience of patients with rheumatoid arthritis. *Journal of Nursing Care Quality*. 2004;19(3):280–289.

99. Jacobi CE, Boshuizen HC, Rupp I et al. Quality of rheumatoid arthritis care: the patient's perspective. *International Journal for Quality in Health Care*. 2004;16(1):73–81.

100. Katz PP, Morris A, Yelin EH. Prevalence and predictors of disability in valued life activities among individuals with rheumatoid arthritis. *Annals of the Rheumatic Diseases*. 2006;65(6):763–769.

101. Kjeken I, Dagfinrud H, Mowinckel P et al. Rheumatology care: involvement in medical decisions, received information, satisfaction with care, and unmet health care needs in patients with rheumatoid arthritis and ankylosing spondylitis. *Arthritis & Rheumatism*. 2006;55(3):394–401.

102. Neame R, Hammond A, Deighton C. Need for information and for involvement in decision making among patients with rheumatoid arthritis: a questionnaire survey. *Arthritis & Rheumatism*. 2005;53(2):249–255.

103. Neugebauer A, Katz PP, Pasch LA. Effect of valued activity disability, social comparisons, and satisfaction with ability on depressive symptoms in rheumatoid arthritis. *Health Psychology*. 2003;22(3):253–262.

104. Rupp I, Boshuizen HC, Jacobi CE et al. Impact of fatigue on health-related quality of life in rheumatoid arthritis. *Arthritis & Rheumatism*. 2004;51(4):578–585.

105. Rupp I, Boshuizen HC, Roorda LD et al. Poor and good health outcomes in rheumatoid arthritis: the role of comorbidity. *Journal of Rheumatology*. 2006;33(8):1488–1495.

106. Rupp I, Boshuizen HC, Dinant HJ et al. Disability and health-related quality of life among patients with rheumatoid arthritis: association with radiographic joint damage, disease activity, pain, and depressive symptoms. *Scandinavian Journal of Rheumatology*. 2006;35(3):175–181.

107. Slatkowsky-Christensen B, Mowinckel P, Loge JH et al. Health-related quality of life in women with symptomatic hand osteoarthritis: A comparison with rheumatoid arthritis patients, healthy controls, and normative data. *Arthritis Care & Research*. 2007;57(8):1404–1409.

108. Katz PP, Morris A. Use of accommodations for valued life activities: prevalence and effects on disability scores. *Arthritis & Rheumatism*. 2007;57(5):730–737.

109. Pouchot J, Le Parc JM, Queffelec L et al. Perceptions in 7700 patients with rheumatoid arthritis compared to their families and physicians. *Joint, Bone, Spine: Revue du Rhumatisme*. 2007;74(6):622–626.

110. Reinseth L, Espnes GA. Women with rheumatoid arthritis: non-vocational activities and quality of life. *Scand J Occup Ther*. 2007;14(2):108–115.

111. Sterba KR, DeVellis RF, Lewis MA et al. Effect of couple illness perception congruence on psychological adjustment in women with rheumatoid arthritis. *Health Psychology*. 2008;27(2):221–229.

112. Strating MMH, van Duijn MAJ, Van Schuur WH et al. The differential effects of rheumatoid arthritis on distress among patients and partners. *Psychology & Health*. 2007;22(3):361–379.

113. Ward V, Hill J, Hale C et al. Patient priorities of care in rheumatology outpatient clinics: a qualitative study. *Musculoskeletal Care*. 2007;5(4):216–228.

114. Uhlig T, Loge JH, Kristiansen IS et al. Quantification of reduced health-related quality of life in patients with rheumatoid arthritis compared to the general population. *Journal of Rheumatology*. 2007;34(6):1241–1247.

115. Williams AE, Nester CJ, Ravey MI. Rheumatoid arthritis patients' experiences of wearing therapeutic footwear – A qualitative investigation. *BMC Musculoskeletal Disorders*. 2007;8

116. Verduin PJ, de Bock GH, Vliet Vlieland TP et al. Purpose in life in patients with rheumatoid arthritis. *Clinical Rheumatology*. 2008;27(7):899–908.

117. Wolfe F, Michaud K. Resistance of rheumatoid arthritis patients to changing therapy: discordance between disease activity and patients' treatment choices. *Arthritis & Rheumatism*. 2007;56(7):2135–2142.

118. Lempp H, Scott D, Kingsley G. The personal impact of rheumatoid arthritis on patients' identity: a qualitative study. *Chronic Illness.* 2006;2(2):109–120.

119. Barlow JH, Cullen LA, Rowe IF. Comparison of knowledge and psychological well-being between patients with a short disease duration (< or = 1 year) and patients with more established rheumatoid arthritis (> or = 10 years duration). *Patient Education & Counseling.* 1999;38(3):195–203.

120. Lempp H, Scott DL, Kingsley GH. Patients' views on the quality of health care for rheumatoid arthritis. *Rheumatology.* 2006;45(12):1522–1528.

121. Chilton F, Collett RA. Treatment choices, preferences and decision-making by patients with rheumatoid arthritis. *Musculoskeletal Care.* 2008;6(1):1–14.

122. Stamm T, Lovelock L, Stew G et al. I have mastered the challenge of living with a chronic disease: Life stories of people with rheumatoid arthritis. *Qualitative Health Research.* 2008;18(5):658–669.

123. Treharne GJ, Lyons AC, Booth DA et al. Psychological well-being across 1 year with rheumatoid arthritis: coping resources as buffers of perceived stress. *British Journal of Health Psychology.* 2007;12(Pt:3):3–45.

124. Veehof MM, Taal E, Willems MJ et al. Determinants of the use of wrist working splints in rheumatoid arthritis. *Arthritis Care & Research.* 2008;59(4):531–536.

125. Burckhardt CS, Lorig K, Moncur C et al. Arthritis and musculoskeletal patient education standards. Arthritis Foundation. *Arthritis Care & Research.* 1994;7(1):1–4.

126. Barlow JH. How to use education as an intervention in osteoarthritis. *Best Practice & Research in Clinical Rheumatology.* 2001;15(4):545–558.

127. National Institute for Health and Clinical Excellence. *Computerised cognitive behaviour therapy for Depression and Anxiety.* (TA97). London: NICE, 2006.

128. Barlow JH, Turner AP, Wright CC. A randomized controlled study of the Arthritis Self-Management Programme in the UK. *Health Education Research.* 2000;15(6):665–680.

129. Barlow JH, Turner AP, Wright CC. Long-term outcomes of an arthritis self-management programme. *British Journal of Rheumatology.* 1998;37(12):1315–1319.

130. National Institute for Health and Clinical Excellence. *Adalimumab, etanercept and infliximab for the treatment of rheumatoid arthritis.* (TA130). London: NICE, 2007.

131. Riemsma RP, Kirwan JR, Taal E et al. Patient education for adults with rheumatoid arthritis. *Cochrane Database Syst Rev.* 2003;(2):CD003688.

132. Brus HL, van de Laar MA, Taal E et al. Effects of patient education on compliance with basic treatment regimens and health in recent onset active rheumatoid arthritis. *Annals of the Rheumatic Diseases.* 1998;57(3):146–151.

133. Freeman K, Hammond A, Lincoln NB. Use of cognitive-behavioural arthritis education programmes in newly diagnosed rheumatoid arthritis. *Clinical Rehabilitation.* 2002;16(8):828–836.

134. Hammond A, Freeman K. One-year outcomes of a randomized controlled trial of an educational-behavioural joint protection programme for people with rheumatoid arthritis. *Rheumatology.* 2001; 40(9):1044–1051.

135. Hammond A, Freeman K. The long-term outcomes from a randomized controlled trial of an educational-behavioural joint protection programme for people with rheumatoid arthritis. *Clinical Rehabilitation.* 2004;18(5):520–528.

136. Hammond A, Young A, Kidao R. A randomised controlled trial of occupational therapy for people with early rheumatoid arthritis. *Annals of the Rheumatic Diseases.* 2004;63(1):23–30.

137. Barlow JH, Pennington DC, Bishop PE. Patient education leaflets for people with rheumatoid arthritis: A controlled study. *Psychology Health & Medicine.* 1997;2(3):221–235.

138. Helliwell PS, O'Hara M, Holdsworth J et al. A 12-month randomized controlled trial of patient education on radiographic changes and quality of life in early rheumatoid arthritis. *Rheumatology.* 1999; 38(4):303–308.

139. Hill J, Bird H, Johnson S. Effect of patient education on adherence to drug treatment for rheumatoid arthritis: a randomised controlled trial. *Annals of the Rheumatic Diseases.* 2001;60(9):869–875.

140. Lindroth Y, Brattstrom M, Bellman I et al. A problem-based education program for patients with rheumatoid arthritis: evaluation after three and twelve months. *Arthritis Care & Research.* 1997;10(5): 325–332.

141. Riemsma RP, Taal E, Rasker JJ. Group education for patients with rheumatoid arthritis and their partners. *Arthritis & Rheumatism.* 2003;49(4):556–566.

142. Riemsma RP, Taal E, Brus HL et al. Coordinated individual education with an arthritis passport for patients with rheumatoid arthritis. *Arthritis Care & Research.* 1997;10(4):238–249.

143. Van Lankveld W, van HT, Naring G et al. Partner participation in cognitive-behavioral self-management group treatment for patients with rheumatoid arthritis. *Journal of Rheumatology.* 2004;31(9):1738–1745.

144. Walker D, Adebajo A, Heslop P et al. Patient education in rheumatoid arthritis: the effectiveness of the ARC booklet and the mind map. *Rheumatology.* 2007;46(10):1593–1596.

145. Giraudet-Le Quintrec JS. Effect of a collective educational program for patients with rheumatoid arthritis: a prospective 12-month randomized controlled trial. *Journal of Rheumatology.* 2007;34(8):1684–1691.

146. Masiero S, Boniolo A, Wassermann L et al. Effects of an educational-behavioral joint protection program on people with moderate to severe rheumatoid arthritis: a randomized controlled trial. *Clinical Rheumatology.* 2007;26(12):2043–2050.

147. Ahlmen M, Sullivan M, Bjelle A. Team versus non-team outpatient care in rheumatoid arthritis. A comprehensive outcome evaluation including an overall health measure. *Arthritis & Rheumatism.* 1988;31(4):471–479.

148. Vliet Vlieland TP, Breedveld FC, Hazes JM. The two-year follow-up of a randomized comparison of in-patient multidisciplinary team care and routine out-patient care for active rheumatoid arthritis. *British Journal of Rheumatology.* 1997;36(1):82–85.

149. Vliet Vlieland TP, Zwinderman AH, Vandenbroucke JP et al. A randomized clinical trial of in-patient multidisciplinary treatment versus routine out-patient care in active rheumatoid arthritis. *Rheumatology.* 1996;35(5):475–482.

150. Scholten C, Brodowicz T, Graninger W et al. Persistent functional and social benefit 5 years after a multidisciplinary arthritis training program. *Archives of Physical Medicine & Rehabilitation.* 1999;80(10): 1282–1287.

151. Schned ES, Doyle MA, Glickstein SL et al. Team managed outpatient care for early onset chronic inflammatory arthritis. *Journal of Rheumatology.* 1995;22(6):1141–1148.

152. Feinberg JR, Brandt KD. Allied health team management of rheumatoid arthritis patients. *American Journal of Occupational Therapy.* 1984;38(9):613–620.

153. Jacobsson LTH, Frithiof M, Olofsson Y et al. Evaluation of a structured multidisciplinary day care program in rheumatoid arthritis. *Scandinavian Journal of Rheumatology.* 1998;27(2):117–124.

154. Prier A, Berenbaum F, Karneff A et al. Multidisciplinary day hospital treatment of rheumatoid arthritis patients. Evaluation after two years. *Revue du Rhumatisme (English Edition).* 1997;64(7–9):443–450.

155. Nordmark B, Blomqvist P, Andersson B et al. A two-year follow-up of work capacity in early rheumatoid arthritis: a study of multidisciplinary team care with emphasis on vocational support. *Scandinavian Journal of Rheumatology.* 2006;35(1):7–14.

156. Van den Hout WB, Tijhuis GJ, Hazes JM et al. Cost effectiveness and cost utility analysis of multi-disciplinary care in patients with rheumatoid arthritis: a randomised comparison of clinical nurse specialist care, inpatient team care, and day patient team care. *Annals of the Rheumatic Diseases.* 2003; 62(4):308–315.

157. Gabriel SE, Wagner JL, Zinsmeister AR et al. Is rheumatoid arthritis care more costly when provided by rheumatologists compared with generalists? *Arthritis & Rheumatism.* 2001;44(7):1504–1514.

158. Li LC, Maetzel A, Davis AM et al. Primary therapist model for patients referred for rheumatoid arthritis rehabilitation: a cost-effectiveness analysis. *Arthritis & Rheumatism.* 2006;55(3):402–410.

159. Sokka T, Hakkinen A, Kautiainen H et al. Physical inactivity in patients with rheumatoid arthritis: data from twenty-one countries in a cross-sectional, international study. *Arthritis & Rheumatism.* 2008; 59(1):42–50.

160. Turesson C, Matteson EL. Cardiovascular risk factors, fitness and physical activity in rheumatic diseases. *Current Opinion in Rheumatology.* 2007;19(2):190–196.

161. World Confederation of Physical Therapists. *World Confederation of Physical Therapists: a message from the WCPT president.* Available from: World Confederation of Physical Therapists. Last accessed on: 2008 July 28.

162. Huusko TM, Korpela M, Karppi P et al. Threefold increased risk of hip fractures with rheumatoid arthritis in Central Finland. *Annals of the Rheumatic Diseases.* 2001;60(5):521–522.

163. Hakkinen A, Sokka T, Kotaniemi A et al. Muscle strength characteristics and central bone mineral density in women with recent onset rheumatoid arthritis compared with healthy controls. *Scandinavian Journal of Rheumatology.* 1999;28(3):145–151.

164. American Academy of Orthopaedic Manual Physical Therapists. *Home page.* Available from: American Academy of Orthopaedic Manual Physical Therapists. Last accessed on: 2008 July 28.

165. Robinson V, Brosseau L, Casimiro L et al. Thermotherapy for treating rheumatoid arthritis. *Cochrane Database Syst Rev.* 2002;(2):CD002826.

166. Brosseau L, Welch V, Wells G et al. Low level laser therapy (classes I, II and III) in the treatment of rheumatoid arthritis. *Cochrane Database Syst Rev.* 2005;(4):CD002049.

167. Brosseau L, Judd MG, Marchand S et al. Transcutaneous electrical nerve stimulation (TENS) for the treatment of rheumatoid arthritis in the hand. *Cochrane Database Syst Rev.* 2003;(2):CD004377.

168. Casimiro L, Brosseau L, Robinson V et al. Therapeutic ultrasound for the treatment of rheumatoid arthritis. *Cochrane Database Syst Rev.* 2002;(3):CD003787.

169. Han A, Robinson V, Judd M et al. Tai chi for treating rheumatoid arthritis. *Cochrane Database Syst Rev.* 2004;(3):CD004849.

170. Bearne LM, Scott DL, Hurley MV. Exercise can reverse quadriceps sensorimotor dysfunction that is associated with rheumatoid arthritis without exacerbating disease activity. *Rheumatology.* 2002;41(2):157–166.

171. Hall J, Skevington SM, Maddison PJ et al. A randomized and controlled trial of hydrotherapy in rheumatoid arthritis. *Arthritis Care & Research.* 1996;9(3):206–215.

172. Harris R, Millard JB. Paraffin-wax baths in the treatment of rheumatoid arthritis. *Annals of the Rheumatic Diseases.* 1955;14(3):278–282.

173. Bell MJ, Lineker SC, Wilkins AL et al. A randomized controlled trial to evaluate the efficacy of community based physical therapy in the treatment of people with rheumatoid arthritis. *Journal of Rheumatology.* 1998;25(2):231–237.

174. Lineker SC, Bell MJ, Wilkins AL et al. Improvements following short term home based physical therapy are maintained at one year in people with moderate to severe rheumatoid arthritis. *Journal of Rheumatology.* 2001;28(1):165–168.

175. Buljina AI, Taljanovic MS, Avdic DM et al. Physical and exercise therapy for treatment of the rheumatoid hand. *Arthritis & Rheumatism.* 2001;45(4):392–397.

176. O'Brien AV, Jones P, Mullis R et al. Conservative hand therapy treatments in rheumatoid arthritis – a randomized controlled trial. *Rheumatology.* 2006;45(5):577–583.

177. Eversden L, Maggs F, Nightingale P et al. A pragmatic randomised controlled trial of hydrotherapy and land exercises on overall well being and quality of life in rheumatoid arthritis. *BMC Musculoskeletal Disorders.* 2007;8:23–29.

178. Hoenig H, Groff G, Pratt K et al. A randomized controlled trial of home exercise on the rheumatoid hand. *Journal of Rheumatology.* 1993;20(5):785–789.

179. De Jong Z, Munneke M, Zwinderman AH et al. Long term high intensity exercise and damage of small joints in rheumatoid arthritis. *Annals of the Rheumatic Diseases.* 2004;63(11):1399–1405.

180. De Jong Z, Munneke M, Lems WF et al. Slowing of bone loss in patients with rheumatoid arthritis by long-term high-intensity exercise: results of a randomized, controlled trial. *Arthritis & Rheumatism.* 2004;50(4):1066–1076.

181. De Jong Z, Munneke M, Zwinderman AH et al. Is a long-term high-intensity exercise program effective and safe in patients with rheumatoid arthritis? Results of a randomized controlled trial. *Arthritis & Rheumatism.* 2003;48(9):2415–2424.

182. Neuberger GB, Aaronson LS, Gajewski B et al. Predictors of exercise and effects of exercise on symptoms, function, aerobic fitness, and disease outcomes of rheumatoid arthritis. *Arthritis & Rheumatism.* 2007; 57(6):943–952.

183. Hansen TM, Hansen G. Longterm physical training in rheumatoid arthritis. A randomized trial with different training programs and blinded observers. *Scandinavian Journal of Rheumatology.* 1993;22(3): 107–112.

184. Van den Berg MH, Ronday HK, Peeters AJ et al. Using internet technology to deliver a home-based physical activity intervention for patients with rheumatoid arthritis: A randomized controlled trial. *Arthritis & Rheumatism.* 2006;55(6):935–945.

185. Hakkinen A, Sokka T, Hannonen P. A home-based two-year strength training period in early rheumatoid arthritis led to good long-term compliance: a five-year followup. *Arthritis & Rheumatism.* 2004;51(1):56–62.

186. Hakkinen A, Sokka T, Lietsalmi AM et al. Effects of dynamic strength training on physical function, Valpar 9 work sample test, and working capacity in patients with recent-onset rheumatoid arthritis. *Arthritis & Rheumatism.* 2003;49(1):71–77.

187. Hakkinen A, Sokka T, Kotaniemi A et al. A randomized two-year study of the effects of dynamic strength training on muscle strength, disease activity, functional capacity, and bone mineral density in early rheumatoid arthritis. *Arthritis & Rheumatism.* 2001;44(3):515–522.

188. Hakkinen A, Sokka T, Kautiainen H et al. Sustained maintenance of exercise induced muscle strength gains and normal bone mineral density in patients with early rheumatoid arthritis: a 5 year follow up. *Annals of the Rheumatic Diseases.* 2004;63(8):910–916.

189. Van den Ende CH, Hazes JM, Le CS et al. Comparison of high and low intensity training in well controlled rheumatoid arthritis. Results of a randomised clinical trial. *Annals of the Rheumatic Diseases.* 1996;55(11):798–805.

190. Van den Ende CH, Breedveld FC, Le CS et al. Effect of intensive exercise on patients with active rheumatoid arthritis: a randomised clinical trial. *Annals of the Rheumatic Diseases.* 2000;59(8): 615–621.

191. Brodin N, Eurenius E, Jensen I et al. Coaching patients with early rheumatoid arthritis to healthy physical activity: A multicenter, randomized, controlled study. *Arthritis Care & Research.* 2008;59(3):325–331.

192. Hirvonen HE, Mikkelsson MK, Kautiainen H et al. Effectiveness of different cryotherapies on pain and disease activity in active rheumatoid arthritis. A randomised single blinded controlled trial. *Clinical & Experimental Rheumatology.* 2006;24(3):295–301.

193. Munneke M, de JZ, Zwinderman AH et al. Effect of a high-intensity weight-bearing exercise program on radiologic damage progression of the large joints in subgroups of patients with rheumatoid arthritis. *Arthritis & Rheumatism.* 2005;53(3):410–417.

194. Van den Hout WB, de JZ, Munneke M et al. Cost-utility and cost-effectiveness analyses of a long-term, high-intensity exercise program compared with conventional physical therapy in patients with rheumatoid arthritis. *Arthritis & Rheumatism.* 2005;53(1):39–47.

195. Eberhardt KB, Fex E. Functional impairment and disability in early rheumatoid arthritis – development over 5 years. *Journal of Rheumatology.* 1995;22(6):1037–1042.

196. Reisine ST, Goodenow C, Grady KE. The impact of rheumatoid arthritis on the homemaker. *Social Science & Medicine.* 1987;25(1):89–95.

197. Jordan JM, Bernard SL, Callahan LF et al. Self-reported arthritis-related disruptions in sleep and daily life and the use of medical, complementary, and self-care strategies for arthritis: the National Survey of Self-care and Aging. *Archives of Family Medicine.* 2000;9(2):143–149.

198. Katz PP, Yelin EH. Life activities of persons with rheumatoid arthritis with and without depressive symptoms. *Arthritis Care & Research.* 1994;7(2):69–77.

199. Fex E, Larsson BM, Nived K et al. Effect of rheumatoid arthritis on work status and social and leisure time activities in patients followed 8 years from onset. *Journal of Rheumatology.* 1998;25(1):44–50.

200. Astin JA, Beckner W, Soeken K et al. Psychological interventions for rheumatoid arthritis: a meta-analysis of randomized controlled trials. *Arthritis & Rheumatism.* 2002;47(3):291–302.

201. Egan M, Brosseau L, Farmer M et al. Splints and orthoses in the treatment of rheumatoid arthritis. *Cochrane Database Syst Rev.* 2001;(4):CD004018.

202. Helewa A, Goldsmith CH, Lee P et al. Effects of occupational therapy home service on patients with rheumatoid arthritis. *Lancet.* 1991;337(8755):1453–1456.

203. Haskett S, Backman C, Porter B et al. A crossover trial of custom-made and commercially available wrist splints in adults with inflammatory arthritis. *Arthritis & Rheumatism.* 2004;51(5):792–799.

204. Evers AW, Kraaimaat FW, van Riel PL et al. Tailored cognitive-behavioral therapy in early rheumatoid arthritis for patients at risk: a randomized controlled trial. *Pain.* 2002;100(1–2):141–153.

205. Parker JC, Frank RG, Beck NC et al. Pain management in rheumatoid arthritis patients. A cognitive-behavioral approach. *Arthritis & Rheumatism.* 1988;31(5):593–601.

206. Pradhan EK, Baumgarten M, Langenberg P et al. Effect of mindfulness-based stress reduction in rheumatoid arthritis patients. *Arthritis & Rheumatism.* 2007;57(7):1134–1142.

207. Sharpe L, Sensky T, Timberlake N et al. Long-term efficacy of a cognitive behavioural treatment from a randomized controlled trial for patients recently diagnosed with rheumatoid arthritis. *Rheumatology.* 2003;42(3):435–441.

208. Sharpe L, Allard S, Sensky T. Five-year followup of a cognitive-behavioral intervention for patients with recently-diagnosed rheumatoid arthritis: Effects on health care utilization. *Arthritis Care & Research.* 2008;59(3):311–316.

209. Zautra AJ, Davis MC, Reich JW et al. Comparison of cognitive behavioral and mindfulness meditation interventions on adaptation to rheumatoid arthritis for patients with and without history of recurrent depression. *Journal of Consulting & Clinical Psychology.* 2008;76(3):408–421.

210. Kjeken I, Moller G, Kvien TK. Use of commercially produced elastic wrist orthoses in chronic arthritis: a controlled study. *Arthritis Care & Research.* 1995;8(2):108–113.

211. National Institute for Health and Clinical Excellence. *Depression (amended): management of depression in primary and secondary care.* (CG23 (amended)). London: NICE, 2007.

212. Michelson J, Easley M, Wigley FM et al. Foot and ankle problems in rheumatoid arthritis. *Foot & Ankle International.* 1994;15(11):608–613.

213. Wickman AM, Pinzur MS, Kadanoff R et al. Health-related quality of life for patients with rheumatoid arthritis foot involvement. *Foot & Ankle International.* 2004;25(1):19–26.

214. Kerry RM, Holt GM, Stockley I. The foot in chronic rheumatoid arthritis: a continuing problem. *Foot.* 1994;4(4):201–203.

215. Redmond AC, Waxman R, Helliwell PS. Provision of foot health services in rheumatology in the UK. *Rheumatology.* 2006;45(5):571–576.

216. Davys HJ, Turner DE, Helliwell PS et al. Debridement of plantar callosities in rheumatoid arthritis: a randomized controlled trial. *Rheumatology.* 2005;44(2):207–210.

217. Woodburn J, Barker S, Helliwell PS. A randomized controlled trial of foot orthoses in rheumatoid arthritis. *Journal of Rheumatology.* 2002;29(7):1377–1383.

218. Williams AE, Rome K, Nester CJ. A clinical trial of specialist footwear for patients with rheumatoid arthritis. *Rheumatology.* 2007;46(2):302–307.

219. Woodburn J, Helliwell PS, Barker S. Changes in 3D joint kinematics support the continuous use of orthoses in the management of painful rearfoot deformity in rheumatoid arthritis. *Journal of Rheumatology.* 2003;30(11):2356–2364.

220. Moncur C, Ward JR. Heat-moldable shoes for management of forefoot problems in rheumatoid arthritis. *Arthritis Care & Research.* 1990;3(4):222–226.

221. Verstappen SM, Jacobs JW, Kruize AA et al. Trends in economic consequences of rheumatoid arthritis over two subsequent years. *Rheumatology.* 2007;46(6):968–974.

222. Nordenskiold U. Evaluation of assistive devices after a course in joint protection. *International Journal of Technology Assessment in Health Care*. 1994;10(2):293–304.

223. Clark H, Rome K, Plant M et al. A critical review of foot orthoses in the rheumatoid arthritic foot. *Rheumatology*. 2006;45(2):139–145.

224. Chalmers AC, Busby C, Goyert J et al. Metatarsalgia and rheumatoid arthritis – a randomized, single blind, sequential trial comparing 2 types of foot orthoses and supportive shoes. *Journal of Rheumatology*. 2000;27(7):1643–1647.

225. Finckh A, Liang MH, van Herckenrode CM et al. Long-term impact of early treatment on radiographic progression in rheumatoid arthritis: A meta-analysis. *Arthritis & Rheumatism*. 2006;55(6):864–872.

226. Anon. A randomized trial of hydroxychloroquine in early rheumatoid arthritis: the HERA Study. *American Journal of Medicine*. 1995;98(2):156–168.

227. Tsakona E, Fitzgerald AA. Consequences of delayed therapy with second-line agents in rheumatoid arthritis: a 3 year followup on the hydroxychloroquine in early rheumatoid arthritis (HERA) study. *Journal of Rheumatology*. 2000;27(3):623–629.

228. Borg G, Allander E, Lund B et al. Auranofin improves outcome in early rheumatoid arthritis. Results from a 2-year, double blind placebo controlled study. *Journal of Rheumatology*. 1988;15(12):1747–1754.

229. Egsmose C, Lund B, Borg G et al. Patients with rheumatoid arthritis benefit from early 2nd line therapy: 5 year followup of a prospective double blind placebo controlled study. *Journal of Rheumatology*. 1995;22(12):2208–2213.

230. Mottonen T, Hannonen P, Korpela M et al. Delay to institution of therapy and induction of remission using single-drug or combination-disease-modifying antirheumatic drug therapy in early rheumatoid arthritis. *Arthritis & Rheumatism*. 2002;46(4):894–898.

231. Van der Heide A, Jacobs JW, Bijlsma JW et al. The effectiveness of early treatment with 'second-line' antirheumatic drugs. A randomized, controlled trial. *Ann Intern Med*. 1996;124(8):699–707.

232. Verstappen SM, Jacobs JW, Bijlsma JW et al. Five-year followup of rheumatoid arthritis patients after early treatment with disease-modifying antirheumatic drugs versus treatment according to the pyramid approach in the first year. *Arthritis & Rheumatism*. 2003;48(7):1797–1807.

233. Buckland-Wright JC, Clarke GS, Chikanza IC et al. Quantitative microfocal radiography detects changes in erosion area in patients with early rheumatoid arthritis treated with myocrisine. *Journal of Rheumatology*. 1993;20(2):243–247.

234. Choy EH, Scott DL, Kingsley GH et al. Treating rheumatoid arthritis early with disease modifying drugs reduces joint damage: a randomised double blind trial of sulphasalazine vs diclofenac sodium. *Clinical & Experimental Rheumatology*. 2002;20(3):351–358.

235. Peltomaa R, Paimela L, Helve T et al. Effect of treatment on the outcome of very early rheumatoid arthritis. *Scandinavian Journal of Rheumatology*. 2001;30(3):143–148.

236. Nell VP, Machold KP, Eberl G et al. Benefit of very early referral and very early therapy with disease-modifying anti-rheumatic drugs in patients with early rheumatoid arthritis. *Rheumatology*. 2004;43(7):906–914.

237. Chen YF, Jobanputra P, Barton P et al. A systematic review of the effectiveness of adalimumab, etanercept and infliximab for the treatment of rheumatoid arthritis in adults and an economic evaluation of their cost-effectiveness. *Health Technology Assessment*. 2006;10(42):iii–iiv.

238. Ryan L, Brooks P. Disease-modifying antirheumatic drugs. *Current Opinion in Rheumatology*. 1999; 11(3):161–166.

239. Spalding JR, Hay J. Cost effectiveness of tumour necrosis factor-alpha inhibitors as first-line agents in rheumatoid arthritis. *Pharmacoeconomics*. 2006;24(12):1221–1232.

240. Yen JH. Treatment of early rheumatoid arthritis in developing countries. Biologics or disease-modifying anti-rheumatic drugs? *Biomedicine & Pharmacotherapy*. 2006;60(10):688–692.

241. Verhoeven AC, Bibo JC, Boers M et al. Cost-effectiveness and cost-utility of combination therapy in early rheumatoid arthritis: randomized comparison of combined step-down prednisolone, methotrexate and sulphasalazine with sulphasalazine alone. COBRA Trial Group. *British Journal of Rheumatology*. 1998; 37(10):1102–1109.

242. Grigor C, Capell H, Stirling A et al. Effect of a treatment strategy of tight control for rheumatoid arthritis (the TICORA study): A single-blind randomised controlled trial. *Lancet.* 2004;364(9430):263–269.

243. Korthals-de Bos I, Van Tulder M, Boers M et al. Indirect and total costs of early rheumatoid arthritis: a randomized comparison of combined step-down prednisolone, methotrexate, and sulfasalazine with sulfasalazine alone. *Journal of Rheumatology.* 2004;31(9):1709–1716.

244. Choy EH, Smith C, Dore CJ et al. A meta-analysis of the efficacy and toxicity of combining disease-modifying anti-rheumatic drugs in rheumatoid arthritis based on patient withdrawal. *Rheumatology.* 2005;44(11):1414–1421.

245. Felson DT, Anderson JJ, Meenan RF. The efficacy and toxicity of combination therapy in rheumatoid arthritis. A meta-analysis. *Arthritis & Rheumatism.* 1994;37(10):1487–1491.

246. Hetland ML, Stengaard-Pedersen K. Combination treatment with methotrexate, cyclosporine, and intraarticular betamethasone compared with methotrexate and intraarticular betamethasone in early active rheumatoid arthritis: an investigator-initiated, multicenter, randomized, double-blind, parallel-group, placebo-controlled study. *Arthritis & Rheumatism.* 2006;54(5):1401–1409.

247. Hetland ML, Stengaard-Pedersen K, Junker P et al. Aggressive combination therapy with intraarticular glucocorticoid injections and conventional DMARDs in early rheumatoid arthritis. Two year clinical and radiographic results from the CIMESTRA study. *Annals of the Rheumatic Diseases.* 2007;66

248. Korpela M, Laasonen L, Hannonen P et al. Retardation of joint damage in patients with early rheumatoid arthritis by initial aggressive treatment with disease-modifying antirheumatic drugs: five-year experience from the FIN-RACo study. *Arthritis & Rheumatism.* 2004;50(7):2072–2081.

249. Makinen H, Kautiainen H, Hannonen P et al. Sustained remission and reduced radiographic progression with combination disease modifying antirheumatic drugs in early rheumatoid arthritis. *Journal of Rheumatology.* 2007;34(2):316–321.

250. Mottonen T, Hannonen P, LeirisaloRepo M et al. Comparison of combination therapy with single-drug therapy in early rheumatoid arthritis: A randomised trial. *Lancet.* 1999;353(9164):1568–1573.

251. Puolakka K. Impact of initial aggressive drug treatment with a combination of disease-modifying antirheumatic drugs on the development of work disability in early rheumatoid arthritis: a five-year randomized followup trial. *Arthritis & Rheumatism.* 2004;50(1):55–62.

252. Van Jaarsveld CH, Jacobs JW, Van der Veen MJ et al. Aggressive treatment in early rheumatoid arthritis: a randomised controlled trial. On behalf of the Rheumatic Research Foundation Utrecht, The Netherlands. *Annals of the Rheumatic Diseases.* 2000;59(6):468–477.

253. Boers M. Randomised comparison of combined step-down prednisolone, methotrexate and sulphasalazine with sulphasalazine alone in early rheumatoid arthritis. *Lancet.* 1997;350(9074):309–318.

254. Landewe RB, Boers M, Verhoeven AC et al. COBRA combination therapy in patients with early rheumatoid arthritis: long-term structural benefits of a brief intervention. *Arthritis & Rheumatism.* 2002;46(2):347–356.

255. Capell HA, Madhok R, Porter DR et al. Combination therapy with sulfasalazine and methotrexate is more effective than either drug alone in patients with rheumatoid arthritis with a suboptimal response to sulfasalazine: results from the double-blind placebo-controlled MASCOT study. *Annals of the Rheumatic Diseases.* 2007;66(2):235–241.

256. Allaart CF, Goekoop-Ruiterman YP, De Vries-Bouwstra JK et al. Aiming at low disease activity in rheumatoid arthritis with initial combination therapy or initial monotherapy strategies: the BeSt study. *Clinical & Experimental Rheumatology.* 2006;24(6 suppl 43):1–77.

257. Goekoop-Ruiterman YP, de Vries BJK, Allaart CF et al. Comparison of treatment strategies in early rheumatoid arthritis: a randomized trial. *Ann Intern Med.* 2007;146(6):406–415.

258. Goekoop-Ruiterman YP, De Vries-Bouwstra JK, Allaart CF et al. Clinical and radiographic outcomes of four different treatment strategies in patients with early rheumatoid arthritis (the best study): A randomized, controlled trial. *Arthritis & Rheumatism.* 2005;52(11):3381–3390.

259. Van der Kooji SM, De Vries-Bouwstra JK, Goekoop-Ruiterman YP et al. Limited efficacy of conventional DMARDs after initial methotrexate failure in patients with recent onset rheumatoid arthritis treated according to the disease activity score. *Annals of the Rheumatic Diseases.* 2007;66(10):1356–1362.

260. Ferraccioli GF, Gremese E, Tomietto P et al. Analysis of improvements, full responses, remission and toxicity in rheumatoid patients treated with step-up combination therapy (methotrexate, cyclosporin A, sulphasalazine) or monotherapy for three years. *Rheumatology.* 2002;41(8):892–898.

261. Choy EH, Smith CM, Farewell V et al. Factorial randomised controlled trial of glucocorticoids and combination disease modifying drugs in early rheumatoid arthritis. *Annals of the Rheumatic Diseases.* 2008;67(5):656–663.

262. Braun J, Kastner P, Flaxenberg P et al. Comparison of the clinical efficacy and safety of subcutaneous versus oral administration of methotrexate in patients with active rheumatoid arthritis: results of a six-month, multicenter, randomized, double-blind, controlled, phase IV trial. *Arthritis & Rheumatism.* 2008;58(1): 73–81.

263. Hider SL, Silman A, Bunn D et al. Comparing the long-term clinical outcome of treatment with methotrexate or sulfasalazine prescribed as the first disease-modifying antirheumatic drug in patients with inflammatory polyarthritis. *Annals of the Rheumatic Diseases.* 2006;65(11):1449–1455.

264. Stenger AA, Van Leeuwen MA, Houtman PM et al. Early effective suppression of inflammation in rheumatoid arthritis reduces radiographic progression. *British Journal of Rheumatology.* 1998;37(11): 1157–1163.

265. Ahern MJ, Hall ND, Case K et al. D-penicillamine withdrawal in rheumatoid arthritis. *Annals of the Rheumatic Diseases.* 1984;43(2):213–217.

266. De Silva M, Hazleman BL. Long-term azathioprine in rheumatoid arthritis: A double-blind study. *Annals of the Rheumatic Diseases.* 1981;40(6):560–563.

267. Gotzsche PC, Hansen M, Stoltenberg M et al. Randomized, placebo controlled trial of withdrawal of slow-acting antirheumatic drugs and of observer bias in rheumatoid arthritis. *Scandinavian Journal of Rheumatology.* 1996;25(4):194–199.

268. Kremer JM, Rynes RI, Bartholomew LE. Severe flare of rheumatoid arthritis after discontinuation of long-term methotrexate therapy. Double-blind study. *American Journal of Medicine.* 1987;82(4):781–786.

269. Ten Wolde S, Breedveld FC, Hermans J et al. Randomised placebo-controlled study of stopping second-line drugs in rheumatoid arthritis. *Lancet.* 1996;347(8998):347–352.

270. Van der Leeden H, Dijkmans BA, Hermans J et al. A double-blind study on the effect of discontinuation of gold therapy in patients with rheumatoid arthritis. *Clinical Rheumatology.* 1986;5(1):56–61.

271. Bacon PA, Myles AB, Beardwell CG et al. Corticosteroid withdrawal in rheumatoid arthritis. *Lancet.* 1966;2(7470):935–937.

272. Tishler M, Caspi D, Yaron M. Methotrexate treatment of rheumatoid arthritis: is a fortnightly maintenance schedule enough? *Annals of the Rheumatic Diseases.* 1992;51(12):1330–1331.

273. Fleischmann RM, Cohen SB, Moreland LW et al. Methotrexate dosage reduction in patients with rheumatoid arthritis beginning therapy with infliximab: the Infliximab Rheumatoid Arthritis Methotrexate Tapering (iRAMT) trial. *Current Medical Research & Opinion.* 2005;21(8):1181–1190.

274. Tengstrand B, Larsson E, Klareskog L et al. Randomized withdrawal of long-term prednisolone treatment in rheumatoid arthritis: effects on inflammation and bone mineral density. *Scandinavian Journal of Rheumatology.* 2007;36(5):351–358.

275. Hansen M, Podenphant J, Florescu A et al. A randomised trial of differentiated prednisolone treatment in active rheumatoid arthritis. Clinical benefits and skeletal side effects. *Annals of the Rheumatic Diseases.* 1999;58(11):713–718.

276. Corkill MM, Kirkham BW, Chikanza IC et al. Intramuscular depot methylprednisolone induction of chrysotherapy in rheumatoid arthritis: a 24-week randomized controlled trial. *British Journal of Rheumatology.* 1990;29(4):274–279.

277. Capell HA, Madhok R, Hunter JA et al. Lack of radiological and clinical benefit over two years of low dose prednisolone for rheumatoid arthritis: results of a randomised controlled trial. *Annals of the Rheumatic Diseases.* 2004;63(7):797–803.

278. Hansen TM, Kryger P, Elling H et al. Double blind placebo controlled trial of pulse treatment with methylprednisolone combined with disease modifying drugs in rheumatoid arthritis. *British Medical Journal.* 1990;301(6746):268–270.

279. Hickling P, Jacoby RK, Kirwan JR et al. Joint destruction after glucocorticoids are withdrawn in early rheumatoid arthritis. *British Journal of Rheumatology*. 1998;37(9):930–936.

280. Kirwan JR, Byron M, Dieppe P et al. The effect of glucocorticoids on joint destruction in rheumatoid arthritis. *New England Journal of Medicine*. 1995;333(3):142–146.

281. Svensson B, Boonen A, Albertsson K et al. Low-dose prednisolone in addition to the initial disease-modifying antirheumatic drug in patients with early active rheumatoid arthritis reduces joint destruction and increases the remission rate: A two-year randomized trial. *Arthritis & Rheumatism*. 2005;52(11): 3360–3370.

282. Van Everdingen AA, Jacobs JW, Siewertsz van Reesema DR et al. Low-dose prednisone therapy for patients with early active rheumatoid arthritis: clinical efficacy, disease-modifying properties, and side effects: a randomized, double-blind, placebo-controlled clinical trial. *Ann Intern Med*. 2002;136(1):1–12.

283. Van Everdingen AA, Siewertsz van Reesema DR, Jacobs JW et al. The clinical effect of glucocorticoids in patients with rheumatoid arthritis may be masked by decreased use of additional therapies. *Arthritis & Rheumatism*. 2004;51(2):233–238.

284. Wassenberg S, Rau R, Steinfeld P et al. Very low-dose prednisolone in early rheumatoid arthritis retards radiographic progression over two years: A multicenter, double-blind, placebo-controlled trial. *Arthritis & Rheumatism*. 2005;52(11):3371–3380.

285. Choy EH, Kingsley GH, Khoshaba B et al. A two year randomised controlled trial of intramuscular depot steroids in patients with established rheumatoid arthritis who have shown an incomplete response to disease modifying antirheumatic drugs. *Annals of the Rheumatic Diseases*. 2005;64(9):1288–1293.

286. Kirwan JR, Hallgren R, Mielants H et al. A randomised placebo controlled 12 week trial of budesonide and prednisolone in rheumatoid arthritis. *Annals of the Rheumatic Diseases*. 2004;63(6):688–695.

287. Van Vliet-Daskalopoulu E, Jentjens T, Scheffer RTC. Intra-articular rimexolone in the rheumatoid knee: A placebo-controlled, double-blind, multicentre trial of three doses. *British Journal of Rheumatology*. 1987;26(6):450–453.

288. Bae SC, Corzillius M, Kuntz KM et al. Cost-effectiveness of low dose corticosteroids versus non-steroidal anti-inflammatory drugs and COX-2 specific inhibitors in the long-term treatment of rheumatoid arthritis. *Rheumatology*. 2003;42(1):46–53.

289. Navarro-Sarabia F, Ariza AR, Hernandez CB et al. Adalimumab for treating rheumatoid arthritis. *Cochrane Database Syst Rev*. 2005;(3):CD005113.

290. Lee YH, Woo JH, Rho YH et al. Meta-analysis of the combination of TNF inhibitors plus MTX compared to MTX monotherapy, and the adjusted indirect comparison of TNF inhibitors in patients suffering from active rheumatoid arthritis. *Rheumatology International*. 2008;28(6):553–559.

291. Weinblatt ME, Keystone EC, Furst DE et al. Adalimumab, a fully human anti-tumor necrosis factor alpha monoclonal antibody, for the treatment of rheumatoid arthritis in patients taking concomitant methotrexate: the ARMADA trial. *Arthritis & Rheumatism*. 2003;48(1):35–45.

292. Klareskog L, Van Der HD, de Jager JP et al. Therapeutic effect of the combination of etanercept and methotrexate compared with each treatment alone in patients with rheumatoid arthritis: double-blind randomised controlled trial. *Lancet*. 2004;363(9410):675–681.

293. Van der Heijde D, Klareskog L, Singh A et al. Patient reported outcomes in a trial of combination therapy with etanercept and methotrexate for rheumatoid arthritis: the TEMPO trial. *Annals of the Rheumatic Diseases*. 2006;65(3):328–334.

294. Keystone EC, Kavanaugh AF, Sharp JT et al. Radiographic, clinical, and functional outcomes of treatment with adalimumab (a human anti-tumor necrosis factor monoclonal antibody) in patients with active rheumatoid arthritis receiving concomitant methotrexate therapy: a randomized, placebo-controlled, 52-week trial. *Arthritis & Rheumatism*. 2004;50(5):1400–1411.

295. Furst DE, Schiff MH, Fleischmann RM et al. Adalimumab, a fully human anti tumor necrosis factor-alpha monoclonal antibody, and concomitant standard antirheumatic therapy for the treatment of rheumatoid arthritis: results of STAR (Safety Trial of Adalimumab in Rheumatoid Arthritis). *Journal of Rheumatology*. 2003;30(12):2563–2571.

296. Combe B, Codreanu C, Fiocco U et al. Etanercept and sulfasalazine, alone and combined, in patients with active rheumatoid arthritis despite receiving sulfasalazine: a double-blind comparison. *Annals of the Rheumatic Diseases.* 2006;65(10):1357–1362.

297. Westhovens R, Yocum D, Han J et al. The safety of infliximab, combined with background treatments, among patients with rheumatoid arthritis and various comorbidities: a large, randomized, placebo-controlled trial. *Arthritis & Rheumatism.* 2006;54(4):1075–1086.

298. Westhovens R, Cole JC, Li T et al. Improved health-related quality of life for rheumatoid arthritis patients treated with abatacept who have inadequate response to anti-TNF therapy in a double-blind, placebo-controlled, multicentre randomized clinical trial. *Rheumatology.* 2006;45(10):1238–1246.

299. Strand V, Balbir GA, Pavelka K et al. Sustained benefit in rheumatoid arthritis following one course of rituximab: improvements in physical function over 2 years. *Rheumatology.* 2006;45(12):1505–1513.

300. Van der Heijde D, Klareskog L, Rodriguez VV et al. Comparison of etanercept and methotrexate, alone and combined, in the treatment of rheumatoid arthritis: two-year clinical and radiographic results from the TEMPO study, a double-blind, randomized trial. *Arthritis & Rheumatism.* 2006;54(4): 1063–1074.

301. Van Riel P, Taggart AJ, Sany J et al. Efficacy and safety of combination etanercept and methotrexate versus etanercept alone in patients with rheumatoid arthritis with an inadequate response to methotrexate: the ADORE study. *Annals of the Rheumatic Diseases.* 2006;65(11):1478–1483.

302. Emery P, Kosinski M, Li T et al. Treatment of rheumatoid arthritis patients with abatacept and methotrexate significantly improved health-related quality of life. *Journal of Rheumatology.* 2006;33(4):681–689.

303. Van der Heijde D, Burmester G, Melo GJ et al. The safety and efficacy of adding etanercept to methotrexate or methotrexate to etanercept in moderately active rheumatoid arthritis patients previously treated with monotherapy. *Annals of the Rheumatic Diseases.* 2008;67(2):182–188.

304. Van der Heijde D, Klareskog L, Landewe R et al. Disease remission and sustained halting of radiographic progression with combination etanercept and methotrexate in patients with rheumatoid arthritis. *Arthritis & Rheumatism.* 2007;56(12):3928–3939.

305. Klareskog L, Gaubitz M, Rodriguez VV et al. A long-term, open-label trial of the safety and efficacy of etanercept (Enbrel) in patients with rheumatoid arthritis not treated with other disease-modifying antirheumatic drugs. *Annals of the Rheumatic Diseases.* 2006;65(12):1578–1584.

306. Choi HK, Seeger JD, Kuntz KM. A cost effectiveness analysis of treatment options for methotrexate-naive rheumatoid arthritis. *Journal of Rheumatology.* 2002;29(6):1156–1165.

307. Brennan A, Bansback N, Reynolds A et al. Modelling the cost-effectiveness of etanercept in adults with rheumatoid arthritis in the UK. *Rheumatology.* 2004;43(1):62–72.

308. Wong JB, Singh G, Kavanaugh A. Estimating the cost-effectiveness of 54 weeks of infliximab for rheumatoid arthritis. *American Journal of Medicine.* 2002;113(5):400–408.

309. Kobelt G, Jonsson L, Young A et al. The cost-effectiveness of infliximab (Remicade) in the treatment of rheumatoid arthritis in Sweden and the United Kingdom based on the ATTRACT study. *Rheumatology.* 2003;42(2):326–335.

310. Kobelt G, Eberhardt K, Geborek P. TNF inhibitors in the treatment of rheumatoid arthritis in clinical practice: costs and outcomes in a follow up study of patients with RA treated with etanercept or infliximab in southern Sweden. *Annals of the Rheumatic Diseases.* 2004;63(1):4–10.

311. Chiou CF, Choi J, Reyes CM. Cost-effectiveness analysis of biological treatments for rheumatoid arthritis. *Expert Review of Pharmacoeconomics and Outcomes Research 4(3)()(pp 307–315), 2004 Date of Publication: Jun 2004.* 2004;(3):307–315.

312. Welsing PM, Severens JL, Hartman M et al. Modeling the 5-year cost effectiveness of treatment strategies including tumor necrosis factor-blocking agents and leflunomide for treating rheumatoid arthritis in the Netherlands. *Arthritis & Rheumatism.* 2004;51(6):964–973.

313. Bansback NJ, Brennan A, Ghatnekar O. Cost effectiveness of adalimumab in the treatment of patients with moderate to severe rheumatoid arthritis in Sweden. *Annals of the Rheumatic Diseases.* 2005; 64(7):995–1002.

314. Kobelt G, Lindgren P, Singh A et al. Cost effectiveness of etanercept (Enbrel) in combination with methotrexate in the treatment of active rheumatoid arthritis based on the TEMPO trial. *Annals of the Rheumatic Diseases.* 2005;64(8):1174–1179.

315. Tanno M, Nakamura I, Ito K et al. Modeling and cost-effectiveness analysis of etanercept in adults with rheumatoid arthritis in Japan: a preliminary analysis. *Modern Rheumatology.* 2006;16(2):77–84.

316. Marra CA, Marion SA, Guh DP et al. Not all 'quality-adjusted life years' are equal. *Journal of Clinical Epidemiology.* 2007;60(6):616–624.

317. Brennan A, Bansback N, Nixon R et al. Modelling the cost effectiveness of TNF-alpha antagonists in the management of rheumatoid arthritis: results from the British Society for Rheumatology Biologics Registry. *Rheumatology.* 2007;46(8):1345–1354.

318. Clark W, Jobanputra P, Barton P et al. The clinical and cost-effectiveness of anakinra for the treatment of rheumatoid arthritis in adults: a systematic review and economic analysis. *Health Technology Assessment.* 2004;8(18):iii–iiv.

319. Cohen SB, Woolley JM, Chan W et al. Interleukin 1 receptor antagonist anakinra improves functional status in patients with rheumatoid arthritis. *Journal of Rheumatology.* 2003;30(2):225–231.

320. Genovese MC, Cohen S, Moreland L et al. Combination therapy with etanercept and anakinra in the treatment of patients with rheumatoid arthritis who have been treated unsuccessfully with methotrexate. *Arthritis & Rheumatism.* 2004;50(5):1412–1419.

321. Fleischmann RM, Tesser J, Schiff MH et al. Safety of extended treatment with anakinra in patients with rheumatoid arthritis. *Annals of the Rheumatic Diseases.* 2006;65(8):1006–1012.

322. Bresnihan B, Newmark R, Robbins S et al. Effects of anakinra monotherapy on joint damage in patients with rheumatoid arthritis. Extension of a 24-week randomized, placebo-controlled trial. *Journal of Rheumatology.* 2004;31(6):1103–1111.

323. Nuki G, Bresnihan B, Bear MB et al. Long-term safety and maintenance of clinical improvement following treatment with anakinra (recombinant human interleukin-1 receptor antagonist) in patients with rheumatoid arthritis: extension phase of a randomized, double-blind, placebo-controlled trial. *Arthritis & Rheumatism.* 2002;46(11):2838–2846.

324. Glowinski J, Boccard E. Placebo-controlled study of the analgesic efficacy of a paracetamol 500 mg/Codeine 30 mg combination together with low-dose vs high-dose diclofenac in rheumatoid arthritis. *Clinical Drug Investigation.* 1999;18(3):189–197.

325. Herrero-Beaumont G, Bjorneboe O, Richarz U. Transdermal fentanyl for the treatment of pain caused by rheumatoid arthritis. *Rheumatology International.* 2004;24(6):325–332.

326. Berliner MN, Giesecke T, Bornhovd KD. Impact of transdermal fentanyl on quality of life in rheumatoid arthritis. *Clinical Journal of Pain.* 2007;23(6):530–534.

327. Seideman P. Additive effect of combined naproxen and paracetamol in rheumatoid arthritis. *British Journal of Rheumatology.* 1993;32(12):1077–1082.

328. Seideman P, Melander A. Equianalgesic effects of paracetamol and indomethacin in rheumatoid arthritis. *British Journal of Rheumatology.* 1988;27(2):117–122.

329. Frank RG, Kashani JH, Parker JC et al. Antidepressant analgesia in rheumatoid arthritis. *Journal of Rheumatology.* 1988;15(11):1632–1638.

330. Emery P, Gibson T. A double-blind study of the simple analgesic nefopam in rheumatoid arthritis. *British Journal of Rheumatology.* 1986;25(1):72–76.

331. Grace EM, Bellamy N, Kassam Y et al. Controlled, double-blind, randomized trial of amitriptyline in relieving articular pain and tenderness in patients with rheumatoid arthritis. *Current Medical Research & Opinion.* 1985;9(6):426–429.

332. Blake DR, Robson P, Ho M et al. Preliminary assessment of the efficacy, tolerability and safety of a cannabis-based medicine (Sativex) in the treatment of pain caused by rheumatoid arthritis. *Rheumatology.* 2006;45(1):50–52.

333. National Institute for Clinical Excellence. *Guidance on the use of cyclo-oxygenase (cox) II selective inhibitors, celecoxib, rofecoxib, meloxicam and etodolac for osteoarthritis and rheumatoid arthritis.* (TA27). London: NICE, 2001.

334. Geusens PP, Truitt K, Sfikakis P et al. A placebo and active comparator-controlled trial of rofecoxib for the treatment of rheumatoid arthritis. *Scandinavian Journal of Rheumatology.* 2002;31(4):230–238.

335. Porzio F. Meta-analysis of two double-blind comparative studies with the sustained-release form of etodolac in rheumatoid arthritis. *Rheumatology International.* 1993;13(2 suppl):1–30.

336. Shi W. Safety and efficacy of oral nonsteroidal anti-inflammatory drugs in patients with rheumatoid arthritis: a six-month randomised study. *Clinical Drug Investigation.* 2004;24(2):89–101.

337. Collantes E, Curtis SP, Lee KW et al. A multinational randomized, controlled, clinical trial of etoricoxib inthetreatment of rheumatoid arthritis. *BMC Family Practice.* 2002;3:1–10.

338. Matsumoto AK, Melian A, Mandel DR et al. A randomized, controlled, clinical trial of etoricoxib in the treatment of rheumatoid arthritis. *Journal of Rheumatology.* 2002;29(8):1623–1630.

339. Bensen W, Weaver A, Espinoza L et al. Efficacy and safety of valdecoxib in treating the signs and symptoms of rheumatoid arthritis: a randomized, controlled comparison with placebo and naproxen. *Rheumatology.* 2002;41(9):1008–1016.

340. Geusens P, Alten R, Rovensky J et al. Efficacy, safety and tolerability of lumiracoxib in patients with rheumatoid arthritis. *International Journal of Clinical Practice.* 2004;58(11):1033–1041.

341. Gibofsky A, Rodrigues J, Fiechtner J et al. Efficacy and tolerability of valdecoxib in treating the signs and symptoms of severe rheumatoid arthritis: a 12-week, multicenter, randomized, double-blind, placebo-controlled study. *Clinical Therapeutics.* 2007;29(6):1071–1085.

342. Krug H, Broadwell LK, Berry M et al. Tolerability and efficacy of nabumetone and naproxen in the treatment of rheumatoid arthritis. *Clinical Therapeutics.* 2000;22(1):40–52.

343. Simon LS, Weaver AL, Graham DY et al. Anti–inflammatory and upper gastrointestinal effects of celecoxib in rheumatoid arthritis: a randomized controlled trial. *Journal of the American Medical Association.* 1999;282(20):1921–1928.

344. Williams GW, Kivitz AJ, Brown MT et al. A comparison of valdecoxib and naproxen in the treatment of rheumatoid arthritis symptoms. *Clinical Therapeutics.* 2006;28(2):204–221.

345. Zhao SZ, Fiechtner JI, Tindall EA et al. Evaluation of health-related quality of life of rheumatoid arthritis patients treated with celecoxib. *Arthritis Care & Research.* 2000;13(2):112–121.

346. Matsumoto A, Melian A, Shah A et al. Etoricoxib versus naproxen in patients with rheumatoid arthritis: a prospective, randomized, comparator-controlled 121-week trial. *Current Medical Research & Opinion.* 2007;23(9):2259–2268.

347. Brown TJ, Hooper L, Elliott RA et al. A comparison of the cost-effectiveness of five strategies for the prevention of non-steroidal anti-inflammatory drug-induced gastrointestinal toxicity: a systematic review with economic modelling. *Health Technology Assessment.* 2006;10(38):iii–xiii, 1.

348. Spiegel BM, Targownik L, Dulai GS et al. The cost-effectiveness of cyclooxygenase-2 selective inhibitors in the management of chronic arthritis. *Ann Intern Med.* 2003;138(10):795–806.

349. Svarvar P, Aly A. Use of the ACCES model to predict the health economic impact of celecoxib in patients with osteoarthritis or rheumatoid arthritis in Norway. *Rheumatology.* 2000;39(suppl 2):43–50.

350. McCabe CJ, Akehurst RL, Kirsch J et al. Choice of NSAID and management strategy in rheumatoid arthritis and osteoarthritis. The impact on costs and outcomes in the UK. *Pharmacoeconomics.* 1998; 14(2):191–199.

351. Maetzel A, Krahn M, Naglie G. The cost effectiveness of rofecoxib and celecoxib in patients with osteoarthritis or rheumatoid arthritis. *Arthritis & Rheumatism.* 2003;49(3):283–292.

352. You JH, Lee KK, Chan TY et al. Arthritis treatment in Hong Kong – cost analysis of celecoxib versus conventional NSAIDS, with or without gastroprotective agents. *Alimentary Pharmacology & Therapeutics.* 2002;16(12):2089–2096.

353. Zabinski RA, Burke TA, Johnson J et al. An economic model for determining the costs and consequences of using various treatment alternatives for the management of arthritis in Canada. *Pharmacoeconomics.* 2001;19(suppl 1):49–58.

354. Fendrick AM, Bandekar RR, Chernew ME et al. Role of initial NSAID choice and patient risk factors in the prevention of NSAID gastropathy: a decision analysis. *Arthritis & Rheumatism.* 2002;47(1):36–43.

355. Chancellor JV, Hunsche E, de CE et al. Economic evaluation of celecoxib, a new cyclo-oxygenase 2 specific inhibitor, in Switzerland. *Pharmacoeconomics.* 2001;19(suppl 1):59–75.

356. El-Serag HB, Graham DY, Richardson P et al. Prevention of complicated ulcer disease among chronic users of nonsteroidal anti-inflammatory drugs: the use of a nomogram in cost-effectiveness analysis. *Archives of Internal Medicine.* 2002;162(18):2105–2110.

357. Fransen J, Moens HB, Speyer I et al. Effectiveness of systematic monitoring of rheumatoid arthritis disease activity in daily practice: a multicentre, cluster randomised controlled trial. *Annals of the Rheumatic Diseases.* 2005;64(9):1294–1298.

358. Verstappen SM, Jacobs JW, Van der Veen MJ et al. Intensive treatment with methotrexate in early rheumatoid arthritis: aiming for remission. Computer Assisted Management in Early Rheumatoid Arthritis (CAMERA, an open-label strategy trial). *Annals of the Rheumatic Diseases.* 2007;66(11):1443–1449.

359. Smolen JS, Breedveld FC, Schiff MH et al. A simplified disease activity index for rheumatoid arthritis for use in clinical practice. *Rheumatology.* 2003;42(2):244–257.

360. Dixon JS, Hayes S, Constable PDL et al. What are the 'best' measurements for monitoring patients during short-term second-line therapy? *British Journal of Rheumatology.* 1988;27(1):37–43.

361. Dixon JS, Bird HA, Sitton NG et al. C-reactive protein in the serial assessment of disease activity in rheumatoid arthritis. *Scandinavian Journal of Rheumatology.* 1984;13(1):39–44.

362. Kalla AA, Smith PR, Brown GM et al. Responsiveness of Keitel functional index compared with laboratory measures of disease activity in rheumatoid arthritis. *British Journal of Rheumatology.* 1995; 34(2):141–149.

363. Van der Heijde D, van't Hof MA, van Riel PL et al. Validity of single variables and composite indices for measuring disease activity in rheumatoid arthritis. *Annals of the Rheumatic Diseases.* 1992;51(2):177–181.

364. Van Leeuwen MA, Van Rijswijk M, Van der Heijde D et al. The acute-phase response in relation to radiographic progression in early rheumatoid arthritis: A prospective study during the first three years of the disease. *British Journal of Rheumatology.* 1993;32(6):9–13.

365. Arthritis and Musculoskeletal Alliance. *Standards of care for people with inflammatory arthritis.* London: ARMA, 2004.

366. Symmons D, Tricker K, Harrison M et al. Patients with stable long-standing rheumatoid arthritis continue to deteriorate despite intensified treatment with traditional disease modifying anti-rheumatic drugs – results of the British Rheumatoid Outcome Study Group randomized controlled clinical trial. *Rheumatology.* 2006;45(5):558–565.

367. Hewlett S, Mitchell K, Haynes J et al. Patient-initiated hospital follow-up for rheumatoid arthritis. *Rheumatology.* 2000;39(9):990–997.

368. Mowat AG, Nichols PJ, Hollings EM et al. A comparison of follow-up regimes in rheumatoid arthritis. *Annals of the Rheumatic Diseases.* 1980;39(1):12–17.

369. Kirwan JR, Mitchell K, Hewlett S et al. Clinical and psychological outcome from a randomized controlled trial of patient-initiated direct-access hospital follow-up for rheumatoid arthritis extended to 4 years. *Rheumatology.* 2003;42(3):422–426.

370. Alderman AK, Ubel PA, Kim HM et al. Surgical management of the rheumatoid hand: consensus and controversy among rheumatologists and hand surgeons. *Journal of Rheumatology.* 2003;30(7):1464–1472.

371. Alderman AK, Arora AS, Kuhn L et al. An analysis of women's and men's surgical priorities and willingness to have rheumatoid hand surgery. *Journal of Hand Surgery – American Volume.* 2006; 31(9):1447–1453.

372. Chung KC, Kotsis SV, Kim HM et al. Reasons why rheumatoid arthritis patients seek surgical treatment for hand deformities. *Journal of Hand Surgery – American Volume.* 2006;31(2):289–294.

373. Loza E, Abasolo L, Clemente D et al. Variability in the use of orthopedic surgery in patients with rheumatoid arthritis in Spain. *Journal of Rheumatology.* 2007;34(7):1485–1490.

374. Mandl LA, Burke FD, Shaw Wilgis EF et al. Could preoperative preferences and expectations influence surgical decision making? Rheumatoid arthritis patients contemplating metacarpophalangeal joint arthroplasty. *Plastic & Reconstructive Surgery.* 2008;121(1):175–180.

375. Hamilton JD, Gordon MM, McInnes IB et al. Improved medical and surgical management of cervical spine disease in patients with rheumatoid arthritis over 10 years. *Annals of the Rheumatic Diseases.* 2000;59(6):434–438.

376. Little C, Parsons T. Herbal therapy for treating rheumatoid arthritis. *Cochrane Database Syst Rev.* 2000;(4):CD002948.

377. Goldberg RJ, Katz J. A meta-analysis of the analgesic effects of omega-3 polyunsaturated fatty acid supplementation for inflammatory joint pain. *Pain.* 2007;129(1–2):210–223.

378. Skoldstam L, Brudin L, Hagfors L et al. Weight reduction is not a major reason for improvement in rheumatoid arthritis from lacto-vegetarian, vegan or Mediterranean diets. *Nutrition Journal.* 2005;4(15)

379. Skoldstam L, Hagfors L, Johansson G. An experimental study of a Mediterranean diet intervention for patients with rheumatoid arthritis. *Annals of the Rheumatic Diseases.* 2003;62(3):208–214.

380. Panush RS, Carter RL, Katz P et al. Diet therapy for rheumatoid arthritis. *Arthritis & Rheumatism.* 1983;26(4):462–471.

381. Hansen GVO, Nielsen L, Kluger E et al. Nutritional status of Danish rheumatoid arthritis patients and effects of a diet adjusted in energy intake, fish-meal, and antioxidants. *Scandinavian Journal of Rheumatology.* 1996;25(5):325–330.

382. Holst-Jensen SE, Pfeiffer-Jensen M, Monsrud M et al. Treatment of rheumatoid arthritis with a peptide diet: a randomized, controlled trial. *Scandinavian Journal of Rheumatology.* 1998;27(5):329–336.

383. Kavanagh R, Workman E, Nash P et al. The effects of elemental diet and subsequent food reintroduction on rheumatoid arthritis. *British Journal of Rheumatology.* 1995;34(3):270–273.

384. Sarzi-Puttini P, Comi D, Boccassini L et al. Diet therapy for rheumatoid arthritis: A controlled double-blind study of two different dietary regimens. *Scandinavian Journal of Rheumatology.* 2000;29(5):302–307.

385. Van de Laar M, van der Korst JK. Food intolerance in rheumatoid arthritis. I. A double blind, controlled trial of the clinical effects of elimination of milk allergens and azo dyes. *Annals of the Rheumatic Diseases.* 1992;51(3):298–302.

386. Edmonds SE, Winyard PG. Putative analgesic activity of repeated oral doses of vitamin E in the treatment of rheumatoid arthritis. Results of a prospective placebo controlled double blind trial. *Annals of the Rheumatic Diseases.* 1997;56(11):649–655.

387. Peretz A, Siderova V, Neve J. Selenium supplementation in rheumatoid arthritis investigated in a double blind, placebo-controlled trial. *Scandinavian Journal of Rheumatology.* 2001;30(4):212.

388. Hafstrom I, Ringertz B, Spangberg A et al. A vegan diet free of gluten improves the signs and symptoms of rheumatoid arthritis: the effects on arthritis correlate with a reduction in antibodies to food antigens. *Rheumatology.* 2001;40(10):1175–1179.

389. Kjeldsen-Kragh J. Haugen M, Borchgrevink CF et al. Vegetarian diet for patients with rheumatoid arthritis – status: two years after introduction of the diet. *Clinical Rheumatology.* 1994;13(3):475–482.

390. Kjeldsen-Kragh J, Mellbye OJ, Haugen M et al. Changes in laboratory variables in rheumatoid arthritis patients during a trial of fasting and one-year vegetarian diet. *Scandinavian Journal of Rheumatology.* 1995;24(2):85–93.

391. Kjeldsen-Kragh J, Haugen M, Borchgrevink CF et al. Controlled trial of fasting and one-year vegetarian diet in rheumatoid arthritis. *Lancet.* 1991;338(8772):899–902.

392. Nenonen MT, Helve TA, Rauma AL et al. Uncooked, lactobacilli-rich, vegan food and rheumatoid arthritis. *British Journal of Rheumatology.* 1998;37(3):274–281.

393. Galarraga B, Ho M, Youssef HM et al. Cod liver oil (n-3 fatty acids) as an non-steroidal anti-inflammatory drug sparing agent in rheumatoid arthritis. *Rheumatology.* 2008;47(5):665–669.

394. Elkan AC, Sjoberg B, Kolsrud B et al. Gluten-free vegan diet induces decreased LDL and oxidized LDL levels and raised atheroprotective natural antibodies against phosphorylcholine in patients with rheumatoid arthritis: A randomized study. *Arthritis Research & Therapy.* 2008;10(2)

395. Ernst E. Musculoskeletal conditions and complementary/alternative medicine. *Best Practice & Research in Clinical Rheumatology.* 2004;18(4):539–556.

396. Casimiro L, Brosseau L, Milne S et al. Acupuncture and electroacupuncture for the treatment of Rheumatoid Arthritis. *Cochrane Database Syst Rev.* 2005;(4):CD003788.

397. Field T, Diego M, Hernandez RM et al. Hand arthritis pain is reduced by massage therapy. *Journal of Bodywork & Movement Therapies.* 2007;11(1):21–24.

398. Gibson RG, Gibson SL, MacNeill AD et al. Homoeopathic therapy in rheumatoid arthritis: evaluation by double-blind clinical therapeutic trial. *British Journal of Clinical Pharmacology.* 1980;9(5):453–459.

399. Gibson RG, Gibson SLM, MacNeill AD et al. The place for non-pharmaceutical therapy in chronic rheumatoid arthritis: A critical study of homoeopathy. *British Homoeopathic Journal.* 1980;69(3):121–133.

400. Freye E, Latasch L. Analgesic therapy of rheumatoid arthritis – Part II: A study of combined allopathic and homeopathic therapy. *Biomedical Therapy.* 2000;18(2):193–196.

401. Kobelt G, Jonsson L, Lindgren P et al. Modeling the progression of rheumatoid arthritis: a two-country model to estimate costs and consequences of rheumatoid arthritis. *Arthritis & Rheumatism.* 2002;46(9):2310–2319.

402. Saunders SA, Capell HA, Stirling A et al. Triple therapy in early active rheumatoid arthritis: a randomized, single-blind, controlled trial comparing step-up and parallel treatment strategies. *Arthritis & Rheumatism.* 2008;58(5):1310–1317.

403. Dougados M, Combe B, Cantagrel A et al. Combination therapy in early rheumatoid arthritis: a randomised, controlled, double blind 52 week clinical trial of sulphasalazine and methotrexate compared with the single components. *Annals of the Rheumatic Diseases.* 1999;58(4):220–225.

404. Gerards AH, Landewe RB, Prins AP et al. Cyclosporin A monotherapy versus cyclosporin A and methotrexate combination therapy in patients with early rheumatoid arthritis: a double blind randomised placebo controlled trial. *Annals of the Rheumatic Diseases.* 2003;62(4):291–296.

405. Miranda JM, varez-Nemegyei J, Saavedra MA et al. A randomized, double-blind, multicenter, controlled clinical trial of cyclosporine plus chloroquine vs. cyclosporine plus placebo in early-onset rheumatoid arthritis. *Archives of Medical Research.* 2004;35(1):36–42.

406. Sarzi-Puttini P, D'Ingianna E, Fumagalli M et al. An open, randomized comparison study of cyclosporine A, cyclosporine A + methotrexate and cyclosporine A + hydroxychloroquine in the treatment of early severe rheumatoid arthritis. *Rheumatology International.* 2005;25(1):15–22.

407. Marchesoni A, Battafarano N, Arreghini M et al. Radiographic progression in early rheumatoid arthritis: a 12-month randomized controlled study comparing the combination of cyclosporin and methotrexate with methotrexate alone. *Rheumatology.* 2003;42(12):1545–1549.

408. Van den Borne B E, Landewe RB, Goei THS et al. Combination therapy in recent onset rheumatoid arthritis: a randomized double blind trial of the addition of low dose cyclosporine to patients treated with low dose chloroquine. *Journal of Rheumatology.* 1998;25(8):1493–1498.

409. Lu G, Ades AE. Combination of direct and indirect evidence in mixed treatment comparisons. *Statistics in Medicine.* 2004;23(20):3105–3124.

410. Caldwell DM, Ades AE, Higgins JP. Simultaneous comparison of multiple treatments: combining direct and indirect evidence. *British Medical Journal.* 2005;331(7521):897–900.

411. Lumley T. Network meta-analysis for indirect treatment comparisons. *Statistics in Medicine.* 2002; 21(16):2313–2324.

412. WinBugs. Cambridge: University of Cambridge;2004.

413. University of Bristol. *Mixed Treatment Comparisons.* Available from: University Of Bristol. Last accessed on: 2008 Nov. 18.

414. Congdon P. *Applied Bayesian Modelling.* Chichester: Wiley Blackwell;2003.

415. McCullagh P, Nelder JA. *Generalized Linear Models.* 2nd ed. London: Chapman & Hall;1989.

416. Bansback N, Ara R, Karnon J et al. Economic evaluations in rheumatoid arthritis: a critical review of measures used to define health States. *Pharmacoeconomics.* 2008;26(5):395–408.

417. Barbieri M, Wong JB, Drummond M. The cost effectiveness of infliximab for severe treatment-resistant rheumatoid arthritis in the UK. *Pharmacoeconomics.* 2005;23(6):607–618.

418. Wailoo AJ, Bansback N, Brennan A et al. Biologic drugs for rheumatoid arthritis in the Medicare program: a cost-effectiveness analysis. *Arthritis & Rheumatism.* 2008;58(4):939–946.

419. Dolan P. Modeling valuations for EuroQol health states. *Medical Care.* 1997;35(11):1095–1108.

420. Hurst NP, Kind P, Ruta D et al. Measuring health-related quality of life in rheumatoid arthritis: validity, responsiveness and reliability of EuroQol (EQ-5D). *British Journal of Rheumatology.* 1997;36(5):551–559.

421. Office of National Statistics. *Standard Interim UK Life Tables.* 2006. London, ONS. www.statistics. gov.uk/StatBase/Product.asp?vlnk=14459